HISTORICAL RECORD

OF THE

EIGHTY-NINTH

PRINCESS VICTORIA'S REGIMENT.

HISTORICAL RECORD

OF THE

EIGHTY-NINTH

PRINCESS VICTORIA'S REGIMENT.

COMPILED BY

ROWLAND BRINCKMAN,

Captain and Adjutant, 2nd Royal Irish Fusiliers.

"Not once or twice in our rough island-story,
  The path of duty was the way to glory."—*Tennyson.*

WITH ILLUSTRATIONS.

1888.

PREFACE.

In order that the General Public might understand more fully the difficulties, and privations that beset the Military Profession in all parts of the World, even during the time of Peace, and the achievements, deeds of valour, and vicissitudes of the Service in time of War; His Majesty King William IV authorized that the Historical Records of each Regiment should be made public.

The following General Order was therefore promulgated:

HORSE GUARDS,
1st *January*, 1836.

His Majesty has been pleased to command that, with the view of doing the fullest justice to Regiments, as well as to Individuals who have distinguished themselves by their bravery in action with the enemy, an account of the Services of every Regiment in the British Army shall be published under the superintendence and direction of the Adjutant General; and that the account shall contain the following particulars, viz:—

—— The Period and Circumstances of the Original Formation of the Regiment; The Stations at which it has from time to time been employed; The Battles, Sieges and other Military Operations in which it has been engaged, particularly specifying any Achievement it may have performed, and the Colours, Trophies, etc., it may have captured from the Enemy.

—— The Names of the Officers, and the Number of Non-commissioned Officers and Privates Killed or Wounded by the Enemy, specifying the Place and Date of the Action.

PREFACE.

—— The Names of those Officers who, in consideration of their Gallant Service, and Meritorious Conduct in Engagements with the Enemy, have been distinguished with Titles, Medals, or other Marks of His Majesty's gracious favour.

—— The Names of all such Officers, Non-commissioned Officers, and Privates, as may have specially signalized themselves in Action.

And,

—— The Badges and Devices which the Regiment may have been permitted to bear, and the Causes on account of which such Badges or Devices, or any other Marks of Distinction, have been granted.

By Command of the Right Honourable
GENERAL LORD HILL,
Commanding-in-Chief.

JOHN MACDONALD,
Adjutant-General.

In consequence of this Order, the work of publication was entrusted to Mr. Richard Cannon (Chief Clerk of the Adjutant-General's Office). This gentleman compiled and published the Histories of many of our Regiments during the years following 1836. On his retirement however, and before the Records of one half of the Regiments in the Service had been printed, the Authorities for some reason decided that the work of publication should be discontinued.

It thus happened that the History of the 89th was never published by authority. Its Records are in no way inferior to those that have already seen the light, and in now submitting them to the Public in general, and to the Regiment in particular, it is hoped that the "Esprit-de-Corps" already great, will be strengthened, and that all Ranks will try to emulate the good example of their predecessors. True "Esprit-de-Corps" should cause the Public

(Civil and Military) to believe that there is no Army in the world like that of Great Britain, and every Soldier that there is no Regiment in that Army like his own. So may it be with those of the "PRINCESS VICTORIA'S."

The Records as here published are given in almost the identical words in which they have been written by each succeeding Commanding Officer, and no embellishment has been attempted. Additional interest it is hoped will be given by the various Rolls of Officers, which form so to speak, a Regimental Army List.

Any Anecdotes connected with the Regiment or those who have served in it, will be very gladly received, and will be embodied in a Second Edition should one be called for.

Also any further information of interest, which will serve to make the "Records of the 89th" more complete, will be exceedingly acceptable. Officers (past and present) are asked to kindly point out any errors in this work that come to their notice, and errors must occur when so many names and dates are brought together as in the various Succession Rolls, and more so as the Old Army Lists from which they were taken were often inaccurate, especially with regard to "Initials" and the "Spelling of Names."

This Volume is dedicated to those of all Ranks who have served in, and passed from the 89th, and to those now serving in it, in the belief that it will not be altogether unacceptable to them.

R. BRINCKMAN, *Captain & Adjutant,*
2nd Batt. Princess Victoria's (R. Irish Fus.)

Dover,
August, 1888.

CONTENTS.

	Page.
The Preface	v
Contents	ix
Index of the Historical Records	xi
List of Plates	xxiv
The Historical Records of the Regiment	1
Stations occupied by the Regiment since 1793	167
The "Colours"	171
Table of "Active Service" seen by the Regiment	173
Succession Roll of Colonels	178
,, ,, Lieut.-Cols. Commanding	179
,, ,, Adjutants	180
,, ,, Quarter-Masters	181
,, ,, Paymasters	182
,, ,, Instructors of Musketry and Assistant Adjutants	183
,, ,, The Staff Officers of the 2nd Battalion of the 89th	184
,, ,, All Officers who have served in the Regiment	185
Alphabetical Index to names mentioned in these "Records"	216

INDEX

OF THE HISTORICAL RECORD.

Year.		Page.
1793	The Regiment raised in Ireland	1
	Placed on the Establishment of the Army, and numbered 89	1
	Facings of the uniform	1
1794	Colonel Handfield appointed to command	1
	Proceeded from Ireland to England	1
	Quartered at Southampton Camp	1
	Expedition to Holland under Lord Moira	1
	Reinforced the Army under the Duke of York	1
	Attack on Alost	1
	Attack on Boxtel	2
	Retreat of the Army through Holland	2
	Embarked for England	2
1795	Landed at Sunderland; marched to Whitby and thence to Whitburn Camp	2
	Gave large drafts to the 87th Regiment or "King's Own"	2
	Officers employed recruiting	2
	Moved to Ireland, Arklow, and afterwards Wexford	2
	Lieut.-Col. William Stewart appointed to command	3
1796	Sent to oppose the French landing at Bantry Bay	3
	Quartered at Loughlinstown Camp, and at Clonmel	3
1797	Quartered at Fermoy	3
1798	The Irish Rebellion	3
	Battle of "Vinegar Hill"	3
	Pursuit of the Rebel Chief. His surrender	3
1799	Embarked for foreign service, in company with the 30th Regiment	4
	Landed at Messina (Sicily)	4
1800	Blockade of La Valetta	4
	Its surrender to General Pigott	4
	The Regiment selected to accompany the Expedition to Egypt	4

Year.		Page.
1801	Landing effected near Alexandria	4
	Action of 13th March	4
	Battle of Alexandria	5
	Death of Sir Ralph Abercrombie	5
	Crossed the Nile, to co-operate with the Army of the Grand Vizier	5
	Sent in advance of the Army on the Right Bank	5
	Action of 9th May	5
	Capture of a convoy in its descent down the Nile	6
	Siege of Cairo. Its capitulation	6
	Under orders to join an Expedition to Corfu	7
	The Expedition countermanded	7
	Proceeded to Gibraltar	7
1802	Proceeded to Ireland	7
	Stationed at Youghall	7
	Moved to Enniskillen	7
	Lieut.-Col. Lord Blayney, assumed the command	7
1803	Quartered at Athlone and Loughrea	7
	A second Battalion raised	7
1804	Quartered at Doneraile and Cork	7
	Embarked for the West Indies, but was countermanded	7
1805	Embarked for Foreign Service	8
	The Expedition to Holland	8
	Shipwreck of the vessel conveying the 89th	8
1806	Returned to England	8
	Received new Colours	8
	Embarked for South America	8
	Outbreak of Opthalmia on board ship	8
	Re-landed at Portsmouth	8
1807	Embarked for Buenos Ayres	8
	Proceeded to the Cape of Good Hope	9
1808	Proceeded from the Cape to Ceylon	9
1809	Colonel Garden assumed command	9
	Detachment sent to Trincomalee	9
	Mutiny in the Madras Army	9
	Moved to Madras	9
1810	Expedition against the "Isle of France"	10
1811	Expedition to "Java"	10
	Action of 5th June	10
	Capture of a Blockhouse	10

Year.		Page.
1811	Half Battalion 89th, formed into a Rifle Battalion	11
	Action near Weltervreeden	11
	Capture of "Fort Cornelius"	11
1812	Expedition to "Sumatra"	11
	Return to Madras	11
	General Order by Sir Samuel Achmuty	11
	General Order by the Governor of Java	12
	General Order by the Commander of Forces in Java	13
	The word "JAVA" authorised for the Regimental Colour	14
	Moved to Poonamallee	14
1813	Returned to Madras	14
	Reviewed by Lord Moira	14
	General Order by Lord Moira	15
1814	Moved to Bangalore	15
1815	Moved to Cannanore	15
1816	Moved to Quilon	15
	The "Second Battalion" disbanded	15

SERVICES OF THE SECOND BATTALION.

1803	Formation of the Second Battalion	16
1812	Embarked for North America	16
	Stationed at Halifax	16
1813	Proceeded to Quebec	16
	War with the United States	16
	Marched to Kingston, the scene of hostilities	16
	Action of 24th August	17
	The Enemy's advance on Montreal	17
	Action of "Christlers Farm"	18
	District General Order by Major-General De Rottenburg	20
	Despatch of Colonel Morrison, commanding the force at "Christler's Farm"	21
	Application to bear "Christlers Farm" on the Regimental Colour	23
	The Commander-in-Chief unable to sanction the request	25
	Storming of "Blackrock"	26
	Despatch of Major-General Riall	27
1814	Pursuit of the United States Army	28
	Severe Action of 4th March	28
	The Enemy make fresh preparations for an attempt on Canada	29
	Battle of "Niagara"	29

xiv   INDEX.

Year.		Page.
1814	The word "NIAGARA" authorised for the Regimental Colour ...	30
	Sir George Provost's despatch to the Secretary of State	30
	Despatch of Lieut.-General Drummond, commanding the Forces at "Niagara"	31
	District General Order by Lieut.-General Drummond	38
	Siege and assault of Fort Erie	39
	Extract from despatch of Lieut.-General Drummond	39
	Despatch of Major-General De Wattville	40
	The Enemy abandon the Canadian side of the St. Lawrence ...	41
	The Second Battalion returned to York	41
1815	Peace concluded with the United States	41
	Return to England	41
1816	The "Second Battalion" disbanded.............................	41

SERVICES OF THE REGIMENT—continued.

1817	Quartered at Quilon	42
1818	Outbreak of the Mahratta War	42
	Six Companies despatched to the Deccan	42
	Capture of "Loghur," "Issapore" and many other strong Fortresses	42
	Bombardment and capture of the "Fort Ryghur"	43
	Brigade Order issued on the capture of "Loghur"	43
	Brigade Order issued on the capture of "Fort Koaree"	44
	Brigade Order on the storming of the Stockades, near "Indapore"	44
	Brigade Order on the capture of "Ryghur"	45
	Letter from Lieut.-Col. Prother (commanding the Force in the Deccan) to the Commander-in-Chief, Bombay	45
1819	Expedition to Sawant Warree States	46
	Assault of the Fortress of Raree	46
	Peace proclaimed	47
	Return of the Detachment to Quilon	47
	Field Order issued on the capture of "Raree"	47
	Extract from General Order by the Governor of Bombay	48
	Copy of Horse Guards' letter to the Commander-in-Chief Calcutta	49
1820	New Colours presented to the Regiment............................	50
	Lieut.-Col. Miles, C.B., assumed command........................	50
1821 1822 }	Remained quartered at Quilon	50
1823	Moved to Cannanore	51

INDEX.

Year.		Page.
1824	War proclaimed with Burmah	51
	Embarked for Madras in two Divisions	51
	Occupied Fort St. George	51
	Outbreak of Cholera in the Regiment	51
	Proceeded to Rangoon	51
	Operations against the Stockades of Kymendine	52
	Pitiable condition of the Regiment as regards food, provisions, native followers, etc.	53
	Severe outbreak of Dysentry	53
	Death of Captain Coates	53
	General Order of General Officer commanding at Rangoon	54
	Detachment sent to attack a Stockade	54
	The Stockades of Kymendine	54
	Lieut.-Col. Mallet appointed a Brigadier	54
	The Regiment detailed to bring under subjection the line of Coast from Martaban to Mergui	55
	Unconditional surrender of the Fort of Tavoy	55
	Goodwill of the Natives	56
	Capture of the Town of Mergui	56
	Return to Rangoon	57
	Divisional Order on the fall of Mergui	57
	Regimental Order on the fall of Mergui	58
	Letter from the Adjutant-General, Calcutta, to the General Officer Commanding at Rangoon	59
	Letter from the Governor-General to the General Officer Commanding at Rangoon	59
	General Order issued on the resumption of hostilities	61
	General attack on the Enemy's Works	62
	Capture of some of the Enemy's Guns	62
	Attack and Capture of Redoubts	62
	General Order by Sir A. Campbell	63
	Extract from Despatch of Sir A. Campbell	63
	General Action with the Enemy, 15th December	64
	General Order issued after the Action	65
	Divisional Order by Lieut.-Col. Miles, C.B.	66
1825	The Regiment embarked in various craft and proceeded up the river with the general advance of the Army	66
	Divisional Order by General Cotton	67
	Extract of Despatch	67
	Attack on the Enemy, March 1st	68
	Attack on the Stockades at Donabew	68
	Death of Captain Rose and Captain Cannon	68

INDEX.

Year.		Page.
1825	Divisional Order after the Attack	69
	Extract from Despatch of General Cotton	69
	General Order previous to final Attack on Donabew	70
	The Enemy abandoned the Works on the death of their General, (Maha Bundoola)	71
	Advance to Prome	71
	Cessation of active hostilities	71
	A short Armistice granted	71
	The Enemy advance in force on Prome	72
	General Attack on the Enemy's Position	72
	Divisional Order issued 3rd December	73
	Divisional Order issued 5th December	74
	The Burmese sue for Peace; an Armistice granted	74
1826	On the expiration of the Armistice, the Town of Pattanagoh stormed, destroyed and burnt	75
	General Order issued 20th January	75
	The English Force advanced	76
	Action at Pegamew: Capture of the Fort	76
	General Order issued 9th February	76
	Peace signed 24th February	77
	The Force broken up, and the Regiment returned to Rangoon, and immediately embarked, and proceeded to Madras	77
	General Order on the termination of the War	77
	The word "Ava" authorised for the Regimental Colour	78
1827	Quartered at Madras	78
1828	Marched to Trichinopoly	78
1829	Extract from a letter from the Adjutant-General	79
1830	Marched to Madras for embarkation to England	79
	The Regiment opened for Volunteers	79
	Farewell Order of the General Officer Commanding Southern Division of the Madras Army	79
1831	Embarked for England, 13th January	80
	Farewell Order of the Governor of Madras	80
	Arrived at Gravesend, 7th May	82
	Proceeded to Canterbury, and later in the year to Plymouth and Devonport	82
1832	Quartered at Devonport	82
1833	New Colours presented by "Princess Victoria"	82
	Moved to Cork	84
	Lieut.-Col. Jones K.H., assumed command	85

INDEX. xvii

Year.		Page.
1834	Marched to Fermoy	85
	Inspected and Reviewed by Sir Hussey Vivian, Commander-in-Chief in Ireland. Regimental Order issued after it	85
	Inspected by Major-General Sir Thomas Arbuthnot. Regimental Order issued after the Inspection	86
	A Turkish Gold Medal presented to the Regiment by Colonel Stewart	86
	Employed in aid of Civil Power	87
	Standing Orders for the Regiment issued by Col. Jones	87
1835	Largely employed in aid of Civil Power	87
	Lieut.-Col. Hartley assumed command, *vice* Jones, exchanged. Colonel Doherty assumed command, *vice* Colonel Hartley, retired	88
	Embarked for the West Indies	88
	Arrived at the Barbadoes. Inspected by Sir Lionel Smith	88
	The Depôt moved to Drogheda	89
1836	Proceeded to Trinadad	89
	Regimental Order by Colonel Doherty, prior to proceeding to England, on leave	90
	Outbreak of yellow fever	91
	The Depôt moved to Omagh	91
1837	Alteration in the clothing	91
	Mutiny of the 1st West Indian Regiment	91
	Sir Charles Bulkeley Egerton, G.C.M.G., K.C.H. appointed Colonel to the Regiment	91
	The Depôt movements	92
1838	Lieut.-Col. Basden, assumed command	92
	Severe outbreak of yellow fever	92
	Death of Captain Pearson, Lieuts. Blunt and Need, and of Surgeon Orr	93
1839	Proceeded from Trinidad to Antigua	93
	Death of Captain Gray and Lieut. McCausland	93
1840	Inspected by General Officer Commanding Windward Isles. General Order issued thereon	94
1841	Proceeded from Antigua to the Barbadoes	95
	Regimental Order issued on arrival at St. Anns	95
	Proceeded to Canada. Quartered at Amherstburg	95
	The Depôt moved to Drogheda	96
1842	Moved from Amherstburg to Chambly	96
	The Regiment received a large reinforcement of Volunteers	96
	The Depôt moved to Naas	96

B

xviii INDEX.

Year.		Page.
1843	Moved from Chambly to Montreal	96
	Lieut.-Col. Aplin assumed command *vice* Col. Basden, retired.	96
	Lieut.-Col. Bouverie assumed command *vice* Col. Aplin, exchanged	97
	Movements of the Depôt	97
1844	Quartered at Montreal	97
	The Depôt moved from Cork to Newbridge	97
1845	Lieut.-Col. Thorp assumed command *vice* Col. Bouverie, deceased	97
	Moved from Montreal to Quebec	97
	Two calamitous Fires in Quebec	98
	General Order after the Conflagration of 28th May	98
	,, ,, ,, of 28th June	99
	The Depôt moved to Carlisle	100
1846	Percussion arms issued to the Regiment	100
	Moved from Quebec to Halifax	100
	Regimental Order on leaving Quebec	101
	Address presented by the Magistrates of Quebec to the Regiment on leaving	101
	Address presented by the Mayor and Council	102
	The Depôt moved to Hull	103
1847	Embarked for England	103
	General Order by G.O.C. Halifax	103
	Arrived in England and proceeded to Chichester	104
	Regimental Order issued on arrival in England	104
	Moved to Ashton-under-lyne	105
	Address from the Corporation of Dover	105
1848	The Chartist Riots. Employed in Manchester, Liverpool, Birkenhead, etc., in aid of Civil Power	106
	Proceeded to Ireland	107
	Employed in many detachments in aid of Civil Power	107
1849	Lieut.-Col. Ferryman assumed command *vice* Col. Thorp exchanged	107
1850	Moved from Birr to Dublin	107
	Address from the inhabitants of Birr to the Regiment on leaving.	107
1851	Moved to Clonmel, giving several detachments	108
1852	Employed in aid of Civil Power	108
	Moved to Templemore and thence to Buttevant	109
	The "Minie" rifle introduced into the service	109

Year.		Page.
1853	Moved to Cork	109
	Furnished with new accoutrements	109
1854	Embarked for Gibraltar	109
	Proceeded to the Crimea	110
	Armed with the Enfield rifle	110
	The Establishment increased	110
	Movements of the Depôt	111
1855	Served with the 3rd Division in the Crimea	111
	Siege of Sebastopol	111
	Death of Capt. A. E. Hill	111
	Casualties in the Crimea	111
	Formation of a Reserve Depôt	111
	A Detachment employed in the Baidar valley, making gabions, fascines, etc	112
	Moved from Sebastopol to the Marine Heights, Balaklava, and employed on fatigue duties	112
	The word "SEVASTOPOL" authorised for the Regimental Colour	112
1856	Inspected on Balaklava Heights	113
	Peace signed 29th March, 1856	113
	Honours and Decorations conferred by Foreign Powers for services in the Crimea	113
	Proceeded to Gibraltar	114
	Proceeded from Gibraltar to the Cape	114
	Expected disturbances in Kaffraria	115
	The Tunic substituted for the Coatee	116
1857	Established a line of Posts on the frontier	116
	Destitute condition of the Kaffirs	116
	Under Orders for New Zealand	117
	Outbreak of the Indian Mutiny	117
	Hurriedly despatched to India	117
	Marched to Ahmedabad	118
	Col. Ferryman appointed Brigadier	118
	The Strength increased to 1000	119
	Death of Sir Charles Bulkeley Egerton, G.C.M.G., K.C.H. Colonel of the Regiment. Succeeded by General Arbuthnot	119
	Movement of the Depôt	119
1858	Field Force under Major Grimes to disarm the Natives	120
	Death of Col. Skynner	120
	Skirmish with Bheels	121
	Suppressing the Rebels in Rajpootana	121

INDEX.

Year.		Page.
1858	Attack on Village of Mondetti	123
	Death of Lieut.-Col. Phillips	123
	Field Force sent from Deesa to protect Oodeypore	123
	The Rebels hunted from place to place	124
	Death of Capts. Nixon and Morris, Lieuts. Lamont and Warburton	125
1859	The Regiment united at Oodeypore	125
	Detachments largely employed in pursuing and suppressing the Rebels in Meywar	126
	Arrival of the Families of the Regiment from the Cape	127
	The Regiment transferred from the Bombay to the Bengal Presidency	127
	Marched from Neemuch to Goonah	128
	The Seronge Field Force. Surprise of the Rebel Camp, Surrender of Chutter Sal	129
	Death of Lieut. Harrison and Ensign Dickson	131
	New Equipment issued to the Regiment	131
	Turkish Medals for the Crimea received	132
	The "Field Exercises and Evolutions of Infantry" first adopted in the Regiment	132
1860	Lieut.-Col. Ferryman exchanged to the 75th Regiment	132
	The Regiment very unhealthy	132
1861	Moved to Jhansi	132
	Lieut.-Col. Boyle assumed command from leave of absence	133
	Outbreak of Cholera	133
	Alteration in the Establishment	133
	Inspected by Sir Hugh Rose, G.C.B	134
	Death of Major Atkinson and Lieut. Sewell	134
1862	Marched to Mooltan	134
	Camp at Umballa under Sir Hugh Rose, G.C.B.	134
1863	Quartered at Mooltan	135
	Death of Captain Selby	135
1864	Detachment sent to Dehra Ismail Khan	135
	Major-General C. Gascoigne appointed "Colonel."	135
1865	Ordered suddenly to England. Sailed in two divisions, both reaching Dover, 8th August; proceeded thence to Shorncliffe	135
	Death of Ensign Jones	136
	Strength of Home Establishment	136
	Furnished with new Arms and Accoutrements	136
	Inspection before H.R.H. the Duke of Cambridge, F.M. C. in Chief	136

Year.		Page.
1866	Moved to Aldershot. Quartered in the North Camp	136
	New "Colours" presented by H.M. the Queen, on 5th April. The Ceremony and Festivities following it	137
	Title of "Princess Victoria's" conferred on the Regiment	140
	A "Princess' Coronet" authorised to be worn as a Badge	140
	A Watercolour Drawing of the Ceremony of presenting the Colours, given to the Regiment by H.M. the Queen	140
	The Old Colours placed in All Saints Church, Aldershot, where a Stained Glass Window was also erected	141
	The fixed Establishment of the Regiment	141
	Field Days and Reviews at Aldershot	141
1867	Armed for the first time with Breechloaders	141
	Sudden Orders to proceed to Ireland. Left Aldershot for the Curragh at 12 hours notice	141
	Employed in aid of Civil Power	142
	Change in Dress	143
1868	Visit of the Prince and Princess of Wales to Ireland	143
	Divided into many Detachments in aid of Civil Power	143
1869	Placed under Orders for India	143
	Volunteers received from other Corps	144
	The whole Regiment moved to Fermoy	144
1870	Departure for India postponed from February	144
	Employed in aid of Civil Power	144
	Many Volunteers received from other Corps, and the Establishment increased for India	145
	Inspected by Major General Campbell	146
	Embarked for India, 29th September, and proceeded viâ Alexandia and Suez	146
	On arrival in India proceeded to Cannanore	146
	The Depôt moved to Bristol	146
	Major General Garvock, K.C.B. appointed Colonel	147
1871	Quartered at Cannanore	147
	Purchase system abolished, and rank of *Ensign* done away with	147
1872	Moved to Bangalore	147
	Volunteers from other Corps	148
	The Depôt returned to Ireland (Fermoy)	148
1873	Colonel Boyle proceeded to England on sick leave	148
	Won the "Bangalore Cup" at the S. Indian Rifle Association meeting	148
	Quarter Master Osborne died	148

xxii   INDEX.

Year.		Page.
1873	Officers' names who joined and left during the year	148
	The Depôt moved to Mullingar	149
1874	The Bangalore Camp of Exercise	149
	Death of Colonel Boyle, C.B.	150
	Death of Major General C. R. Egerton, Colonel of the Regiment Succeeded by Lieut.-Gen. Lord Henry Percy, V.C., K.C.B.	150
	Won the "Bangalore Cup" for a second time	150
1875	Moved from Bangalore to Madras	150
	Detachment sent to the Andaman Isles	151
	Visit of the Prince of Wales to India	151
	The Regiment complimented by Sir Frederick Haines	151
	Death of Lieut. Ormsby Cox	151
1876	Proceeded to British Burmah, and quartered at Thayetmyo and Tonghoo	151
	Lieut.-Col. Penton assumed command	152
	The Depôt moved to Armagh	152
1877	Inspected by Major General Knox Gore	152
	Moved to Rangoon	153
	The Silver Medal to commemorate H.M. the Queen's assumption of the title "Empress of India," presented to the Sergeant-Major	153
	Martini-Henry Rifles issued in lieu of Snider	153
	The "Princess Victoria's Coronet" sanctioned to be worn as a Badge on the Tunic	153
	The rank of "Sub-Lieutenant" abolished and that of "2nd Lieutenant" substituted	153
1878	Inspected by Major General Knox Gore	153
	Lieut.-Col. Penton proceeded to England on sick leave	154
	Capt. Richmond joined the Army Pay Department	154
	Outbreak of Cholera	154
	Lieut. Harman appointed Adjutant	154
1879	Changes among the Officers	154
	Death of Quarter-Master Archer, succeeded by Sergeant-Major J. Watkins	155
	Half Battalion proceeded to Tayrangoon	155
1880	For a Fourth time inspected by Major General Knox Gore	156
	The Half Battalion from Tayrangoon rejoined Head Quarters at Rangoon	156
	General Lambert appointed Colonel	156
	Death of Capt. Cuthbert	159

INDEX. xxiii

Year.		Page.
	Embarked at Rangoon for India	156
	Prevalence of Intermittent Fever	156
1881	Disembarked at Vingorla, and marched to Belgaum	156
	Colonel Penton appointed a Brigadier in the Kandahar Field Force	157
	Detachment sent to Kolapore	157
	Lieut. Rogers appointed Adjutant	157
	Changes in the Organization, Title, and Uniform of July 1st	157
	Amalgamated with the 87th Royal Irish Fusiliers, and called the 2nd Battalion Princess Victoria's (Royal Irish Fusiliers)	157
	Rank of 2nd Lieutenant abolished	157
	Establishment of the Battalion	157
	Colonel Penton gave up the command to Lieut. Colonel Robinson	158
1882	Camp at Batchee for Field Firing	158
	Inspected by Brigadier General Brice	158
	Success of the Rifle Team at Poona	159
1883	Death of Captain Brown	159
	Transfer of men to the 1st Battalion	159
	Inspected by the C. in C. Bombay Presidency	159
1884	Departure from Belgaum for England	159
	Slight outbreak of Small pox	160
	Embarked at Vingorla on H.M.S. "Jumna"	160
	Intercepted at Aden, and received orders for active service at Suakim	160
	Campaign in the Soudan under Lieut.-Gen. Sir Gerald Graham, V.C., K.C.B	160
	Occupation of Fort Baker	160
	Battle of El-Teb (29th Feb.)	160
	Relief of Tokar	160
	Battle of Tamai (13th March)	162
	Expedition to Tamanieb	163
	Embarked for England on H.M.S. "Jumna"	163
	Landed in England and remained quartered at Portsmouth	163
	Presentation of Medals for the Soudan	164
	The word and date "EGYPT, 1884," authorised for the Regimental Colour	164
1885	Lieut.-Col. Dunn assumed command	164
1886	Moved from Portsmouth to Aldershot	165
	Lieut. Brinckman appointed Adjutant	165
	The Establishment increased	165

Year.		Page.
1886	Large number of Recruits received	165
	Quarter-Master Watkins specially promoted to the rank of Honorary Captain	165
1887	Jubilee Review at Aldershot before H.M. the Queen	165
	Took part in a brigade "Flying Column"	166
	Colonel G. Cox assumed command *vice* Colonel J. Dunn, retired	166
	General Ferryman, C.B., appointed "Colonel" *vice* General Lambert deceased	166
	Rank of 2nd Lieutenant again created	166
1888	Moved from Aldershot to Dover	166
	Standing orders for the Regiment published	166

LIST OF PLATES.

	To face page
Uniform of the Regiment 1794	FRONTIS
Silhouette of Lieut.-Gen. Sir Charles Bulkeley Egerton, G.C.M.G., K.C.H.	91
Uniform of the Regiment 1854	111
The "Colours"	140
Uniform of the Regiment 1887	166

Uniform of the 89th Regt 1794.

Lt General Sir Charles Bulkeley Egerton. G.C.M.G. K.C.H.
Colonel of the 89th Regt 1837 to 1857.

Taken from a Silhouette drawn about 1845.

Uniform of the Regiment in 1854.

Queen's Colour

Colours of the 89th Regiment.
Presented by H.M. Queen Victoria, April 5th 1866.

Regimental Colour.

Colours of the 89th Regiment
Presented by H.M. Queen Victoria, April 5th 1866.

PRESENT UNIFORM, 1887.

HISTORICAL RECORD

OF THE

EIGHTY-NINTH REGIMENT OF FOOT,

CONTAINING AN ACCOUNT OF

THE FORMATION OF THE REGIMENT IN 1793,

AND OF

ITS SUBSEQUENT SERVICES.

THE

EIGHTY-NINTH REGIMENT OF FOOT

BEARS ON ITS COLOURS

"THE SPHINX."

"EGYPT."   "JAVA."

"NIAGARA."   "AVA."

"SEVASTOPOL."

HISTORICAL RECORD

OF THE

EIGHTY-NINTH REGIMENT OF FOOT.

THE Eighty-ninth Regiment was raised in Ireland, by Major-General William Crosbie in the year 1793, at the augmentation to the Army, consequent on the breaking out of the French Revolutionary War.

1793.
IRELAND.

The regiment was placed on the Establishment of the Army in the month of December the same year, and numbered "Eighty-nine." Its facings were black, those of the officers being velvet.

Early this year the regiment embarked for England under the command of Lieutenant-Colonel Charles Handfield, and landing at Bristol, marched to Southampton Camp. It was here the 89th Regiment first received the rudiments of discipline, and scarcely had the men learned their exercise, when the regiment was ordered (with the other corps encamped) to embark for the Continent, forming part of the Force of 7,000 men under the command of Major-General the Earl of Moira, destined to reinforce the Army under the Duke of York in Holland.

1794.
SOUTHAMPTON CAMP.

The expedition landed at Ostend on the 26th June, and, after a forced march conducted with great ability in the face of a superior enemy, His Lordship effected a junction with the Duke of York, at Malines, on the 9th July, having gallantly repulsed an attack made upon him by the French at Alost, on the 6th July.

HOLLAND.

1794. HOLLAND.	No general action occurred in the subsequent campaign, in which the British were forced to retire before an enemy greatly superior in numbers. It was a warfare of Posts, in which the 89th gallantly bore its part, especially at Boxtel, Tiet, and Schener. In the affair at Boxtel the regiment suffered very severely.

The memorable retreat through Holland in the winter of 1794, and the subsequent embarkation of the army for England, closed this unfortunate campaign.

There is no record to show the number of officers, non-commissioned officers and privates killed, wounded, or taken prisoners, on this expedition, but the casualties would appear to have been very great, as on the return of the regiment to England in the spring of 1795, it was reduced to a mere skeleton.

1795. WHITBURN CAMP.	The regiment landed at Sunderland in April 1795, and marched thence to Scarborough, and Whitby. The corps much reduced in numbers

was here recruited by drafts from the newly raised levies, and when completed, the regiment marched to Whitburn Camp near Sunderland, where the 87th, or* King's Own, were preparing to embark for the West Indies, and being very thin in numbers, received large drafts from the 89th Regiment. The staff with a few of the officers returned to Scarborough, and the remainder were dispersed over England and Ireland (principally the latter place) to recruit.

ARKLOW. WEXFORD.	Towards the end of the year, the regiment went over to Ireland, and had its head-quarters fixed at Arklow whence in a short time it removed to Wexford; here the corps had its numbers quickly completed by recruits and by volunteers from the English and Scotch Fencibles.

---

* The manuscript record gives "King's Own," but it is probably a mistake for "Prince's Own," which was then the title of the 87th Foot.

Lieutenant-Colonel William Stewart assumed command of the regiment at the time, and very shortly brought it to a high state of discipline, and efficiency.

1795.
WEXFORD.

On the appearance of the French Fleet at Bantry Bay, in December 1796, the 89th Regiment with other corps, marched in a most severe season to oppose the landing of their troops; the destruction of their fleet, however, prevented the necessity of further operations against them on this occasion.

The regiment was stationed this year at Loughlinstown Camp near Dublin, and at Clonmel.

1796.
LOUGHLINSTOWN.
CAMP.

The regiment occupied Fermoy where it encamped during the season.

1797.
FERMOY.

The rebellion in Ireland breaking out in this year the regiment proceeded to the county of Limerick (one of the disturbed districts) where it was dispersed in various detachments. In the course of the year the rebels having collected in great strength in the County of Wexford, a large force under the command of General Lake marched to oppose them. The 89th was one of the Corps employed on this service, and was present at the battle of "Vinegar Hill," where the rebels were defeated with immense loss. The regiment suffered but slightly in this affair.

After this defeat, which gave the death blow to the rebellion, the 89th was ordered by Lord Lake in pursuit of the rebel chief, and his remaining adherents, who had taken refuge among the wilds and fastnesses of the County of Wicklow, and were carrying on a guerrilla warfare in those mountainous districts. This was a most harassing and unpleasant service, and occupied some months, but it was successfully brought to a close, resulting in the surrender of the rebel chief and the dispersion of his forces.

1798.
COUNTY LIMERICK.

1799.

The regiment marched to Cork and embarked for foreign service on the 3rd January, 1799. The 30th Regiment embarked at the same time.

SICILY.

The force after touching at Gibraltar and Minorca, landed at Messina in Sicily on the 18th of March. The two Corps continued here the remainder of the year under the command of Colonel Graham, 90th Regiment.

1800.
MALTA.

In the beginning of this year the 89th and 30th Regiments proceeded to the blockade of La Valetta and its dependencies, at this time garrisoned by 5000 French troops. The two British Corps, a small detachment of Marines and Neapolitans, assisted by the natives, formed the Blockade, the whole under the command of Colonel Graham. The enemy did not venture on a sortie, and confined himself to an occasional cannonade, which did but little execution.

The French garrison being at length reduced to extremity, surrendered on the 4th September to General Pigott, who had in the meantime arrived with reinforcements.

On the arrival about this time of Lieutenant-General Sir Ralph Abercrombie with the army destined for Egypt, the 89th had the good fortune to be one of the few Corps selected by him to accompany the expedition.

1801.
EGYPT.

The expedition sailed from Malta on the 20th December 1800, but having been driven by stress of weather into the Bay of Mamorice, it was not until the 2nd March, 1801, that the fleet came to anchor in the Bay of Aboukir. The landing was gallantly effected on the 8th, and on the 9th the army advanced.

The 89th Regiment was stationed in the 2nd line in the Brigade commanded by Brigadier-General Doyle. On the morning of the 13th the French made a vigorous attack on the British during the march. The 89th were closely engaged during the day, and were exposed to a severe fire, particularly in the advance of General Doyle's Brigade on the bridge. The enemy were repulsed at all points, and driven with great loss to the entrenched camp before Alexandria.

1801.
EGYPT.

The loss the regiment sustained in this affair was comparatively small.

The British took up a position three miles in front of Alexandria.

On the morning of the 21st of March, before daybreak, the enemy attacked the British camp in great force, the grand effort was directed against the right flank of the army, which they repeatedly attempted to turn. After a sanguinary contest in which both sides displayed distinguished valour, victory declared for the British, clouded however by the loss of their gallant and lamented Commander-in-Chief.

There is no record to shew the loss of the regiment on this memorable day.

The 89th was now detached to Rosetta, where it crossed the Nile under the command of Lieutenant-Colonel Stewart, to co-operate with the army of the Grand Vizier.

On the 9th May, the army arrived in front of Rahamanie.

The 89th regiment, a party of Artillery, a detachment of Turks, and the gunboats which were placed under the command of Colonel Stewart, had received orders to move by the right bank of the Nile (the Delta) so as to keep at all times about 3 miles in advance of the army.

At daylight, a strong patrol of the French Cavalry were discovered on the opposite side of the river. The gunboats opened a smart fire upon them, and they left the river immediately.

The position of the enemy being seen, Colonel Stewart halted his force, just out of the reach of their guns; but the boats moved on and opened a brisk cannonade upon their batteries.

1801.
EGYPT.

The army now approaching, Colonel Stewart received orders to turn their right and protect the left flank of the army.

A large detachment of the enemy having crossed the river, seemed disposed to await the attack, but on the advance of the regiment, etc., they made a sudden rush for their boats, closely pursued to the bank of the river, and took shelter under the fire of their batteries, not distant more than 250 yards. They must have suffered very considerably; the 89th had 8 men killed and 11 wounded. The Artillery, Turks and gunboats likewise suffered some loss.

After a cannonade of some continuance, the enemy's fire ceased, as their position was completely turned, though our force was separated from them by the river. The enemy retreated towards Cairo during the night.

On the 14th May, at daylight, a large convoy of boats, &c., which came down the Nile from Cairo, and had unintentionally passed the French Army during its retreat, were captured by the 89th Regiment, &c., they made a sharp resistance for a short time.

In the beginning of June, the 30th Regiment joined Colonel Stewart's force, on the famous canal of Minsuf, and at the latter end of June, all the troops in the Delta joined the army of the grand Vizier, about 30 miles from Cairo. On the position being occupied before Cairo by the English and Turkish Armies, a bridge of boats was established to secure a communication between them. The 30th and 89th Regiments were particularly charged with the care of it, as apprehensions were entertained, that the enemy then occupying Cairo would make strenuous efforts to destroy it.

The capitulation followed.

On the surrender of the French at Cairo, the 89th took possession of the Citadel, which it occupied until the return of the British Army to

PRINCESS VICTORIA'S REGIMENT.

the camp before Alexandria, which took place on the 4th September, 1801.   1801. EGYPT.

On the embarkation of the army, the 89th was one of the corps placed under the command of Major-General Cradock, destined against Corfu. At sea, the expedition was countermanded, and directed to proceed to Malta, and thence to Gibraltar, there to await orders from England.

Peace being now proclaimed, the 89th Regiment was ordered to Ireland, and landed in the Cove of Cork on the 28th January, 1802.   1802. IRELAND.

The regiment was first stationed at Youghall, where it was reduced to the Peace establishment. From this station the regiment marched to Enniskillen, and remained there till the end of the year. At this period, Lieutenant-Colonel Lord Blayney* assumed the command of the regiment on the retirement of Lieutenant-Colonel Stewart, an officer under whose care the 89th had become a pattern to the service.   ENNISKILLEN.

The regiment occupied Athlone and Loughrea.   1803. ATHLONE.
At Loughrea, a 2nd battalion was added to the regiment.

The regiment occupied Doneraile and Cork.   1804. DONERAILE.
On the 13th July, the regiment embarked at the Cove of Cork for the West Indies, but received counter orders, re-landed and marched to Kinsale.

---

* It was from this officer that the regiment obtained the soubriquet of "*Lord Blayney's Bloodhounds,*" a name by which it is still well known. Though very little mention is made of Lord Blayney in the records, it is evident that he must have made himself well known, and have thoroughly identified himself with the regiment. He joined the 89th as a Major on its formation in 1793, served with it throughout the Campaigns in Holland and Egypt, and obtained the command in 1802. Although he did not finally leave the regiment until 1814, yet he handed over the command to the next senior officer, Colonel Garden, in 1809; the reason of this being, that in all probability he was given some appointment or command, as early in 1810 he was promoted Major-General in the army.

1805.
KINSALE.

The regiment this year again embarked for foreign service, and arriving in the Downs, joined an expedition under the command of Lord Cathcart, intended for the Continent.

The expedition sailed for the Weser on the 7th December, but encountering a violent storm was forced back with the loss of several ships. Unfortunately the head-quarter ship of the 89th was one of the number, being wrecked on the coast of Holland on the night of 13th December; many lives were lost on this disastrous occasion, together with the colours, band, mess plate, and regimental books and papers. Those who were so fortunate as to escape with their lives, were made prisoners by the Dutch.

1806.
HOLLAND.

The remainder of the regiment proceeded to the Weser, where the expedition landed on the 5th January, 1806, and went into cantonment.

The army remained here about a month, when it was suddenly embarked at two hours' notice for England.

MARGATE.

The regiment landed at Ramsgate, and proceeded to Margate. The officers and men made prisoners on the coast of Holland having been exchanged, rejoined at this station.

OSPRINGE.

The regiment moved to Ospringe on the 2nd April, and while there was reviewed by the Duke of York, meeting with His Royal Highness' entire approbation. At this station the regiment received new colours.

PORTSMOUTH.

The 89th embarked at Ramsgate on the 14th September for South America, but opthalmia breaking out with great violence on board ship, the regiment was landed at Portsmouth, and sent to Cumberland Fort for recovery, whence it removed to Gosport.

1807.
SOUTH AMERICA.

The opthalmia being entirely subdued, the regiment embarked once more for South America on the 23rd February, 1807, commanded by

Colonel Lord Blayney, to join the force under Lieutenant-General Whitelock, destined against Buenos Ayres.

1807.
SOUTH AMERICA.

After a tedious voyage of five months, the regiment arrived at Monte Video. In the interim, the failure at Buenos Ayres had taken place, and the army was then preparing to evacuate the country. In the general distribution, the 89th was directed to proceed to the Cape, and arrived there in the month of October.

THE CAPE.

On the 27th September, 1808, the 89th regiment embarked at Cape Town under the command of Major Hilliard for Ceylon, and arrived at Trincomalee on the 12th December, where it was landed and remained for ten weeks; it then embarked for Colombo.

1808.
CEYLON.

The regiment arrived at Colombo on the 11th March. Colonel Garden took command of the 89th while at this station.

1809.
CEYLON.

On the 19th April, a detachment under the command of Captain Hall was sent to Point-de-Galle, and then to Trincomalee, to relieve the 66th Regiment, ordered to the coast. This detachment rejoined head-quarters at Madras on the 19th March, 1810.

On the breaking out of the mutiny in the Madras Army during this year, a detachment of 300 men of the 89th regiment under command of Major McBean, suddenly embarked for Madras, where it arrived on the 5th of August, and immediately took the field, under the command of Colonel Conran, (Royals). After some severe marches in which the detachment visited Gooby, and Bangalore, it returned to Fort St. George, Madras, on the 23rd March, 1810.

In December, 1809, the seven remaining companies of the 89th, and head-quarters, under the command of Lieutenant-Colonel Garden, embarked at Colombo for Travancore, and marched across the Peninsula to Madras.

c 2

1810.
MADRAS.

By the 20th April, 1810, the entire regiment was assembled at Fort St. George, Madras.

On the 17th September, a detachment of 300 rank and file, under the command of Major Butler, sailed with the expedition under the command of Major-General the Honourable John Abercrombie against the Isle of France.

This service happily concluded, the detachment having received the thanks of the Commander-in-Chief, returned to Madras on the 15th March, 1811. The regiment during the latter part of this year, was commanded by Lieutenant-Colonel McBean.

1811.
JAVA.

In February, 1811, a detachment of the regiment, 200 strong, embarked at Madras, under the command of Captain Oakes, and proceeded to the coast of Java, where it was actively employed. On the 5th of June, part of the detachment, with two companies of the 14th Regiment, and some marines, repelled an attack of about 1,800 of the enemy, who attempted to cut off a party left on shore near the town of Bantam, to secure water, and to keep up communications with the natives, who were friendly. The enemy left on the ground 5 officers and 49 men killed, the number of their wounded could not be ascertained.

In July, one of the companies of the 89th Regiment, with the detachment 14th Regiment, were landed against a blockhouse with a battery of 12 guns, which surrendered at discretion. On the 1st August, the same party assisted at the capture of six large gunboats.

On the 4th August, the expedition under Sir Samuel Achmuty, arrived from Madras, and with it three more companies of the 89th Regiment under Major Butler, who took command of the 5 companies of the regiment now united.

The detachment 89th Regiment, under Major Butler, was formed by the Commander-in-Chief,

PRINCESS VICTORIA'S REGIMENT

into a Rifle Battalion. They were clothed in "*green*," and placed in advance of the army, under the command of Major-General Gillespie.

On the 10th August, near Weltervreeden, while leading the advance, the detachment forced and drove in the enemy from a very strong position, and captured 4 of their guns. The loss of the detachment in this affair amounted to 8 men killed, 3 officers and 36 rank and file wounded, the loss of the French was very great.

The detachment also bore a distinguished part in the capture of Fort Cornelius by storm, losing on that occasion only 4 men killed, 5 officers, 3 sergeants, one drummer, and 22 rank and file wounded.

Shortly after, this detachment was ordered up the country to Bintenzorg, with the Cavalry, and part of the Horse Artillery.

The head-quarters of the regiment were this year under command of Lieutenant-Colonel McBean and Captain St. Leger.

1811.
JAVA.

In March 1812 the 5 companies now under command of Major French, left Batavia with an expedition commanded by Major-General Gillespie, against Palembang on the Coast of Sumatra, where a Dutch Garrison had been massacred by the Sultan, who fled from his capital on the approach of the force sent against him.

In July the detachment returned to Batavia, and in September embarked for Madras, where they arrived in October, and rejoined head-quarters.

The following Government and General Orders bear most gratifying testimony, as well to the gallantry of this detachment before the enemy, as to their exemplary and soldier-like conduct on all occasions :—

1812.
SUMATRA.

MADRAS.

General Orders by His Excellency Lieutenant-

1812.
MADRAS.

General Sir Samuel Achmuty, Commander-in-Chief:—

> "*Head-quarters, Choultry Plain,*
> "10*th October*, 1812.

"The return of the detachment of H.M.'s 89th "Regiment from Java, affords His Excellency the "Commander-in-Chief, an opportunity which he "gladly embraces of assuring them that their "conduct since their separation from the head-"quarters of the regiment, has been highly "creditable to themselves as soldiers, has con-"ferred honour on that excellent and distin-"guished corps of which they form a part, and "holds out to the Army at large an example of "zeal, gallantry, and subordination that has "never been surpassed.

"The behaviour of the detachment under "Major Butler during the operations which "ended in the capture of Java, though eminently "conspicuous, has been *already* noticed, and the "Commander-in-Chief should not have thought "it necessary to repeat his thanks for their "services on that occasion. The detachment of "H.M.'s 22nd Dragoons, the 69th Regiment, "and the detachment of Pioneers on their return "to the coast, would equally with them require "his warm and grateful acknowledgements. It "is their uniform good behaviour in several "trying situations since that event, when com-"manded by Major French, that now induces "His Excellency to notice them in this public "manner, and to direct that the General Orders "by the Lieutenant-Governor of Java and by "Major-General Gillespie commanding the forces, "on the occasion of their departure from that "Island, may be published to the Army under "this Presidency."

General Order by the Honorable The Lieu-tenant-Governor of Java in Council:—

"*Batavia, 15th August,* 1812.

1812.
MADRAS.

" On the departure of the detachment of H.M.'s 89th Regiment, the Lieutenant-Governor in Council has much satisfaction in bearing testimony to the high sense which he entertains of the meritorious services of that distinguished corps, and although its gallantry has been already most honourably recorded on the memorable conquest of the Island, the Lieutenant-Governor considers it still incumbent on him to communicate to the Supreme Government of Fort St. George, the sentiments of approbation entertained by this Government, and his satisfaction at the honourable, and successful termination of the service on which the detachment was ordered from the latter Presidency.

"By order of the Honourable the Lieutenant-Governor in Council.

"(Signed)   T. O. TRAVERS,
     "*Asst. Sec. to the Gov. Milty. Dept.*"

General Order by Major-General Gillespie, Commander of the Forces in Java:—

"*Weltervreeden, 21st August,* 1812.

"The detachment of His Majesty's 89th Regiment, under the command of Major French, being on the eve of embarkation to join the head-quarters of their corps at Madras, the commander of the forces cannot permit their departure without marking his regret at losing the service of a body of men, who have on all occasions so eminently distinguished themselves.

"Boldness, conspicuous prompt and ardent desire to meet the enemy when an opportunity offered, have marked the character of this detachment since it first trod on the shores of Java under the command of Major Butler.

"His Excellency Sir Samuel Achmuty placed them in the advance of the army under the com-

1812.
MADRAS.

"mand of Colonel Gillespie and during the late service marked their gallantry. Having such dignified and high authority to support him, Major-General Gillespie can with more confidence contribute his humble mite of applause, and on the present occasion has the satisfaction to express to Major French, the officers, non-commissioned officers, and privates, his grateful sense of their former as well as subsequent soldier-like conduct.

"Praise is often unthinkingly lavished when it is perhaps not strictly deserved. On the present occasion it is distinctly, pure and deservedly, a tribute to a corps, from an officer who has so often seen it face death with intrepidity and cheerfulness, and to maintain the honor of their beloved King and Country at the point of the bayonet."

In commemoration of the distinguished services of the wing of the 89th Regiment as above detailed, in the capture of Java on the 10th September, 1811, and subsequent operations, His Royal Highness the Prince Regent was pleased to command that the word "JAVA" should be borne on the colours and appointments of the regiment.—Authority dated 24th June, 1818.

The regiment was commanded during this year by Major Hall, and Lieutenant-Colonel Sewell.

POONAMALLEE.

On the detachment from Java joining headquarters, the regiment received orders to march to Poonamallee, and left Fort St. George on the 12th October.

1813.
MADRAS.

On the 4th January this year the regiment was ordered to return to Fort St. George, Madras.

The Earl of Moira, Governor-General and Commander-in-Chief of India, having touched at Madras in September, reviewed the troops in the garrison and his recognition of the regiment in the General Order issued on the occasion, and allusion to their services in 1794, under his

Lordship's Command in Holland, could not fail to be gratifying to the corps.

1813
MADRAS.

"*Head-quarters, Madras,*
"16*th September,* 1813.

"The veteran and truly military air of H.M.'s "89th Regiment, was peculiarly pleasing to Lord "Moira, who cannot forget that he had the "happiness of witnessing the earliest pledge of "that zeal and intrepidity which have always "distinguished the regiment.

"(Signed) T. H. CONWAY,
"*Adjutant-General of the Army.*"

On the 7th March, 1814, the regiment marched out of Fort St. George under command of Major Hall, *en route* to Bangalore, and arrived there on the 30th March.

1814.
BANGALORE.

The regiment remained at Bangalore until the 13th May, 1815, when orders were received to proceed to Cannanore, where it arrived on the 3rd of June under the command of Major French.

1815.
CANNANORE.

The 89th Regiment continued to occupy Cannanore until the 5th October, when the regiment marched for Quilon under the command of Major Hall, and arrived there on the 6th of November.

1816.
QUILON.

In the middle of November, 1816, the 2nd Battalion of the 89th Regiment was disbanded.

At this point, it will therefore be proper to return some few years in the Record, in order to recount the history of that portion of the regiment, and it will be found that while the 1st Battalion was reaping laurels in the East, their brethren of the 2nd Battalion were rendering in the "Far West" equally effective and distinguished service against the enemies of their King and Country, and were in no wise inferior to them in daring deeds, in discipline, endurance, or any other quality of good and gallant soldiers.

SERVICES OF THE 2nd BATTALION 89th REGIMENT.

1803.	At the rupture of the peace of Amiens in 1803, when Napoleon was meditating the invasion of England, and great additions were in consequence made to the army, a 2nd Battalion was added to the 89th Regiment.
	There are no records in possession of the regiment connected with the history of the 2nd Battalion of earlier date than 1812. Up to that time they were principally employed on home service.
1812. NORTH AMERICA (HALIFAX.)	In August, 1812, when the United States of America declared War against Britain the 2nd Battalion of the 89th Regiment was embarked at Portsmouth under the command of Colonel Morrison, for North America, and arrived at Halifax on the 13th of October.
1813. QUEBEC.	Having remained in garrison at Halifax until the spring was sufficiently advanced to render navigation open, the battalion embarked on the 19th of May for Quebec, and arrived there on 5th of June.
CANADA.	The regiment was immediately landed, and without loss of time was pushed on to the Upper Province, then the scene of hostilities. The battalion marched in two divisions on the 7th June, and reached Kingston, in Upper Canada, a distance of about 400 miles in nineteen days.

PRINCESS VICTORIA'S REGIMENT.

On the arrival of the 2nd Battalion at Kingston, the Light Company was attached to a demi Brigade of Light Infantry, and soon after marched to the Frontiers higher up the province to join the army in the field under the command of Major-General De Rottenberg, at that time encamped near the Fort George, where the enemy had retired after his defeat by Brigadier-General Vincent at Stoney Creek.

1813.
CANADA.

On the 24th August a demonstration was made upon the enemy, and the Light Company was warmly engaged, unfortunately losing their captain and 3 rank and file killed, and 5 rank and file wounded. The enemy's outposts were driven in with great precipitation and loss of about 60 men.

Killed:
Captain Annesley.

The Commander-in-Chief, Sir George Provost, was pleased to express his admiration of the conduct of the company on this occasion in General Orders.

The head-quarters and remaining companies 2nd Battalion 89th, continued to garrison Kingston, upon which place it was expected an attack would be made by a strong force the enemy had collected at Tacketts Harbour, commanded by General Wilkinson, supported by a powerful squadron on Lake Ontario under Commodore Chauncey.

The enemy having completed his arrangements, rendezvoused his forces at Grenadier Island, and being joined there by a division from Fort George, the expedition in all 6,000 strong and well equipped, set forward about the 1st November to make another desperate effort for the conquest of Canada. Kingston, however, proved not to be the point of attack. Making a feint only upon that place, the enemy's flotilla dropped down the St. Lawrence with the view of attacking Montreal, and cutting off the communication between the Upper and Lower Province, in which event the former must of necessity have

1813.
CANADA.

fallen, all their supplies being drawn from Lower Canada. Montreal was at this time without defences, and without a garrison of regular troops, indeed there appeared to be nothing to arrest the progress of the invader, and the general alarm was proportionate.

A second American Corps under General Hampton, of about 5,000 men, was also on its march from Lake Champlain, intended to form a junction with General Wilkinson's army before Montreal.

On the 7th of November, a small force consisting of the 2nd Battalion of the 89th (with the exception of the light company already brigaded), eight companies of the 49th (both regiments very weak in numbers) and two 6 pounders, the whole under the command of Lieutenant-Colonel Morrison 89th Regiment, was detached from the garrison of Kingston to act as a corps of observation, and if possible to harass the rear of General Wilkinson's army.

The troops embarked on board the "Beresford" and "Sir Sidney Smith" schooners, together with some gun boats, and batteaux; the flotilla being commanded by Captain Mulcaster, R.N. In defiance of the American covering squadron, that officer proceeded with his convoy down the river to Fort Wellington. Colonel Morrison here received a reinforcement to his division, of the remainder of the 49th Regiment, and some Militia, together with another 6 pounder.

The schooners drawing too much water, the troops were transferred to batteaux, and again advanced without delay. On the 9th the force was landed at Point Troquois, on the Canadian side of the St. Lawrence, and after an extraordinary rapid march, and some skirmishing on the 9th and 10th, came up with a division of the enemy at Christler's Farm on the morning of the 11th.

The enemy's forces consisted of two brigades of infantry, and a regiment of cavalry, amounting to between 3,000 and 4,000 men, supported by six field pieces, the whole under the command of Major-General Boyd.

Lieutenant-Colonel Morrison's corps did not exceed 800 in all. The situation was critical with so great a disproportion in numbers, and the almost impossibility of retreat in case of failure; but that officer proved equal to the emergency, and having selected his ground, and made the best disposition his little band would admit of, he awaited the enemy's attack.

The course of the action is fully detailed in Colonel Morrison's despatch, as well as the distinguished part borne in it by the 2nd Battalion 89th Regiment.

" So steady was the firing, and so prompt and "regular the movements of Colonel Morrison's "little corps, that on their part it resembled a "field day rather than a destructive battle. Their "opponents although threefold in number fell "before them."—*Vide James' American War.*

The results which followed this brilliant victory were of the very highest importance. The enemy embarked his troops that evening and proceeded down the river, and on the night of the 12th encamped near Cornwall. With the first daylight on the morning of the 12th, Colonel Morrison with his victorious troops, now reduced to about 620 rank and file continued their march down the river, but were not again afforded the opportunity of closing with the enemy, as General Wilkinson on the 13th crossed his whole force to the American side, taking up a position at French Mills, on the Salmon River, where he proceeded to entrench himself and place his army in winter quarters, abandoning altogether the attack on Montreal and other objects, for which the expedition was with enormous pains and expense fitted out.

1813.

CANADA.

Killed:
1 Drummer, 4 Rank and File.

Wounded:
Captain Browne,
Ensign Leader,
3 Sergeants, 57 Rank and File.

Received Medals:
Lieut.-Col. Morrison,
Major Clifford.

1813.
CANADA.

The feeling at Montreal, and indeed throughout the Canadas, on the receipt of this intelligence, was enthusiastic towards the troops engaged; the thanks of the house of Assembly was voted to them, and the *2nd Battalion 89th Regiment* which bore so conspicious a part in the honors of the day, was held high in the estimation of the public, military, naval and civil.

Lieutenant-Colonel Morrison now occupied Cornwall where the 89th remained some months.

"*Kingston, November 14th,* 1813.

"DISTRICT GENERAL ORDERS.

"His Honor Major-General De Rottenburg has "received the following despatch from Lieutenant-"Colonel Morrison, commanding a detachment "of the centre division, following up the American "Army commanded by General Wilkinson, while "moving down the St. Lawrence for the avowed "purpose of invading Lower Canada.

"The Major-General feels the highest satisfac-"tion in announcing this glorious event to the "troops in Upper Canada.

"The greatest praise is due to Lieutenant-"Colonel Morrison for his gallant conduct, and "judicious dispositions, as well as to those dis-"tinguished Officers, Lieutenant-Colonel Harvey, "Deputy Adjutant-General, Lieutenant-Colonel "Pearson, Lieutenant-Colonel Plenderleath, "49th Regiment, Majors Clifford, 89th Regiment, "and Harriot, Canadian Voltigeurs, as well as to "every other Officer, and to the non-commissioned "Officers and Soldiers engaged in this brilliant "affair, to whose gallant and distinguished "exertions against a force immensely superior, "the successful issue of this severe contest is to "be attributed. They have betrayed the true "spirits of British soldiers, which can never fail "of asserting its superiority over the enemy "whenever he has the temerity to risk a trial."

"*Christlers, Williamsburg,*
            "*Upper Canada, Nov. 12th,* 1813.
"SIR,

1813.
CANADA.

"I have the heartfelt gratification to report "the brilliant and gallant conduct of the detach- "ment of the centre division of the army, as "yesterday displayed in repulsing and defeating "a division of the enemy's force, consisting of two "brigades of infantry and a regiment of cavalry, "amounting to between three and four thousand "men, who moved forward about two o'clock in "the afternoon from Christlers Point, and attacked "our advance, which gradually fell back to the "position selected for the detachment to occupy; "the right resting on the river, and the left on a "pine-wood exhibiting a front of about 700 yards. "The ground being open, the troops were thus "disposed; the flank companies of the 49th "Regiment, the detachment of the Canadian "Fencibles with one field piece, under Lieutenant- "Colonel Pearson, on the right, a little advanced "on the road; three companies of the 89th "Regiment under Captain Barnes with a gun, "formed echelon with the advance on its left "supporting it; the 49th and 89th thrown more "to the rear with a gun, formed the main body "and reserve, extending to the woods on the left "which were occupied by the Voltigeurs under "Major Harriot, and the Indians under Lieutenant "Anderson. At about half past two the "action became general, when the enemy "endeavoured by moving forward a brigade from "his right, to turn our left, but was repulsed by "the 89th forming en-potence with the 49th, and "both corps moving forward occasionally, "firing by platoons. His efforts were now directed "against our right, and to repulse this movement "the 49th took ground in that direction in echelon "followed by the 89th; when within half musket "shot the line formed under a heavy but irregular "fire from the enemy. The 49th were then

1813.
CANADA.

"directed to charge the gun posted opposite to "ours, but it became necessary when within a "short distance of it to check the forward move- "ment in consequence of a charge from their "cavalry on the right, lest they should wheel "about and fall upon the rear; but they were re- "ceived so gallantly by the companies of the 89th "under Captain Barnes, and the well directed fire "of the artillery, that they quickly retreated, and "by an immediate charge from those companies, "one gun was gained ; the enemy immediately "concentrated their force to check our advance, "but such was the steady countenance and well "directed fire of the troops and artillery, that at "about half past four they gave way at all points "from an exceeding strong position, endeavouring "by their light cavalry to cover their retreat, "these were soon driven away by a judicious "movement made by Lieutenant-Colonel Pearson. "The detachment for the night occupied the "ground from which the enemy had been driven "and are now moving forward in pursuit.

"I regret to find our loss in killed and "wounded has been so considerable, but I hope a "most essential service has been rendered to the "country, as the whole of the enemy's infantry "after the action precipitately retired to their "own shores. It is now my grateful duty to "point out to your Honor the benefit the "service has received from the ability, judge- "ment, and active exertions of Lieutenant- "Colonel Harvey the Deputy Adjutant-General, "for sparing whom to accompany the detach- "ment I must again publicly express my "acknowledgements. To the cordial co-operation "and exertions of Lieutenant-Colonel Pearson "commanding the detachment from Prescott, "Lieutentant-Colonel Plenderleath of the 49th, "Major Clifford 89th, Major Harriott of the "Voltigeurs, and Captain Jackson of the Royal "Artillery, combined with the gallantry of the "troops our great success may be attributed.

"*Every man did his duty*, and I believe I cannot more strongly speak their merits than in mentioning that our small force did not exceed 800 rank and file. To Captains Daines and Skinner of the Quarter-Master-General's Department, I am under the greatest obligations for the assistance I have received from them, their zeal and activity has been unremitting; Lieutenant Hagerman of the Militia has also for his services deserved my public acknowledgement, as has also Lieutenant Anderson of the Indian Department. As the prisoners are hourly being brought in, I am unable to furnish your Honor with a correct return of them, but upwards of 100 are in our possession, neither of the ordnance stores taken, as the whole have not yet been collected.

1813.
CANADA.

"(Signed) I. W. MORRISON,
"*Lieutenant-Colonel, 89th,*
"*Commanding Corps of Observation.*

"To
"Major-General De Rottenburg,
"&c. &c. &c."

At a subsequent period the following letter was written to Colonel Sir George Beckwith to obtain his Majesty's permission for the regiment to bear the words "Christlers" on the colours of the regiment:—

"*Quilon in Travancore,*
"*July 8th,* 1819.

"SIR,
"In submitting the enclosed copies of general orders and despatches for your consideration, I

1813.
CANADA.

"am induced on the part of the regiment I have
"the honor to command, to solicit your exertions
"and support to have them laid before the Prince
"Regent, with the view that the 89th Regiment
"may be permitted to bear on their colours and
"appointments, the word "CHRISTLERS" in com-
"memoration of the distinguished valor of
"conduct, displayed by the late 2nd Battalion of
"the Corps on the 11th November, 1813, when a
"large force of the American Army was repulsed
"and defeated. in their moving down the river
"St. Lawrence to invade Lower Canada; on this
"occasion the officer who commanded the small
"British force (Lieutenant-Colonel Morrison) and
"the officers in command of the 49th and 89th
"Regiments received medals for their conduct.
"This small force had also the thanks of the
"House of Assembly at Quebec voted and pre-
"sented to them for this service; the result of
"the action, considered brilliant in itself from
"the very great and extraordinary disparity of
"the two opposing forces and though composed
"of so very small a British force, was allowed to
"be important in its consequences at the moment,
"and frustrated the object of an expedition formed
"by the enemy with every prospect of success on
"their part, from the time, expense and zeal with
"which they equipped it.

"On this occasion it is necessary to explain why
"the application for the honorary distinction was
"not made before by the commander of the forces
"in America. The circumstance of Sir George
"Provost's return to England before the con-
"clusion of the war, and the occupation of his
"time and mind in preparing for a general court-
"martial, prevented his making it at that time,
"but he declared that as soon as the court-
"martial was over he would not fail to bring the
"conduct of the 2nd battalion 89th Regiment
"before the notice of the Prince Regent, for the
"honorary badge now solicited, and which, if

"obtained will prove most gratifying to the corps.

"I have the honor to be,
"(Signed) W. H. RAINSFORD,
"*Lieutenant-Colonel,*
"*Commanding 89th Regiment.*

"To
"Sir George Beckwith, G.C.B.,
"&c.,   &c.,
"Of H.M.'s 89th Regiment."

The annexed reply from the Adjutant-General, Horse Guards, will show the request made could not be complied with:—

"*Horse Guards,*
"*War Office,*
"*25th July,* 1820.

"SIR,
"I have had the honor to lay before the Commander-in-Chief your Excellency's letter of the 19th inst. with its enclosures, and have it in command to observe in reply, that His Royal Highness is perfectly sensible of the services of the late 2nd battalion 89th Regiment in Canada, which were very meritorious and such as might have been expected from the battalion, but as it did not happen to be the fortune of the battalion to be engaged in the description of actions, for which it has been usual to grant honorary distinction, His Royal Highness does not feel that he can consistently with the principles hitherto acted upon, recommend the request of the 89th Regiment to the favorable consideration of the Prince Regent.

"The Commander-in-Chief would at the same time regret if this decision should be thought in any degree to countenance the conclusion, that the action in which the 2nd battalion 89th Regiment bore a share in Canada, was under-

1813.
CANADA.

1813.
CANADA.

"valued, because it happened to be of a less splendid character than others that occurred under different circumstances, and His Royal Highness would still further and more deeply regret, if ever the idea should go abroad or prevail in the army, that the gallantry of a regiment could be in any degree questionable, or its situation be considered irksome, because the fate of war had not afforded it equal opportunities of acquiring distinctions, and obtaining those Insignia of merit, which other more fortunate, but perhaps not more deserving corps, have become entitled to.

"I have the honor, &c.,
"(Signed) H. CALVERT,
"*Adjutant-General.*

"To
"General Sir G. Beckwith, G.C.B.,
"Colonel of 89th Regiment."

Promoted to Brevet Majority:
Captain Basden.

Killed:
3 rank and file.

Wounded:
5 rank and file.

On the 30th of December, the Light Company (which had remained on the Niagara Frontier) proceeded with a force sent under Major-General Riall, to seize upon the fortifications at Blackrock, in the town of Buffalo. On this occasion they formed the advance, and were so fortunate as to surprise the whole of the enemy's picquets, and to make them prisoners; following up their success they stormed and carried a battery of 5 guns, killing or making prisoners every soul who defended it, among the latter was an Aide-de-Camp of the American General.

Two of the guns (6 pounders) taken on this occasion were afterwards called "the 89th guns" in compliment to the company, and the Commander-in-Chief was pleased again to thank the company in public orders.

Extracts from despatch of Major-General Riall to Lieutenant-General Drummond:—

" Niagara Frontier, near   1814.
           " Fort Erie,   CANADA.
        " 1st January, 1814.

" The troops completed their landing about " 12 o'clock, nearly 2 miles below Blackrock.

" The Light Infantry of the 89th in advance " surprised and captured the greater part of a " picquet of the enemy, and secured the bridge " over the Conguichity Creek, the boards of which " had been loosened, and were ready to be carried " off had time been given for it. * * * *

" At daybreak I moved forward, the King's " Regiment and Light Infantry of the 89th " leading ; the 41st and Grenadiers of the 100th " Regiment being in the reserve. * * * *
" * * The King's and 89th having in the mean- " time gained the town, commenced a very " spirited attack upon the enemy who were in " great force and very strongly posted. * * *

" The enemy maintained his position with very " considerable obstinacy for some time, but such " was the spirited and determined advance of " our troops, he was at last compelled to give " way. * * * * * * * * * *

" In obedience to your further instructions " I have directed Lieutenant-Colonel Gordon to " move down the river to Fort Niagara with a " party of the 19th Light Dragoons, under Major " Lisle, a detachment of the Royal Scots, and " the 89th Light Company, and destroy the " remaining cover of the enemy upon the frontier, " which he has reported to have effectually " done. * * * * * * * * *

" I have great satisfaction in stating to you " the good conduct of the whole of the Regular " Troops and Volunteer Militia, but I must " particularly mention the steadiness and bravery " of the Kings' Regiment and 89th Light " Infantry. * * * Captain Basden of the " 89th, and Captain Brunter of the King's Light

1814.
CANADA.

" Infantry Companies, conducted themselves in
" a most exemplary manner. * * * * *

"(Signed) P. RIALL,
"*Major-General.*"

In the beginning of February, Major-General Wilkinson broke up his cantonments at French Mills, and having burned 300 river craft, 12 gun boats, and all his huts, blockhouses, &c., commenced a retreat upon Plattsburg. Colonel Scott of the 103rd Regiment with a small force, of which the 89th Regiment gave a portion, on hearing this intelligence, crossed the ice from Cornwall, and arrived on the Salmon river in time to press upon Colonel Wilkinson's rear guard, and capture 100 sleigh loads of stores and provisions.

Having extended his patrol to within a few miles of Plattsburg, without encountering further opposition, he returned to Cornwall.

The 89th now returned to Kingston, Upper Canada, and shortly afterwards moved on to York.

During the month of February, the Light Company of the 89th was detached (together with the two flank companies of the Royal Scots) to the village of Delaware on the river Thames, for the purpose of repelling the continued aggressions made by the American Garrison of Detroit, upon the hitherto defenceless shores of Lake Erie, and on the 4th of March was engaged in a very severe affair with a strong patrol of the enemy, who had taken up a commanding position in the "Longwood" and strongly entrenched themselves behind a breast-work of fallen trees. The detachment gallantly led by Captain Basden, crossed a deep ravine and dashed up the opposite height to within a few yards of the log entrenchment; but so securely was the enemy posted, and with such deadly effect did his fire tell upon our troops, that no

Killed:
Lieutenant Graeme.
18 rank and file.

Wounded:
Captain Basden,
severely.
29 rank and file.

impression could be made, until after repeated efforts the enemy at length abandoned his position, and retreated with but little loss to Detroit.

1814.
CANADA.

The Commander-in-Chief published his thanks in General Orders, and complimented the company highly on their conspicuous gallantry, regretting the severe loss sustained in brave officers and men.

After some months hard marching, the Light Company was ordered to rejoin the battalion at York.

The enemy was now preparing to make another strenuous attempt upon Upper Canada, and on the 3rd of July a force 5,000 strong under Major-General Brown, crossed the Niagara and seized Fort Erie, and a few days later worsted Major-General Riall's division at Streets Creek.

In consequence of this intelligence Lieutenant-General Drummond hastened to the scene of action from York, taking with him the 89th and other troops.

The battalion embarked at York on the 24th of July, and was conveyed across the lake with all despatch to Fort George, where they arrived at daylight on the 25th, and were disembarked and marched immediately to Queenstown.

After a short halt there they were hastened forward in the direction of Niagara, near which place the enemy was posted in most imposing force.

The enemy was met at Lundy's Lane and an action commenced at 6 o'clock the same evening, and continued with little intermission until 10 o'clock next morning, when the enemy retired with precipitation to Fort Erie, having thrown the greater portion of his baggage and stores into the rapids.

As the public despatch affords the best information as to the share which the battalion had in this glorious action, that and the other public documents connected with it are given.

1814.
CANADA.

His Majesty was most graciously pleased to order that the 89th Regiment should bear the word "NIAGARA" on its colours and appointments, in commemoration of the distinguished conduct of the 2nd battalion on that trying occasion.

The remains of the 2nd battalion now reduced to a skeleton, were after the action sent to form the garrison of Fort George and Mississaga (the fresh troops at those posts being moved up to the field), with the exception of the Light Company, which remained with General Drummond's force now proceeding to invest Fort Erie.

From Lieutenant-General Sir George Provost, to Earl Bathurst, Secretary of State :—

"*Head-quarters,*
"*Montreal,*
"*5th August,* 1814.

" I have the satisfaction of transmitting to your
" Lordship Lieutenant-General Drummond's
" detail of the distinguished exertions of that
" division of the army near the falls of Niagara
" on the 25th of last month, when the skill of His
" Majesty's General, and valor and discipline of
" his troops, were eminently conspicuous, and I
" beg leave to join the Lieutenant-General in
" humbly soliciting His Royal Highness the Prince
" Regent's gracious consideration of the meritori-
" ous services of the officers particularized in this
" report.

" This despatch will be delivered to your Lord-
" ship by Captain Jervoise, Aide-de-Camp to
" Lieutenant-General Drummond. Having shared
" in the events of the 25th, he can satisfy your
" Lordship's enquiries respecting them, and is well
" calculated from his local knowledge to give your
" Lordship full information upon the state of the
" upper Province."

From Lieutenant-General Drummond, to Sir George Provost:—

1814.
CANADA.

> "*Head-quarters,*
> "*Niagara Falls,*
> "*July 27th,* 1814.

"SIR,

"I embarked on board His Majesty's schooner, "Netley," at York on Sunday evening the 24th inst., and reached Niagara at day-break the following morning. Finding from Lieutenant-Colonel Tucker, that Major-General Riall was understood to be moving towards the Falls of Niagara to support the advance of his division, which he had pushed on to that place the preceding evening, I ordered Lieutenant-Colonel Morrison with the 89th Regiment, and a detachment of the Royals and Kings, drawn from Fort George and Mississaga, to proceed to the same place, in order that with the united force I might act against the enemy (posted in Streets Creek with his advance at Chippeway) on my arrival, if it should be found expedient. I ordered Lieutenant-Colonel Tucker at the same time to proceed up the right bank of the river, with 300 of the 41st, about 200 of the Royal Scots, and a body of Indian Warriors, supported (on the river) by a party of armed seamen; the object of this movement was to disperse, or capture a body of the enemy encamped at Lewiston. Some unavoidable delay having occurred in the march of the troops up the right bank, the enemy had moved off previous to Lieutenant-Colonel Tucker's arrival. I have to express myself satisfied with the exertions of that officer.

"Having refreshed the troops at Kingston, and having brought across the 41st Royals and Indians, I sent back the 41st and 100th Regiments to form the garrisons of Fort George and Mississaga and Niagara, under Lieutenant-Colonel Tucker, and moved with the 89th and

1814.
CANADA.

"detachments of the Royals and Kings, and Light Company of the 41st, in all about 800 men, to join Major-General Riall's division at the Falls.

"When arrived within a few miles of that position, I met a report from Major-General Riall, that the enemy was advancing in great force. I immediately pushed on and joined the head of Lieutenant-Colonel Morrison's column, just as it reached the road leading to Beaver's Dam, over the summit of the hill at Lundy's Lane. Instead of the whole of Major-General Riall's division, which I expected to have found occupying this position, I found it almost in the occupation of the enemy, whose columns were within 600 yards of the top of the hill, and the surrounding woods filled with his light troops. The advance of Major-General Riall's Division, consisting of the Glengarry Light Infantry, and Incorporated Militia, having commenced a retreat upon Fort George, I countermanded those corps, and formed the 89th Regiment, the Royal Scots detachment, and the 41st Light Company in the rear of the hill, their left resting on the great road, my two 24 pounder brass field guns a little advanced in front of the centre on the summit of the hill, the Glengarry Light Infantry on the right, the battalion of Incorporated Militia and detachment of Kings Regiment on the left of the great road, the squadron of the 19th Light Dragoons in the rear of the left on the road. I had scarcely completed this movement when the whole front was warmly and closely engaged, the enemy's principal efforts were directed against our left and centre ; after repeated attacks the troops on the left were partially forced back, and the enemy gained a momentary possession of the road, this gave him however no material advantage, as the troops which had been forced back formed in rear of the 89th Regiment fronting the road and

"securing the flank. It was during this short
"interval that Major-General Riall, having re-
"ceived a severe wound was intercepted as he was
"passing the rear by a party of the enemy's
"cavalry, and taken prisoner. In the centre, the
"repeated and determined attacks of the enemy
"were met by the 89th Regiment, the detach-
"ments of the Royals and Kings, and the Light
"Company of the 41st Regiment, with the most
"perfect steadiness and intrepid gallantry, and
"the enemy was constantly repulsed with very
"heavy loss. In so determined a manner were
"their attacks directed against our guns, that our
"Artillerymen were bayonetted while in the act
"of loading, and the muzzles of the enemy's guns
"were advanced within a few yards of ours. The
"darkness of the night during this extraordinary
"conflict, occasioned several uncommon incidents.
"Our troops having for a moment been pushed
"back, some of our guns remained for a few
"minutes in the enemy's hands, they, however,
"were not only quickly recovered, but the 2 pieces
"(a 6 pounder and a $5\frac{1}{2}$ howitzer) which the
"enemy brought up were captured by us, together
"with several tumbrils, and in limbering up our
"guns at one period, one of the enemy's 6 pounders
"was put by mistake on a limber of ours, and one
"of our 6 pounders limbered on one of his, by
"which means the pieces were exchanged, and
"thus, though we captured two of his guns, yet,
"as he obtained one of ours, we have gained only
"one gun.

"About 9 o'clock (the action having commenced
"at 6), there was a short intermission of firing,
"during which it appears the enemy was employed
"in bringing up the whole of his remaining force,
"and he shortly afterwards renewed his attack
"with fresh troops, but was everywhere repulsed
"with equal gallantry and success. About this
"period, the remainder of Major-General Riall's
"division, which had been ordered to retire on the

1814.
CANADA.

1814.
CANADA.

"advance of the enemy, consisting of the 103rd
"Regiment under Colonel Scott, the head-quarter
"division of the Royal Scots, the head-quarter
"division of the 8th or Kings, the flank companies
"of the 104th, and some detachments of the
"Militia, under Lieutenant-Colonel Hamilton,
"inspecting field officer, joined the troops engaged,
"and I placed them in a second line, with the
"exceptions of the Royal Scots and flank com-
"panies of the 104th, with which I prolonged my
"line in front to the right, where I was apprehensive
"of the enemy outflanking me.

"The enemy's efforts to carry the hill were con-
"tinued till about midnight, when he had suffered
"so severely from the superior steadiness and
"discipline of His Majesty's troops, that he gave
"up the contest, and retreated with great precip-
"itation to his camp beyond the Chippeway.

"On the following day he abandoned his camp,
"threw the greater part of his baggage, camp
"equipage and provisions into the rapids, and
"having set fire to Streets mill, and destroyed
"the bridge at Chippeway, continued his retreat
"in great disorder towards Fort Erie. My Light
"Troops, Cavalry, and Indians are detached in
"pursuit, and to harass his retreat, which I
"doubt not he will continue until he reaches
"his own shore.

"The loss sustained by the enemy in this severe
"action cannot be estimated at less than 1,500
"men, including several hundreds of prisoners left
"in our hands, his two Commanding Generals
"Brown and Scott, are said to be wounded; his
"whole force, which has never been rated at less
"than 5,000, having been engaged.

"Enclosed I have the honour to transmit a
"return of our loss which has been very consider-
"able. The number of troops under my command
"did not for the first three hours exceed 1,600
"men, and the addition of troops under Colonel

"Scott, did not increase it to more than 2,800 of every description.

"A very difficult, but at the same time a most gratifying duty remains, that of endeavouring to do justice to the merit of the officers and soldiers, by whose valor and discipline this important success has been obtained.

"I was very early in the action deprived of the service of Major-General Riall, who fell a prisoner into the enemy's hands, and who I regret to learn has since suffered the amputation of his arm; his bravery, zeal, and activity have always been conspicuous.

"To Lieutenant-Colonel Harvey, Deputy-Adjutant-General, I am so deeply indebted for his valuable assistance previous to, as well as his able and energetic exertions during this severe contest, that I feel myself called upon to point your Excellency's attention to the distinguished merits of this highly deserving officer, whose services have been conspicuous in every affair that has taken place since his arrival in this province. The zeal and intelligence displayed by Major Glegg, Assistant-Adjutant-General, deserves my warmest approbation. I much regret the loss of a very intelligent and promising young officer, Lieutenant Moorson, 104th Regiment, Deputy-Assistant-Adjutant-General, who was killed towards the close of the action. The active exertions of Captain Elliott, Deputy-Assistant Quarter-Master-General, of whose gallantry and conduct I had on two former instances to remark, were conspicuous. Major-General Maule, and Lieutenant Le Breton of the Quarter-Master-General's Department were extremely useful to me, the latter was severely wounded.

"Amongst the officers, from whose active exertions I derived the greatest assistance, I cannot omit to mention my Aides-de-Camp Captains Jervoise and Loring, and Captain

1814.
CANADA.

1814.
CANADA.

"Holland Aide-de-Camp to Major-General Riall. Captain Loring was unfortunately taken prisoner by some of the enemy's Dragoons whilst in the execution of an order.

"In reviewing the action from its commencement, the first object which presents itself as deserving of notice, is the steadiness and good countenance of the squadron of the 19th Light Dragoons under Major Lisle, and the very creditable and excellent defence made by the Incorporated Militia Battalion under Lieutenant-Colonel Robinson, who was dangerously wounded, and a detachment of the 8th King's Regiment under Colonel Campbell; Major Kirby succeeded Lieutenant-Colonel Robinson in command of the Incorporated Militia Battalion, and continued very gallantly to direct its efforts. This battalion has only been organised a few months, and, much to the credit of Captain Robinson of the King's Regiment (Provincial Lieutenant-Colonel), has attained a highly respectable degree of discipline."

"In the reiterated and determined attacks which the enemy made on our centre, for the purpose of gaining, at once, the crest of the position and our guns, the steadiness and intrepidity displayed by the troops allotted for the defence of that post were never surpassed; they consisted of the 2nd Battalion 89th Regiment, commanded by Lieutenant-Colonel Morrison, and, after the Lieutenant-Colonel had been obliged to retire from the field by a severe wound, by Major Clifford; a detachment of the Royal Scots under Lieutenant-Colonel Hemphill, and after he was killed, Lieutenant Frazer; a detachment of the 8th (or King's) under Captain Campbell, Light Company 41st Regiment under Captain Glew, with some detachments of Militia under Lieutenant-Colonel Parry 103rd Regiment. These troops repeatedly, when hard pressed formed round the colours of the 89th

"Regiment, and invariably repulsed the desper-
"ate efforts made against them. On the right,
"the steadiness and good countenance of the
"1st Battalion Royal Scots, under Lieutenant-
"Colonel Gordon, on some very trying occasions,
"excited my admiration. The King's Regiment
"1st Battalion under Major Evans, behaved with
"equal firmness and gallantry, as did the Light
"Company of the Royals detached under Captain
"Stewart, the Grenadiers of the 103rd detached
"under Captain Brown, and flank companies of
"the 104th Regiment under Captain Leonard;
"the Glengarry Light Infantry under Lieu-
"tenant-Colonel Battersby, displayed valuable
"qualities as Light Troops. Colonel Scott,
"Major Smelt and the Officers of the 103rd
"Regiment, deserve credit for their exertions in
"rallying that regiment after it had been thrown
"into momentary disorder.

"Lieutenant-Colonel Pearson, Inspecting Field
"Officer, directed the advance with great intelli-
"gence, and Lieutenant-Colonel Drummond of the
"104th, having gone forward with my permission
"early in the day, made himself actively useful in
"different parts of the Field, under my direction.
"These Officers are entitled to my best thanks, as
"is Lieutenant-Colonel Hamilton, Inspecting
"Field Officer, for his exertions after his arrival
"with the troops under Colonel Scott.

"The Field Artillery so long as there was light,
"was well served, the credit of its efficient state
"is due to Captain Mackonachie, who has had
"charge of it since his arrival with this Division.
"Captain Mc.Laughlan, who has charge of the
"batteries at Mississaga Fort, volunteered his
"services in the field on this occasion; he was
"severely wounded. Lieutenant Tomkins deserves
"much credit for the way in which the two brass
"24 Pounders, of which he had charge, were
"served, as does Sergeant Austin of the Rocket
"Company, who directed the Congreve rockets

1814.
CANADA.

1814.
CANADA.

"which did much execution. The zeal, loyalty,
"and bravery with which the Militia of this part
"of the province had come forward to co-operate
"with his Majesty's troops in the expulsion of
"the enemy, and their conspicuous gallantry in
"this, and the action of the 5th instant, claim
"my warmest thanks.

"I cannot conclude this despatch, without
"recommending in the strongest terms the
"following officers whose conduct during the late
"operations has called for marked approbation,
"and I am induced to hope that your Excellency
"will be pleased to submit their names for pro-
"motion to the most favorable consideration of
"His Royal Highness the Prince Regent, viz.,
"Captain Jervoise, my Aide-de-Camp, Captain
"Robinson, 8th (King's) Regiment (Provincial
"Lieutenant-Colonel) Commanding the Incor-
"porated Militia, Captain Elliot, Deputy-Assistant-
"Quarter-Master-General, Captain Holland, Aide-
"de-Camp to Major-General Riall, and Captain
"Glew, 41st Regiment.

"This dispatch will be delivered to you by
"Captain Jervoise my Aide-de-Camp, who is fully
"competent to give your Excellency every further
"information you may require.

"I have the honor to be,
"GORDON DRUMMOND,
"*Lieutenant-General.*

"His Excellency,
"Sir George Provost,
"&c., &c., &c."

"*Head-quarters,*
"*Falls of Niagara,*
"26*th, July,* 1814.
"D.G. ORDERS.

"Lieutenant-General Drummond offers his
"sincerest and warmest thanks to the troops and
"Militia engaged yesterday, for their exemplary

PRINCESS VICTORIA'S REGIMENT. 39

"steadiness, gallantry, and discipline in repulsing
" all the efforts of a numerous and determined
" enemy to carry the position of Lundy's Lane near
" the Falls of Niagara. Their exertions have been
" crowned with success, by the defeat of the enemy
" and his retreat to the position of Chippeway, with
" the loss of two of his guns, and an immense
" number of killed and wounded, and several
" hundred prisoners. Where all have behaved so
" nobly, it is unnecessary to hold up particular
" instances of merit in corps, or individuals.

" The Lieutenant-General however cannot
" refrain from expressing in the strongest manner,
" his admiration of the gallantry and steadiness of
" the 89th Regiment, under Lieutenant-Colonel
" Morrison, and Major Clifford, (who ably and
" gallantly supplied the place of the Lieutenant-
" Colonel after being wounded)."

The enemy after the action at Lundy's Lane
having retired to Fort Erie, Lieutenant-General
Drummond proceeded to invest that fortress, and
the Light Company, 89th Regiment was actively
employed in several operations of the siege.

On the 3rd August they were detached with
a force under Colonel Tucker, against some
batteries on the American side of the river, and
were sharply engaged with the enemy, and again
on the 6th, when in the trenches they took part in
repulsing a sortie from the garrison.

On the 15th August the assault took place
again, and the company formed part of the
Storming Column, which, under the command of
Lieutenant-Colonel Fischer of De-Wattville's
Regiment was directed against Snake Hill, the left
flank of the enemy's works. This attack failed,
the works being found impracticable, but the
gallantry of the troops engaged could not be
surpassed.

Extract of Despatch from Lieutenant-General
Drummond, to Sir George Provost :—

1814.
CANADA.

Killed:
4 rank and file.

Wounded:
Captain Barney.
Severely:
7 rank and file.

1814.
CANADA.

"*Camp before Fort Erie,*
"*August* 15*th,* 1814.

"My thanks are due to the undermentioned "officers, viz: Lieutenant-Colonel Fischer, who "commanded the night attack, to Major Coore "Aide-de-Camp to your Excellency, who accom- "panied that column, Major Evans, of the King's, "commanding the advance, Major Vallatte of "De-Wattville's Regiment, Captain Basden, "Light Company, 89th Regiment.

"Nor can I omit mentioning in the strongest "terms of approbation, the zealous, active, and "useful exertions of Captain Elliot of the 103rd "Regiment, Deputy-Assistant-Quarter-Master "General, who was unfortunately wounded and "taken prisoner, and Captain Barney of the 89th "Regiment who had volunteered his service as a "temporary assistant in the Engineer Depart- "ment, and conducted the centre column to the "attack, in which he received two dangerous "wounds.

"(Signed) GORDON DRUMMOND,
"*Lieutenant-General.*"

From Major-General De Wattville, to Lieutenant-General Drummond:—

"*Camp before Fort Erie,*
"*September* 19*th,* 1814.

" As soon as the alarm was given, the 1st Brigade "being next for support, composed of the Royal "Scots, the 82nd and 89th Regiments under "Lieutenant-Colonel Gordon, received orders to "march forward, and also the Light Demi Brigade "under Lieutenant-Colonel Pearson, the 6th Regi- "ment remaining in reserve under Lieutenant- "Colonel Campbell. From the Concession road, "the Royal Scots, and 89th as support, moved "by the new road and met the enemy near the "block house on the right of No. 3 battery whom "they engaged, and by their steady and intrepid "conduct checked his further progress.

"The enemy being then repulsed at every point, were forced to retire with precipitation to their works, leaving several prisoners, and a number of their wounded in our hands. By five o'clock the entrenchments were again occupied, and the line of picquets established, as it had been previously to the enemy's attack.

> "I have the honor to be, &c.,
> "(Signed) L. DE WATTVILLE,
> "*Major-General.*"

On the 5th of November the enemy abandoned the Canadian side of the St. Lawrence, and the 2nd Battalion shortly after returned to York.

1814.
CANADA.

Peace was concluded with America at the beginning of this year. The 2nd Battalion 89th Regiment moved in February from York to Ernest Town, and after a short stay from thence to William Henry. In May the battalion moved to Quebec, and on the 4th June embarked for England, and arriving in Portsmouth in the month of August, proceeded to Chichester.

1815.
CHICHESTER.

The battalion marched from Chichester to Portsmouth, but during the summer was moved to Sheerness.

A very considerable reduction to the army having been ordered consequent upon the General Peace, in the month of November, the 2nd Battalion 89th Regiment was disbanded, those men fit for service whose term had not expired, being handed over to the 1st Battalion.

1816.
SHEERNESS.

HISTORY OF THE 1st BATTALION 89th REGIMENT—*Continued.*

The services of both battalions having been now recorded up to the close of the year 1816, when the 2nd Battalion was disbanded, the history of the regiment is resumed from that period.

1817.
QUILON.

The Regiment remained at Quilon commanded by Lieutenant-Colonel Rainsford.

1818.
THE DECCAN.

A portion of the regiment was this year once more called to the field—during the latter months of 1817, war having broken out with the Mahrattas; some of the minor native powers in the Bombay Territory, supported by their vicinity to Poonah, and induced by intrigues of the Peishwa, seized the opportunity to revolt.

The Bombay Government being much embarrassed, the European troops of that Presidency having already taken the field, and there being no adequate force at their disposal to meet the danger, made application for assistance to Madras, and accordingly 6 strong companies of the 89th, under command of Major Hall, were embarked with all despatch, and proceeded by sea to Bombay. The detachment left Quilon on the 14th January, and arrived at Bombay on the 14th February. They were disembarked the same day, and on the 22nd February proceeded with a force under command of Lieutenant-Colonel Prother, to Panwell, and from thence marched to attack Loghur, and other Fortresses in the South Concan.

The forces of the native Princes offered but feeble resistance to our troops, and their fortresses, and stockades, fell in quick succession, though many of them were capable of being defended for months, being for the most part of considerable strength, and built on rocks or isolated hills of great height, accessible only by winding and narrow steps.

1818.

THE DECCAN.

Loghur, Issapoor, Teecoonah, and Toomgee were soon taken, and the detachment moved on to invest the strong fort of Koaree, which surrendered after 8 days open trenches. Gunghur, Tella, and Goosella shared the same fate. Some stockades near Indapore offered a smart resistance, but were stormed and taken on the 16th April, the assaulting party being under the command of Captain Rose 89th Regiment, who received the thanks of the Governor in Council for his conduct on this occasion.

The detachment next proceeded to invest the almost impregnable fortress of Ryghur, which was captured after a bombardment of 16 days.

Wounded:

1 Sergeant, 7 Rank and File.

The whole country being now reduced, the detachment returned to Bombay on the 23rd of May.

The following orders were issued during this period expressive of the gallantry and good conduct of the detachment :—

"*Camp at Ambergaum,*
"*7th March,* 1818.

"BRIGADE ORDERS.

"Lieutenant-Colonel Prother, with every satis-"faction congratulates the force under his com-"mand, on the early possession and fall of "Loghur, and Issapoor."

"*Camp Koaree,*
"*15th March,* 1818.

"BRIGADE ORDERS.

"Lieutenant-Colonel Prother is much gratified "in announcing to the force the fall of Koaree,

1818.
THE DECCAN.

"which he has reported to His Excellency, the
"Commander-in-Chief—as being brought about by
"the zeal, exertions and spirit of the troops, when
"suffering great fatigue.

"The same conspicuous merit is due to those
"whom the commanding officer has before men-
"tioned. But it would be unjust to omit the
"praise which is due to the gallantry and exertions
"of the reconnoitering party, on the 12th, under
"Captain Rose, H.M.'s 89th Regiment, to whom,
"together with the officers, European and Native,
"non-commissioned officers and privates, Lieut-
"enant-Colonel Prother returns his thanks."

"*Camp Indapore,*
"*17th April,* 1818.

"BRIGADE ORDERS.

"The commanding officer with sentiments of
"satisfaction announces to the force for general
"information, the following particulars of the
"attack of the stockades on a range of hills, in
"shape somewhat like a half crescent; at the two
"flanks were the right and left, and at the centre,
"the main stockade. Captain Rose divided his
"detachment into three parts, one under Captain
"Hutchinson and Lieutenant Crosbie, another
"under Lieutenant Bellassis and Lieutenant
"Dowdall, the third under his personal command
"with Lieutenant Philan. The enemy were
"in number 500, under the "superintend-
"ence of a Dewan, with rocket batteries
"and two small guns. The detachment of Poonah
"Auxiliary Horse supported the infantry. The
"attack on the flank stockades commenced nearly
"at the same time, under a heavy fire of rockets
"and musketry, and were carried in a very gallant
"style by Captain Hutchinson and Lieutenant
"Bellassis; the enemy abandoned the post, im-
"mediately on perceiving which, Captain Rose who
"had restrained the centre for the purpose of

"supporting the flanking parties, gallantly pushed
"on, and carried the main stockade and captured
"the two guns."

1818.
THE DECCAN.

"*Camp Ryghur,*
"*12th May,* 1818.
"BRIGADE ORDERS.
"The surrender of the forces of Ryghur having
"closed the operations, the commanding officer
"has peculiar pleasure in offering a public acknow-
"ledgement to the merit by which this event has
"been so much accelerated; and, in returning
"his thanks to the commanding officers for their
"support, Lieutenant-Colonel Prother requests
"Major Hall, commanding the detachment 89th
"Regiment, to express his approbation to the
"officers, non-commissioned officers, and privates
"for their laudable exertions."

"*Camp near Pallee,*
"*27th May,* 1818.
"SIR,
"I have taken the liberty of addressing Your
"Excellency a few lines, which I trust will be as
"satisfactory to you to receive, as gratifying to
"me to send, expressive of the pleasure I derive
"in bringing to your notice Major Hall, com-
"manding the detachment H.M.'s 89th Regiment,
"serving with the force, as a meritorious and
"deserving officer, and in every way worthy of
"being brought to your Excellency's notice.
"During the time the detachment H.M.'s 89th
"Regiment was with the field force, I always had
"the opportunities of personally observing and
"noticing the attention the officers uniformly paid
"to their duties, and I do not hesitate in pro-
"nouncing them to be as fine and gallant a set of
"young men as ever I served with.
"The men too are very well behaved, and
"remarkably clean and attentive, and excepting
"a single occasion, of no moment, there has not

1818.
THE DECCAN.

" been a Line or Regimental General Court-martial
" assembled since their service with the force, and
" in that instance the Court recommended it, and
" the offence was passed over.

" In short, the conduct of the detachment has
" been exemplary, and reflects the highest degree
" of credit on Major Hall, an officer whom I
" recommend in the strongest terms to Your
" Excellency's approbation.

> " I have the honor to remain,
> " With every respect,
> " Your Excellency's
> " Most Obdt. Humble Servant,
> " J. PROTHER,
> " *Lieut.-Colonel.*

" To His Excellency,
" Lieut.-General
" Sir Miles Nightingale, K.C.B.,
" Commander-in-Chief, Bombay."

1819.

On the close of the monsoon, the detachment now commanded by Lieutenant-Colonel Clifford, C.B. late 2nd Battalion (Major Hall having been compelled by ill-health to return to Europe), was ordered on service under Major-General Sir William Grant Keir to the Sawant Warree States where several forts still held out. The 6 companies embarked at Bombay on 12th January, and were landed at Malwan on the 14th of the same month, and proceeded to Chokee. On the 25th of January the expedition set forward, and very shortly captured the strong forts of Newtee and Waree, and then proceeded against Raree, the Gibraltar of this part of India where every hill is a fort.

Killed:
2 Rank and File.
Wounded:
Lts. Naylor & Dowdall,
3 Rank and File.

This place offered considerable resistance, and gave the detachment an opportunity of distinguishing itself. It was carried by assault on 13th February. The other forts which had refused to surrender to the summons of General

Grant Keir, on hearing of the fate of a place which they considered impregnable, wisely concluded that it would be in vain to make opposition, and surrendered at discretion.

1819.
THE DECCAN.

The detachment occupied a standing camp until 2nd of May, when peace having succeeded all over India, it was embarked for Quillon, and rejoined the head-quarters of the regiment at that station on the 11th May, 1819.

The despatches, public orders, and other documents are here given to show how highly the Governor of Bombay, and the officers under whose orders the detachment served, appreciated their gallantry and conspicuous good conduct.

Field Orders by Major-General Sir William Grant Keir:—

"*Camp Raree,*
"*14th February,* 1819.

" PAROLE—" MULWAN."

" The Major-General congratulates the troops "on the successful termination of the operations "against the Fort of Raree, and begs that the "officers and men will believe him highly sensible "of their exemplary good conduct and exertions "during the siege.

" The whole of the troops have conducted them"selves with credit, but it has fallen more particu"larly to the lot of the detachment which stormed "the Pettah and out-works of the Fort, to display "that gallantry which the Major-General is per"suaded is common to all. He begs to offer his "tribute and applause to Lieutenant-Colonel "Clifford, C.B. for the spirit and judgment and "decision manifested by him on that occasion. " The Major-General deems it an act of justice to " the gallant troops engaged yesterday, to publish " the following extract from the report of Lieu" tenant-Colonel Clifford :—

" On this occasion I have to regret the loss of

1819

THE DECCAN.

89th Foot:
2 Privates killed.
2 Lieutenants and 3 Privates wounded.

"the men killed and wounded, although infinitely "less than could have been expected on such a "service, amongst the latter are Lieutenants "Naylor and Dowdall of H.M.'s 89th Regiment, "two fine gallant young men, that promised fair "to be an ornament to their profession, although "both are severely wounded, yet I trust and hope "that the army will not be deprived of their "future services.

"I formed up the detachment in two divisions, "Captain Sanderson, 89th Regiment commanded "one, and Captain Garroway, 2nd battalion 9th "Regiment the other. I have every reason to be "satisfied with their conduct and example.

"To my Brigade-Major and Quarter-master of "Brigade, Lieutenants A. B. Taylor and Pearse, "of H.M.'s 89th Regiment, I feel much indebted "for their support and zeal.

"I have had the honour to serve in the four "quarters of the world, and on no occasion was "the conduct of the troops, both Europeans and "Natives, more conspicuous for gallantry and de- "votion to the service than on the present "occasion.

"(Signed) E. J. STANNERS,
"*Assisting Adjutant-General.*

"(Signed) Major A. B. Taylor,
"Major of Brigade 1st Bde."

Extracts from General Orders by The Right Hon. The Governor in Council:—

"*Bombay Castle,*
"*9th March,* 1819.

"The services of the detachment H.M.'s 89th "Regiment being no longer required under this "Presidency, The Rt. Hon. The Governor in "Council is pleased to direct that it should "embark at Mulwan, on board The Hon. "Company's Ship "Ernaad," and proceed to join "the head-quarters of the regiment at Quilon.

"On the return of this detachment to the
"Presidency to which it belongs, the Governor
"in council performs a very gratifying duty, in
"recording the high sense he entertains of the
"zeal and activity, displayed both by the officers
"and men throughout the whole of the harassing
"operations, conducted by the force under the
"command of Lieutenant-Colonel Prother in the
"reduction of the Southern Concan, as well as
"during the operations against the Sawant
"Warree States, under the command of Major-
"General Sir William Grant Keir, and the
"Governor in Council requests that the officers
"and men composing the detachment will accept
"his sincere acknowledgements for their services
"on these occasions, as well as for their exemplary
"conduct in Garrison.

> "By order of
> "The Rt. Hon. The Governor in Council.
> > "(Signed)   J. FARISH,
> > > "*Secretary for Government.*"

1819.

THE DECCAN.

> "*Head-quarters,*
"No. 5197.   "*Calcutta,*
"SIR,   "*9th June,* 1820.

"The enclosed copy of a letter from the
"Adjutant General of the Forces, Horse Guards,
"I am instructed by the Most Noble the Com-
"mander-in-Chief, to transmit for your Excel-
"lency's information and for communication to
"H.M.'s 89th Regiment.

> "I have the honor to be, Sir,
> > "Your Excellency's most obedient
> > > "Humble Servant,
> > "(Signed)   THOMAS McMAHON,
> > > "*Colonel, Adjutant-General.*

"His Excellency,
"Lt.-Gen. Sir Thos. Hislop, Bt.,
> "G.C.B.,
> > "Madras."

1819.

THE DECCAN.

> "*Horse Guards,*
> "30*th Nov.*, 1819.
>
> "MY LORD,
>
> "I have not failed to submit to the Commander-in-Chief, your Lordship's letter of the 31st March last, No. 4040, with the accompanying return of casualties, which have occurred in the portion of the 89th Regiment detached to the Bombay establishment, on a successful attack on the out-works of the Fort of Raree, on the 13th February, and I am commanded to signify His Royal Highness's approbation of the personal good conduct and management therein reported of Brevet-Lieutenant-Colonel Clifford, who commanded the detachment on the above operation, as also the several officers mentioned by the Lieutenant-Colonel, as having distinguished themselves on the occasion alluded to.
>
> "I have, &c.,
> "(Signed) H. CALVERT,
> "*Adjutant General.*

"General
"The Marquis of Hastings, K.G.,
    "&c., &c., &c.,
        "Calcutta."

The regiment was this year under command of Lieutenant-Colonel Rainsford.

1820.

QUILON.

The regiment remained at Quilon. On the 17th May, a new pair of colours was presented to the regiment.

In October, Lieutenant-Colonel Miles, C.B. assumed the command.

1821 & 1822.

QUILON.

The regiment still remained at Quilon, Colonel Rainsford having been promoted to Major-General, Lieutenant-Colonel Malet was appointed to the regiment in his stead.

On the 6th of January, the regiment under command of Lieutenant Colonel Miles, left Quilon *en route* to Cannanore, where it arrived on 5th February.

1823.
CANNANORE.

Early in the year 1824, war having been proclaimed against the Burman Empire, a large European Force was ordered to proceed against Rangoon, and the 89th having the good fortune to be named for that service, H.M.'s 20th Regiment was despatched from Bombay to replace it. On the arrival of the first ship on the 26th April, at Cannanore, the 1st Division of the 89th was embarked, and by the 30th, the whole regiment was on board ship in high health, not a single man was left behind, nor was there a man in Hospital so ill as not to be able to march to the point of embarkation.

1824.
CANNANORE.

After a short passage of nine days, the 89th, disembarked at Madras, on the 9th and 10th of May, and took up the quarters vacated by H.M.'s 69th Regiment, at Fort George.

Disembarked:
29 officers, 31 sergeants, 21 drummers, 782 rank and file.

The regiment had not been there many days, when spasmodic cholera attacked the corps, in a very general and virulent form; so rapid and alarming was the progress of the disease, that the Commander-in-Chief, after having looked at the regiment on the Island in review order on the 15th May, called on the medical board for its opinion, as to the best mode of staying the epidemic, and by the advice of that body, the regiment was hastened on board ship, only a few hours notice being given, to proceed to Rangoon.

MADRAS.

At this time the regiment was without followers of any description, for service, nor could any be procured prior to embarkation, which subsequently proved an incalculable misfortune to it.

RANGOON.

On the 4th of June the regiment entered the Irrawaddy, having previously rendezvoused at the Great Andaman, where Sir Edward Miles' Brigade assembled, and on the 5th and 6th was disembarked at Rangoon.

Disembarked:
32 officers, 40 sergeants, 20 drummers, 723 rank and file.

1824.

RANGOON.

Brevet Lieut.-Colonel M. Clifford, (had to return, being sick.)
Major J. L. Basden (succeeded Lieut.-Col. Clifford, in the command.)
Bt-Major H. R. Gore.
Captain Richard Rose.
  „ W. Pearse.
  „ C. Redmond.
  „ C. Cannon.
Lieut. A. Dowdall.
  „ J. Moore.
  „ J. L. Molloney.
  „ P. McKie.
  „ W. J. King.
  „ W. Kennedy.
  „ C. G. King.
Ensign J. M. McLean.
  „ W. Olperts.
Surgeon. R. Dawn.
Adjutant. E. Kenny.

On the 10th of June, 4 days subsequent to the disembarkation of the 89th at Rangoon, operations on a very extensive scale both by land and by water, were commenced against the important and strongly garrisoned and stockaded post of Kymendine, about 3 miles above Rangoon, where it fully commanded the river. Five hundred rank and file of the regiment, with the officers named in the margin, were employed on this service during the night of the 9th and until the morning of the 11th June, when the companies which had been left at Rangoon, were ordered to join head quarters before Kymendine, so as to take part in the expected escalade of that place. The regiment had undergone excessive fatigue up to the morning of the 11th, having been employed in dragging two 18-pounders from Rangoon, through unusually heavy and uneven ground, but looked forward to the prominent share in the general attack which Sir Archibald Campbell had allotted to them as a full indemnity for their labour and privation; disappointment therefore was great indeed when the regiment formed at daybreak, and expecting anxiously the order to move forward, found that the enemy had stolen off through the right face of the stockade during the night.

The regiment returned to Rangoon on the evening of the 11th June.

* Cr.-Sergeant Sibbald.

BURMAH.

Wounded:
2 *Privates.*

On the 14th, a detachment of 1 *sergeant, 2 corporals, and 20 privates were sent on board the "Mercury," gun brig, and on their being relieved the Commander bore the most honorable testimony to their conduct, both for discipline and gallantry.

Captain Rose.
Lieut. Young, M.B.
  „ Dowdall.
  „ Hewson.
  „ W. J. King.
  „ C. G. King.

On the 14th June the two flank companies with their officers were sent across the river to Dalla, and proceeded many miles in search of the enemy, through the most harassing description of country, but fruitlessly. They returned to Rangoon the same day.

On the 14th the regiment was ordered in advance to the great Dagan Pagoda, where a line of defence, full three-quarters-of-a-mile in extent, was entrusted to its care. The Burmese picquets were within musket shot of the quarters occupied by the regiment, which caused great additional fatigue to all ranks, as on every partial attack by the enemy, a great portion of the regiment was turned out. Our most advanced sentries in some parts of the line, were not more than two or three hundred yards in advance of the men's barracks. Here also disease soon made most rapid and devastating strides, brought about by many concurring causes. The men had come from quarters where cooks and followers of all sorts were in constant attendance upon them, and where their provisions were most excellent of their kind, and ample in quantity. At this period they not only had to bring their provisions from a distance of nearly two miles daily, but when arrived they had to forage for wood, water, &c., and then to cook them, duties which under a Tropical sun cannot be performed by Europeans with impunity, but what was infinitely more prejudicial than all, to the health of the troops, the provisions themselves were such, that none but men reduced to a state of downright want would use them. The ration meat was literally rotten, and covered with white maggots, and the only addition to this was an allowance of rice. The result was dysentry, and the deaths began to reach six, seven, and even eight in a day.

Lieutenant-Colonel Clifford and Captain Coates proceeded to Madras on sick certificate on the 16th June, where the last named died.

1824.
BURMAH.

1824.
BURMAH.

"*Head-quarters,*
"*Rangoon,*
"26*th June,* 1824.

" GENERAL ORDERS.

" Brigadier-General Sir A. Campbell has great
" pleasure in announcing to the army under his
" command, the expression of the highest appro-
" bation and applause of the Right Honourable
" The Governor General in Council, of their
" conduct in the recent capture of Rangoon, and
" its dependencies, which has been conveyed to
" him in a despatch lately received from
" Calcutta."

Captain Pearse.
Lieut. Dougan.
Ensign McClean.

July the 5th, a detachment of 100 rank and file with officers and sergeants in proportion, joined other troops, and made an attack on a stockade of the enemy about midway between the Dagan Pagoda and Kymendine. They returned to their lines, after accomplishing the object sought, on the same evening.

1 Man killed. 1 Man wounded.

On the 8th July 250 rank and file with officers and non-commissioned officers in propor- tion under the command of Brevet-Major Gore, proceeded with a considerable force of Europeans and natives, under the personal superintendence of Brigadier-General McBean, to a strong line of stockades, seven in number on the left flank, and a little in rear of Kymendine. It fell to the lot of the Grenadier company to have an opportunity of distinguishing itself on this occasion.

3 Privates wounded.

On the 26th July Lieutenant-Colonel Malet was appointed to the command of a brigade, and Major Basden assumed the command of the regiment.

The nature of the service at this time was most discouraging and trying, the weather was bad in the extreme, the rain fell in torrents, and whenever a few hours dry weather occurred, a strong detachment was invariably ordered to make its way into some one of the surrounding jungles by some narrow unfrequented path, to beat up the quarters of the enemy, and destroy their stockades and breastworks. It seldom happened that ever the soldier had even this poor satisfaction, for it generally so turned out, that after being several hours marching in wet, and mire under foot, and abundance of rain falling from the heavens, the information proved false, or an impassable Nullah obstructed the course of the column. In this manner did the half starved European return to his comfortless quarters, and to his honor be it remembered that under every privation, his wish to meet the enemy was as ardent as on the day of landing, and at no period was the regiment more conspicuous for steady discipline.

1824.
BURMAH.

Towards the middle of August, Sir A. Campbell having determined to send a force eastwards to bring under subjection the whole line of coasts, from Martaban to Mergui, the command was entrusted to Sir Edward Miles, C.B., and K.I.S. (the Lieutenant-Colonel of the regiment). As many of the 89th as were deemed fit for great exertion were ordered for the service, and embarked on the 16th August.

The expedition arrived at the mouth of the Tavoy River on 3rd September, and removed into light craft consisting of gun-boats, flats, Honourable Company's cruisers, and small brigs, on the 4th.

Owing to the extent of the flotilla, and want of good information as to the channel, (it having to be sounded and buoyed the whole way by officers of the Marines) the force was not in a condition to attack the fort till the 9th. Having cast anchor that morning within musket range of their ramparts, the troops were ready to dart to the point of attack, when a flag of truce caused a pause. An unconditional surrender of the fort with all it contained of public property, and all its dependencies, deprived the troops of a most

1824.
BURMAH.

excellent opportunity of reaping a rich harvest of laurels, though it no doubt saved the lives of a large number of all ranks, the fort being excessively strong and capable of a good defence.

By the 11th the whole of the force had disembarked, and here the men gained new life and spirits. Matters had been so managed that the inhabitants returned to their homes where they enjoyed the most ample protection, and the provisions became at once abundant and very moderate in price.

The soldiers soon became on the most friendly footing with the natives, who on their part readily conformed to the habits of the Europeans, and supplied their wants with much good-will.

Captain Jones.
Lieutenant O'Neil.
2 sergeants.
5 corporals.
2 drummers.
72 privates.

The regiment re-embarked on the 25th, leaving a detail as per margin to form the Garrison conjointly with Madras Sepoys. The residue of the force having got on board the ships at the mouth of the river, the expedition sailed for Mergui, before which place the armed vessels dropped anchor on the 6th of October, so as to be opposed to the several batteries on the front face. After a short communication between the Governor and Sir Edward Miles, the troops landed in quick succession, commencing with the 89th, and a front and flank attack was promptly arranged, and executed within a very short space of time by escalade.

Killed:
6 privates.
Wounded:
Lieutenant Kennedy, (of which he died.)
Lieutenant Mc.Kie.
7 sergeants, 2 corporals, 1 drummer, 12 privates.

With the exception of a few casualties on board the armed vessels, and amongst a party of seamen who were landed and attempted one of the wharfs in front, the loss, which was comparatively very small, fell upon the 89th.

The orders issued on this occasion will best shew how the regiment conducted itself on this service.

4 sergeants, 2 corporals
2 drummers, 26 privates
Ensign McLean in charge.

On the 20th October the regiment once more got on board ship, leaving a detail of sick and wounded for their more effectual recovery, and on the 3rd November reached Tavoy, and landed on the same day, but re-embarked on the 14th. After a number of mishaps to the head quarter ship, those on board were landed at Rangoon on the 22nd November, the remainder of the corps having arrived five days previously.

> "*Head-quarters,*
> "*Mergui,*
> "*6th October,* 1824.

"DIVISION EVENING ORDERS.

"The officer commanding the force will avail "himself of the earliest opportunity of recording "the high gratification he has received this day "from the gallant conduct of the troops. The "devotion shewn by every officer and man, and "the high spirit exhibited throughout a most "trying and arduous period, was never more "conspicuous than in the assault on the "enemy's works. The greater share of the attack "fell upon H.M.'s 89th Regiment, it being im- "practicable to land the whole of the troops, and "Lieutenant-Colonel Miles begs Major Basden "and the officers and men will accept his best "thanks; their numbers were but few, but the "determination of every individual made up for "every deficiency.

"Lieutenant-Colonel Miles will not fail to "express to his superiors, the impression on his "mind of the exemplary good conduct of every "one composing this Division, both naval and "military.

"Lieut.-Colonel Miles regrets very sincerely "the loss he fears he shall sustain for some "protracted period, of the services of Lieutenant "Kennedy and many men of the 89th Regiment, "who have been severely wounded, and he is "only surprised from the very heavy fire kept "up from the enemy, that the loss in killed and "wounded was not much more severe."

1824.
BURMAH.

1824.
BURMAH.

Extracts from Regimental Orders:—

"*Mergui,*
"*9th October,* 1824.

"Major Basden considers the present moment one of the happiest of his existence, as it affords him the opportunity of expressing his sentiments on the spirited, and truly gallant conduct of the officers and men engaged in the attack on the Enemy's Gate Way on the 6th inst., in which the Major had the good fortune of being a partaker, and he requests that every individual of the regiment concerned, will accept his warm and grateful thanks, for the exertions that led to so brilliant and decisive a termination.

"The promptitude and energy displayed on the arrival of the scaling ladders, is beyond all praise, it was evidently the key to success, and the commanding officer has peculiar gratification in recording the names of Captain Cannon, Lieutenant and Adjutant Kenny, Lieutenants C. King, and McKie, also Corporal Hamilton of No. 2, Private Andrew Murphy, of No. 7, and Private John Lacey, of No. 10, who surmounted all obstacles, opened the gate from the inside, and admitted their equally eager comrades.

"The commanding officer is fully sensible of the loss he sustained when Lieutenant Kennedy was wounded, and in like manner he regrets being deprived of the non-commissioned officers and privates who were borne from the field in a similar manner, and he has to express a sincere wish for their speedy recovery.

"For those brave fellows of H.M.'s 89th Regiment who were killed, there can be but one sentiment."

"Adjutant General's Office,   1824.
           "Fort William,   BURMAH.
              "11th November, 1824.

" No. 1948.

" SIR,

"I have the honor by direction of the Com-"mander-in-Chief to acknowledge the receipt of "your letter of the 23rd ultimo, transmitting "copies of the several reports, returns, &c., "forwarded by you to the Secretary to Govern-"ment in the secret and political department, "relative to the capture of the towns of Tavoy "and Mergui, and at the same time to express "His Excellency's satisfaction at the intelligence "of success so important in their character, and "which Sir Edward Paget observes reflects the "highest credit on the professional talent and "judgment of Colonel Miles the Commanding "Officer, in planning out the previous arrange-"ments, and in the persevering gallantry and "devotion to the service of the officers and men "under his command, during the whole of the "operations.

         "I have the honor to be,
            " &c., &c.,
              "(Signed) JAS. NICHOLL,
               " *Adjutant-General of the Army.*

"Brigadier General
   "Sir A. Campbell,
      "Comdg. the troops at Rangoon."

To Brigadier-General Sir A. Campbell, K.C.B., &c., &c. :—

" SECT. DEPT.

" SIR,

"I have had the honor to receive and submit "to the Governor-General in Council, your

1824.
BURMAH.

"despatch, No. 23, date 23rd ultimo, enclosing
"Lieutenant-Colonel Miles' Reports of the
"capture of Tavoy and Mergui.

"His Lordship in Council has perused these
"reports with satisfaction, and desires that you
"will be pleased to convey to that officer and to
"Captain Hardy of the Honorable Company's
"Marine, who commanded the Naval part of the
"expedition, as well as to all the officers employed
"under the orders of Lieutenant-Colonel Miles,
"the expression of his unqualified approbation
"of the judgment and skill with which the
"attacks were planned, and of the gallantry
"and zeal which were displayed in the execu-
"tion of them. In the capture of Tavoy,
"the Governor General in Council has not failed
"to remark the honorable testimony borne by
"Lieutenant-Colonel Miles to the conduct of the
"Brigade-Major, Captain Young of His Majesty's
"89th Regiment, and the Deputy Assistant
"Quarter-Master-General, Captain Spicer of the
"12th Regiment Native Infantry, and to both
"of those Officers Lieutenant-Colonel Miles has
"expressed his obligation, for their equally able
"and zealous assistance at the storm of Mergui,
"and generally on all occasions when their services
"were called into action.

"The terms in which Lieutenant-Colonel Miles
"has spoken of every individual at the capture
"of Mergui reflects the highest credit on their
"gallantry and exemplary conduct; indeed upon
"no occasion during the present arduous and
"harassing conflict, have the heroism and devo-
"tion of the British soldier been more strikingly
"exhibited, than in the assault of the above
"mentioned fort, under every circumstance of
"annoyance, and disadvantage from the un-
"favourable state of the weather and country.
"Amongst those officers whose names are more
"prominently brought forward, the Governor
"General in Council observes Lieutenant-Colonel

"Commandant M'Dowell of the 7th Native
"Infantry, and Major Basden, commanding
"H.M.'s 89th Regiment.

> "I have the honor to be,
> "&c., &c.
> "(Signed) GEORGE SWINTON,
> "*Sec. to Government.*

"Fort William,
   "19th Nov., 1824."

The enemy having assumed a very imposing and threatening attitude towards the close of November, Sir A. Campbell was no sooner reinforced by the 89th Regiment, than he commenced to give effect to his previously concerted plans. The following General Order was issued on the resumption of active operations.

> "*Head-quarters,*
>   "*Rangoon,*
>   "*2nd December,* 1824.

"GENERAL ORDERS.

"The commander of the forces has now the "long looked-for pleasure of congratulating the "troops under his command, upon the opportu- "nity at length afforded them of punishing "the many insults, cruelties, and aggressions, "of an arrogant and barbarous enemy.

"The much vaunted Bundoolah has arrived to "witness what the discipline and valour of British "soldiers can achieve, and the commander of the "forces confidently leaves to his troops, the task "of tearing from his brow, the laurels with which "vanity and presumption has encircled it."

The regiment (as well as the whole army) was drawn out, and kept at their several positions without cover, as if in a state of alarm for several days. This feint had its desired effect. The enemy drew the cord tighter, and brought

1824.

BURMAH.

Brevet-Major Gore, Captain Redmond and Lieutenant McKie, 3 Sergeants, 2 Drummers, 50 Rank and File.

*Captain Rose, Lieutenants Hewson and King, 3 Sergeants, 2 Drummers, 50 Rank and File.
1 Sergeant killed.
Captain Rose and 3 Privates wounded.*

Captain Jones, Ensigns Forbes and Olphert, 5 Sergeants, 2 Drummers, 100 Rank and File.

*Captain Pearse, Lieutenants Taylor, Dowdall, C. G. King, O'Neil, and Macleod, Adjutant Kenny, Assistant Surgeon Walsh, 5 Sergeants, 2 Drummers, 100 Rank and File.
Wounded: 3 Privates.*

*Captain Cannon, Lieutenants A.B.Taylor, Dowdall, Dongan, C. G. King, Adjutant Kenny, and Assistant Surgeon Walsh, 3 Sergeants, 1 Drummer, 50 Rank and File.
Assistant Surgeon Walsh wounded.*

*Major Basden, Lieutenant O'neil, Ensigns Forbes and Olpherts, 8 Sergeants, 3 drummers, 150 Rank and File.
Killed: 1 Private.
Wounded: Lieutenants Taylor and Dowdall, 3 Sergeants, 3 Corporals, 19 Privates.*

up all his guns, and in several places pushed his sap (as in the neighbourhood of the Dagan Pagoda) to within 50 yards of our position.

On the 4th, a party of the 89th joined a force sent forward to make reconnaissance.

On the 5th, another party was sent out to join other troops, in an operation against the enemy's extreme left. On this occasion there were a few casualties.

On the 7th and 8th, there was a combined general attack on the enemy's position, with a view to capture their field ordnance and other material. There were two columns formed from the 89th on this occasion. The loss was very small indeed, owing to the columns being exposed to fire only a few seconds, till they got into the enemy's trenches.

On the evening of the 8th, a party was sent to Dalla, across the river after dark, to capture some guns planted in a redoubt, which did much damage to the British shipping. The duty was successfully executed.

On the 9th, a considerable reinforcement from the 89th Regiment crossed the river, to join the before named party, when a very spirited attack was made on some mud redoubts, three in number, constructed so as to flank each other. The enemy was promptly driven out, and pursued for several miles. The 89th had several casualties in the affair.

The regiment returned to their usual quarters on the evening of the 10th, not having had their accoutrements off since the morning of the 1st.

"*Head-quarters,*
  "*Rangoon,*
  "12*th December,* 1824.

1824.
BURMAH.

" GENERAL ORDERS.

" It is with the most heartfelt satisfaction, Sir
" A. Campbell reverts to the G. O. issued on the
" 2nd instant. The operations of the Army com-
" mencing on the 1st, and their final result on the
" 10th, have fully shown how well his confidence
" was placed in the discipline and valour of the
" troops he has the honor to command. Where all
" have conducted themselves with such devotion
" and enthusiasm, it is needless to particularise,
" and he therefore begs that all engaged, from the
" highest rank to the lowest, without exception,
" will accept his most cordial thanks for their
" steady obedience to, and the prompt and
" effective execution of all his orders."

Extract from a Despatch dated 10th December,
1824, to the Deputy Adjutant-General of the
Forces in Ava :—

" I directed immediately after my arrival a
" small party consisting of 20 men of the Light
" Infantry of H.M.'s 89th Regiment, and 30 men
" of the Light Infantry of the 30th Regiment
" N.I., under the command of Lieutenant Taylor
" 89th Regiment, to be thrown out a little to our
" front to reconnoitre. The advance party of the
" enemy hid by the thickness of the Jungle,
" almost immediately commenced a sharp fire,
" which was returned with much spirit by
" Lieutenant Taylor (an officer who twice
" distinguished himself during the day), but
" finding two or three of H.M.'s 89th Regiment
" wounded, one I fear dangerously, as well as a
" sepoy of the 30th Regiment, I considered it a
" useless waste of life to expose valuable men to
" be picked off by an unseen enemy, I therefore
" recalled them to our post.

" Immediately the column debouched on the

1824.
BURMAH.

"plain, the Light Companies were, I am informed, brought into action by their respective officers in a very handsome manner, whilst Major Basden pushed on the division in gallant style to a breast-work a little in front and on the left, where the enemy made considerable opposition, but was driven out by this instantaneous and spirited attack.

"I should rob Major Basden of the credit which is so justly his due, did I not attribute our success to his most excellent conduct, as he not only led the advance with his usual gallantry, but from his able advice and experience, I received the greatest assistance in the dispositions that were requisite previous to, and after our moving out.

"(Signed)   BROOKE BRYDGES PARLBY,
   "*Lieutenant-Colonel Commanding.*"

The enemy having failed in his attack on Rangoon, concentrated his immense force at Cockain, and thence sent detachments which annoyed the whole British line by keeping it constantly on the alert. Sir A. Campbell prepared to drive them to a more convenient distance, and accordingly on the 15th he moved from the lines with nearly all his disposable force. The 89th (leaving a small detail to protect the line entrusted to its care, which was situated on the verge of a thick wood), joined that part of the army under the immediate command of Sir A. Campbell, and in a brief space of time arrived in the presence of the enemy, who occupied a range of hills, in considerable strength: the base was stockaded and defended by a very deep and wide trench, with pointed abatis and trous-de-loup, covering a space of thirty yards in width along its whole front. It fell to the 89th to attack the left angle of the front face, supported by Sepoys and part

DETAIL OF 89TH.
Major Basden, Comdg. Captains Rose, Pearse, & Cannon; Lieutenants C. G. King, O'Neil & Macleod; Ensigns Forbes Olpherts, & Gray; Adjt. Kenny; Asst.-Surgeon Walsh; 250 rank & file; Sergeants & Drummers in proportion.

of the Madras European Regiment, all under the command of Sir Edward Miles.

1824.
BURMAH.

The column reached the point of attack with great precision, and on the signal rushed forward, and in a few minutes overcame every obstacle. Considering the heavy flank and front fire to which the attacking column was exposed, the casualties were few.

1 Drummer, 1 Private killed; 18 Privates wounded.

"*Head-quarters,*
"*Rangoon,*
"18*th December,* 1824.

"GENERAL ORDERS.

"The Brigadier-General commanding the force "feels that any thing he could say would but ill "express his admiration of the cool and enthusi-"astic valor conducted by the most perfect order "of discipline, with which the troops employed on "the 15th advanced and carried the enemy's "position, yet he cannot refrain from offering his "most grateful thanks to every officer and soldier "he had that day the honor to command, and to "assure them that it will be to him a most "gratifying duty to bring their heroic conduct to "the notice of the Right Honorable the Governor "in Council, and to the Commander-in-Chief. "What need he say more than that 1300 British "soldiers supported by a small detachment of "Artillery, and two troops of the Governor-"General's Body-Guard, nobly stormed and "carried by assault, amost formidable entrench-"ment, and stockaded camp, defended by, from "20,000 to 25,000 men, who but a few minutes "ago treated their appearance with derision and "contempt from the security they felt in their "own strength and position. They ought from "experience to have known better the Troops "they had to contend with."

Divisional Orders by Lieutenant-Colonel Miles, C.B., & K.I.S. :—

1824. BURMAH.	*"Rangoon, 24th December,* 1824. "Lieutenant-Colonel Miles trusts that his "health will permit him to rejoin the Madras "division, but he cannot relinquish the command "without recording his admiration of the "gallantry before the enemy, and the regularity "and subordination in quarters, which have been "so eminently displayed by every regiment "(Europeans and Natives), composing the "division of the Madras army on foreign service."
1825. Captain Redmond Lieutenant Aplin. Ensign Gray. Adjutant Kenny. 5 Sergeants, 2 Drummers 100 Rank and File. No casualties.	February the 5th a detachment under the command of Captain Redmond as per margin, embarked with other troops under the command of Lieutenant-Colonel Godwin, H.M.'s 41st Regiment, and proceeded to Tautobien, where some stockades were taken, and the course of that branch of the river explored; this force returned on the evening of the 8th instant.
	February the 14th, the army commenced a general movement in advance. The 89th being destined to form the principal part of the force
Major Basden, Commanding, Brevet-Major Gore, Captains Rose, Pearce, Redmond, and Cannon. Lieutenants Aplin, A. B. Taylor, W. J. King, C. G. King O'Neil, McKie, Macleod, Currie, McLean, and Forbes. Ensigns Arrow and Gray. Pay-Master Grant. Adjutant Kenny. Quarter-Master Edwards. Assistant Surgeons Orr & Walsh. 36 Sergeants, 29 Corporals, 15 Drummers, 444 Privates.	by water, embarked as per margin, on the 16th February, in small craft of various kinds from the gun-boat to the common Burmese canoe. Each boat carried its own provisions, which were issued daily by guess-work, being unprovided with either weights or measures; very great difficulty was also experienced in cooking on board such small craft, and the men were so crowded that not half the complement of each boat had room to lie down at the same time. Nothing could exceed the hardships endured by the men during the two months they continued on board, but it was borne with cheerfulness and good-will. The column proceeded leisurely up the river, and on its way took Panlang and many other stockades, having encountered considerable and well planned opposition from the enemy. When in a narrow part of the river, an attempt was made by them to burn the

flotilla, by floating a large number of fire rafts of a most formidable description down the stream upon them, but the cool intrepidity of our sailors rendered their efforts quite innocuous, and next day the flotilla entered the grand stream of the Irrawaddy, and proceeded towards Donabew.

1825.
BURMAH.

"*Head-quarters, Panlang,*
"19*th February,* 1825.

" DIVISION ORDERS.

" Brigadier General Cotton congratulates the " troops on the success that has attended their " exertions in the attack on the Panlang stockades. " He begs to thank the officers and men collect- " ively and individually, for the great alacrity and " courage they have manifested.

" The attack having been made in two columns, " he begs Lieutenant-Colonel O'Donoghue of H.M.'s " 47th Regiment, and Major Basden, of H.M.'s " 89th Regiment, who conducted them, will accept " his best thanks for the gallantry and zeal they " displayed in leading the different columns."

" EXTRACT :—

"*Dated Panlang,* 24*th February,* 1825.

"On the morning of the 18th, I directed Major " Basden, commanding the advance, to recon- " noitre the right bank, and burn another stockade " we had discovered the evening before, which was " done, and the flotilla proceeded up the river.

"Two columns of attack were formed on the " right and left banks, (the left under Major " Basden) with orders to attack stockades, situa- " ted on their respective banks, and then advance " according to circumstances after their reduction.

"To Lieutenant-Colonel O'Donoghue, 47th " Regiment, and Major Basden, 89th Regiment, " who as I before stated conducted the attacks, I " wish to offer my strong acknowledgements for " the gallantry and zeal they displayed in lead- " ing them."

1825.
BURMAH.

Early on the 1st of March, the enemy made demonstrations, as if they had determined to arrest our progress, with this view they made choice of a position on the left bank of the river, opposite to an island, which rendered the channel on either side very narrow. Their war boats occupying these channels made a very imposing appearance, and mutually gave and received protection from the troops, who were down at right angles to the course of the river, following the direction of a deep and wide Nullah. In this position, a portion of the 89th having promptly landed, encountered them, and inflicted a considerable loss upon them at a trifling expense. The flotilla continued its course and established itself in a secure anchorage, to await the arrival of the heavy vessels.

5 men wounded.

On the 6th of March the force reached Donabew, and after a close reconnaissance by the Military and Naval Commanders, operations were deferred till the 7th instant, on which morning the 89th landed about 500 yards short of the small or white Pagoda stockade, and being quickly formed into two columns proceeded to storm that work at two different points. The attack was completely successful, and the enemy's loss in killed, wounded, and prisoners, was unusually great. The regiment now moved forward to the attack of the principal stockade, but the defence proved too strong to be practicable, and no impression could be made.

The operation of the day cost the 89th Regiment very dear. In the fall of Captains Rose and Cannon, the regiment sustained a severe loss; they were brave and experienced officers; several gallant non-commissioned officers and men also fell nobly in the discharge of their duty.

Killed:
Captain Rose,
  „   Cannon,
1 Sergeant,
1 Corporal,
8 Privates.

Wounded:
Lieut. C. G. King,
  „   W. J. King,
  „   James Currie,
1 Sergeant,
3 Drummers,
54 Privates.

The General, and the Commodore of H.M.'s Naval Forces, agreed that the enemy was too numerous and strongly posted, to be disturbed by so small a force, now reduced to about

400 bayonets, without in an imminent degree
hazarding the command of the river, and thereby
exposing Rangoon itself, the only magazine and
base of operations, to the enterprises of so active
and numerous an enemy. The troops were
therefore re-embarked in the course of the
night, and dropped down the river some hundred
yards, so as to be clear of the enemy's long range
guns, in which position the force remained until
the 26th, sustaining night after night the efforts
of the enemy, both by land and water, to force
the line and push for Rangoon, which at this
time was most inadequately garrisoned.

1825.
BURMAH.

" DIVISION ORDERS.

"*8th March*, 1825.

" Brigadier-General Cotton returns his warmest
" thanks to the officers and men who composed the
" two columns, who were so ably led by Lieutenant-
" Colonel O'Donoghoe, and Major Basden, for the
" gallantry with which they carried the strong
" positions of the enemy at the Pagoda yesterday,
" and he requests these officers will accept his best
" acknowledgments for the manner in which they
" executed the order of the attack.

" It is impossible to feel stronger than the
" Brigadier-General does, the necessity that existed
" for the re-embarkation of troops, from the
" strength of the enemy's works and force, and
" the limited means the column possesses. He
" confidently trusts that a speedy opportunity will
" arise, for the exertions of the soldier being
" crowned with the success they deservedly merit."

Extract dated Yanginchunar, entrance to the
Great Irrawaddy:—

"*March 9th*, 1825.

" Preparations were accordingly made to
" commence with the Pagoda stockade, and at
" sunrise on the 7th instant five hundred bayo-
" nets were disembarked one mile below the

1825.
BURMAH.

"Pagoda. The men were formed into two columns of equal strength, under the command of Lieutenant-Colonel O'Donoghoe 47th, and Major Basden, 89th Regiment.

"The gallantry and perseverance displayed deserve that I should mention them to you in the most favorable terms. To Lieutenant-Colonel O'Donoghoe and Major Basden, I beg to draw your attention in the strongest way, for the able manner and gallant style they conducted their respective columns to the point of attack at the Pagoda Stockade.

"(Signed)
"WM. COTTON,
"*Brigadier-General.*"

"GENERAL ORDERS.
"*Head-quarters,*
"*Camp near Donabew,*
"31*st March*, 1825.

"Sir A. Campbell regrets the necessity of the severe call for duty, on the troops under his command, but long experience of their high and spirited feeling as soldiers, assures to him a cheerful co-operation for a few hours more in the preparations going on, for affording himself and them a gratifying opportunity of humbling a cruel and arrogant foe."

On the 26th a communication having been opened with the land column, measures were taken to concentrate the whole force above the line of stockades, leaving barely as many men as were necessary to protect the gun boats and vessels below the works, to prevent the enemy's design on Rangoon.

Ground was forthwith broken before the place, and parallels opened in the usual way.

On the morning of the 2nd April at daylight, the breaching batteries opened their fire, and in less than four hours had made a sufficient breach.

At an early hour the men were called upon to get their breakfasts, and be ready to fall in. At 9 o'clock it was found that the enemy had abandoned the works during the night. This was a disappointment. It was ascertained from the few prisoners who were found in the stockade, that General Maha Bundoola, the life and soul of the Burman Army, had been killed the day previously by a rocket whilst making his usual daily examination of the approaches.

As the Burman soldiers had not sufficient confidence in any other of their chiefs, they promptly resolved to abandon what they now despaired of defending, and most admirably did they carry the resolve into effect, as will be evident from the fact above stated, namely, that the British were not aware of their departure before 9 o'clock in the morning.

By the 6th the regiment had re-embarked, and the advance to Prome (its destined quarters) was resumed. On the 1st May, the last party of the corps arrived, the land force under Sir A. Campbell having established themselves there without loss some days previously.

The Monsoon being now fast approaching, and the commander of the forces deeming it impracticable to proceed further, without exposing his troops to the heavy and incessant rains, and the consequent diseases of the country, he established his quarters at Prome, and as the enemy had retired to a considerable distance, nothing happened to disturb or annoy the troops until nearly the close of the rainy season, when the enemy having sued for peace, an armistice was granted, and negotiations to that effect entered into accordingly. Commissioners from the Court of Ava, and those on the part of the British Government, having met in conference on the 2nd October, the former solicited a prolongation of the armistice until the 2nd November, which they

1825.
BURMAH.

1825.
BURMAH.

stated to be necessary that the terms agreed on might receive the final sanction of the King of Ava, though it proved only a device to gain time, and enable him to collect his troops.

On the 20th October Sir A. Campbell gained intelligence that the enemy were in full force marching on Prome, with a view to a general attack on the British position, in conjunction with a large and imposing fleet of war boats, many of which had already passed down the river to a village some miles below the line of demarkation recognised in the terms of the armistice, where, after putting many of the peaceable inhabitants to death they had set fire to their dwellings. The enemy having premeditatedly committed such hostile and provoking acts, the British force commenced to break up its cantonment, and on the 17th November took up a position about one mile in advance of Prome, in daily expectation of being attacked, the troops being in consequence kept constantly under arms.

The 89th, under Major Gore, occupied a central position a little in advance of the line. By the latter end of November the enemy had established himself in several very strong stockaded and entrenched works, about 6 miles in advance of the British position.

On the 1st of December, everything being in readiness for the opening campaign, Sir Archibald Campbell determined to make the first onset, and accordingly the whole Army moved forward to the attack in two divisions; the Madras Division, of which the 89th formed part, under Brigadier-General Cotton, and the Bengal Division under the personal command of Major-General Sir A. Campbell. About 10 o'clock the Madras Division came up with the enemy at Zeope, and in a short time carried the whole line of defence without much loss, though the enemy suffered very considerably, and many officers of distinction were killed.

3 Privates wounded.

About two o'clock the same day the Bengal Division was engaged, but nothing very material was effected until the morning of the 2nd, when the Burmese having concentrated their troops and taken up a very strong position upon the heights above Prome, were attacked and driven from them with great slaughter. From the very formidable attitude of the enemy, the number and situation of his defences, and the very intricate nature of the country it was not until the 5th December that he was completely driven from his positions, although in each successive attack he was forced from point to point with considerable loss, in particular on the 1st, 2nd, and 5th December, on the latter day the 89th with other corps of the Madras Division under Brigadier-General Cotton were again actively engaged.

A considerable body of the enemy had made a stand on the right bank of the river, and some adjacent hills. The division crossed the river at 3 o'clock in the morning, and after traversing a thick jungle for some time, fell in with the enemy and dislodged them from every post that they made an attempt to defend. After completing this service the troops returned to camp a little before sunset.

On the same day a considerable body of the enemy was cut off in their retreat by the Light Brigade; the loss of the British in these operations was trifling, considering they had to contend with a hidden enemy in a thick woody country.

1825.
BURMAH.

89th:
One private killed,
Four privates wounded.

"*Camp, 3rd Dec.*, 1825.

" DIVISION ORDERS.

" Brigadier-General Cotton requests that the "officers and men of the Madras Division, whom "he had the honor of commanding on the "1st of the month, at the capture of those stock-"ades which were so gallantly carried, will accept "his highest encomiums for their spirited conduct "on the occasion."

1825.

BURMAH.

"*Camp near Prome,*
5th December, 1825.

"DIVISION ORDERS.

"It is with the most satisfactory sensation that Brigadier-General Cotton has it again his duty to express to the Madras Division his most sincere thanks and congratulations upon the operations of this day, which renders him fully confident, that whatever the numbers of the enemy may be, and strength of their situation, the result will always be their discomfiture. When everybody exerts himself to the utmost, it is difficult to exemplify, but General Cotton has only again to remark that it is utterly impossible for any operations to have been more manly seconded, than those of the 1st and present occasion have been."

The army prosecuted its march on the 13th, and met with no interruptions until it reached Meady on the 19th December, where the enemy made a stand, but soon gave way without much resistance. The force again moved on, and several strong stockades were vacated as the British approached, some in an unfinished state, and others the enemy endeavoured to burn, in fact so closely were the Burmese pursued, that in their haste they abandoned many materials, carts, &c., as well as many of their sick.

The force arrived at Pattanagoh on the 29th December, and the enemy having crossed over to the other side of the river, established himself at Mallown, a strong and important position on the right bank. On the arrival of the British troops who came up in time to prevent the advance of their boats, the enemy were thrown into great confusion, and commenced embarking military stores, women, and children, and many boats attempted to push forward but were prevented. Being driven to this extremity the Burmese again sued for peace, and a cessation of hostilites took place, till the 19th January, in order that negotiations might be entered upon.

A treaty of peace was signed by the commissioners of both powers on the 3rd January, 1826, and sent to Ava for confirmation by the King. The time allowed for the truce being nearly ended, Sir A. Campbell prepared to storm the works, and on the forenoon of the 19th at 11 o'clock, the day on which the armistice expired, the British opened their batteries, and about 2 o'clock the same day (a breach having been made) the town was stormed and carried.

The 89th on this occasion was detailed in the first instance for the storming party, but afterwards, owing to some subsequent arrangement, was ordered with other regiments to cross the river and land above the town, with a view to cut off the retreat of the enemy.

The force re-crossed the river the same evening, and on the 21st and 22nd the whole fortification was destroyed, and the town burnt to the ground.

> "*Head-quarters,*
> "*Camp Pattanagoh,*
> "*20th January,* 1826.

"GENERAL ORDERS.

"The infatuation of the Burmese Government "has forced upon the Major-General, the task of "congratulating his army on another victory; the "duty, which common prudence and sincerity "ought to have spared them, has been performed "by the troops to his entire satisfaction. Of the "troops destined for the decisive onset, one "brigade alone had the good fortune to be "engaged; of the two regiments of which it is "composed, it is enough to say, that their conduct "was in the spirit of the best days of their "honorable service in this country.

"Circumstances which no forethought could "obviate, deprived the rest of the force embarked, "of the full participation of this fresh success.

1826.
BURMAH.

"The commander of the forces cannot however, "withold his thanks from those troops and their "commanders for their spirited endeavours, which "he also deems a peculiarly gratifying portion of "his duty."

On the 26th of January, the force again moved forward, from which period till the 8th February nothing happened to impede its march. In the course of the night of the 8th, Sir Archibald Campbell got information that the Burmese had strongly entrenched themselves about four miles from Pegamew, and instantly communicated the intelligence to Brigadier-General Cotton, who, with the Madras Division (89th included) moved forward at one o'clock a.m. on the 9th, and after a march of about 25 miles came up with the enemy, who for the first time attacked the British outside the main position, thus for once deviating from their usual system of warfare; but the result proved as on all former occasions, they were shortly driven from the field in great disorder, and pursued even to the very gates of the fort of Pegamew, from whence also they made a precipitate retreat, leaving behind them a quantity of ordnance, warlike and other stores, and a vast number of cattle.

"GENERAL ORDERS.

"*Head-quarters, Pegamew,*
"*9th February,* 1826.

"Providence has once more blessed with success "the British arms in this country, and in the "decisive defeat of the imposing force posted "under and within the walls of Pegamew, the "Major-General recognises a fresh display of the "military virtues which have characterized his "troops from the commencement of the war.

"Early on this day the enemy departing from "the cautious system of defence behind field works "and entrenchments, which forms their usual

"device of war, and relying on their great
"numerical superiority and singular advantages
"of ground, ventured on a succession of bold
"manœuvres on the flanks and front of the
"British columns. This false confidence has
"been rebuked by a reverse, severe, signal and
"disastrous.

"Their troops of either arm were repelled at
"every point, and their masses driven with con-
"fusion within their city.

"The storm of Pegamew which followed, ex-
"hibited the same features of intrepidity and self
"devotion.

"The frequencies of these acts of spirited
"soldiership on the part of his troops, renders it
"difficult for the Major-General to vary the terms
"of his praise, but he offers to every officer and
"soldier engaged this day, the tribute of his thanks,
"at once with the affection of a commander and
"the cordiality of a comrade."

1826.
BURMAH.

On the 12th of February the army was again put in motion, and proceeded as far as Yandaboo, where on the 24th of the same month a treaty of peace was signed, and on the 8th of March the force was broken up, and the 89th returned in boats to Rangoon, where the corps arrived on 27th March; they were embarked on board the transport "Sullimany" and "William Money" the same day, and proceeded to Madras, at which place the head-quarters of the regiment under the command of Major Basden arrived on the 28th April, followed by the 2nd division on the 19th of May, thus concluding a most harassing service of two years, less a few days.

Brevet Major Gore, Capts. Young, Pearse, and Aplin. Lieutenants C. G. King, Arrow, Prendergast, Ensigns, Gray, & Hope. Pay-Master Grant, Qr.-Master Edwards, Assistant-Surgeon Orr, Lt. Hewson, Act. Adjt., 30 Sergeants, 22 Corpls., 14 Drummers, and 233 Privates.

"*Head-quarters,*
"*Camp Yandaboo,*
"*5th March,* 1826.

"GENERAL ORDERS.

"The happy termination in this encampment of
"the contest in behalf of the national honor,

1826.
BURMAH.

"reminds the Major-General of the near approach
"of the period of his separation from this force,
"the officers and soldiers of which will shortly he
"trusts, return to enjoy an unbroken portion of
"repose after their prolonged labours, happy he
"doubts not in the society of those most dear to
"them, from whom they have been now little
"short of two years separated.

"The army that has deserved so well of the
"State which it serves, cannot fail to have
"endeared itself to its General. He will part
"from it, whenever the moment arrives, with an
"impression of satisfaction, deep and indelible, as
"regards its conduct as a body, and he can
"assure every individual in the ranks with a
"perfect sincerity, that it will hereafter be a
"source of pride and gratification to him, to be
"enabled to promote in any way the happiness
"and interest of any soldier or officer who
"has served under him in Ava."

MADRAS.

The regiment moved on the 15th October from Fort St. George to St. Thomas' Mount.

In consideration of the distinguished part borne by the regiment in the war in Burmah, His Majesty was pleased to issue his Royal authority under date 29th November, 1826, that the 89th Regiment should thenceforth bear the word "Ava" on its Colours and Appointments.

1827.
MADRAS.

On the 3rd August, 1827, the 89th returned to Fort St. George, Madras.

1828.
TRICHINOPOLY.

The right wing of the regiment moved into camp, near Palaveram, on the 9th of September, and was followed by the left wing on the 11th.

On the 21st of September the regiment commenced its march for Trichinopoly, where it arrived on the 24th October.

1829.
TRICHINOPOLY.

The regiment remained at Trichinopoly.

Extracts from a letter from the Adjutant-General of the Forces, dated Horse Guards, 4th June, 1829 :—

"Lord Hill considers the reports of the 30th, 41st, 46th, and 89th Regiments as very satisfactory, and that of the last mentioned corps as particularly creditable to Lieutenant-Colonel McCaskill.

"(Signed)   H. TAYLOR,
Adjutant General."

1830.
MADRAS.

The 89th Regiment marched on 2nd August, 1830, from Trichinopoly *en route* to Madras for embarkation to England, and on the 30th of the same month went into camp near the cantonment of St. Thomas' Mount, where they remained during the month of September.

On the 9th, 10th, 11th, 21st, 22nd, 23rd, and 25th September the regiment was opened for volunteers, and 3 sergeants, 19 corporals, 4 drummers, 384 privates extended their services to various of His Majesty's Regiments remaining in India.

On the 9th of October the regiment moved into quarters in Fort St. George.

The following order was issued by the Major-General Commanding the Southern Division of the Madras Army on the departure of the regiment from Trichinopoly :—

"*Deputy Assistant-Adjutant-General's*
"*Office,*
"*Head-quarters Southern Division,*
"*Point Callemere,*
"*27th July,* 1830.

"Division Orders by Major-General the Right Honorable the Earl of Carnworth :—

1830.
MADRAS

"The Major-General views with much regret the removal from his command of H.M.'s 89th Regiment; he has however, the satisfaction to know that the movement will be shortly followed by an order for its embarkation to Europe, when he trusts a speedy arrival in old England, and happy re-union with kindred and friends, will amply compensate the corps for the privations it has sustained in its long and arduous service in India.

"It is a most gratifying part of the Major-General's duty, to record in public orders his entire approbation of the conduct of the regiment whilst under his command, and which has enabled him to report most favourably of it to head-quarters.

"In now taking leave of the corps, he thinks it due to Lieutenant-Colonel McCaskill and the officers under his orders, to state, that he is enabled to assure them and the regiment that its orderly soldierlike conduct since it has been quartered in Trichinopoly, has gained for it the respect and esteem of the inhabitants, European, and native, and it has afforded his Lordship the greatest satisfaction to have heard the expressions of these feelings. It now only remains for him to assure the corps that it will take with it his most sincere esteem, and in whatever part of the world its service may be required, his best wishes will attend it, and he will always feel deeply interested in the honor and welfare of the regiment."

1831.

On the 13th January, 1831, the 89th Regiment embarked at Madras on their return to England.

The following very gratifying order was issued on the occasion by the Governor of Madras in Council :—

"*Fort St. George,*
"*7th January,* 1831.

"G.O. BY GOVERNMENT, No. 6.

"The officers and men of H.M.'s 89th Regiment

"being on the eve of embarkation for their native
" country, the Right Honourable the Governor in
" Council performs a very pleasing part of his duty
" in bearing public testimony to the merits of that
" corps.

1831.
MADRAS.

" During the last 21 years, there has scarcely a
" service of importance been performed by the
" army of this establishment, in which H.M.'s
" 89th Regiment has not borne a prominent and
" distinguished part.

" At the capture of the Isle of France, at the
" reduction of the island of Java, in the Deccan, in
" the Southern Concan, and in Ava, their gallantry
" and steadiness were the admiration of their com-
" panions in arms, and obtained for them the
" thanks of the highest authorities, and the Right
" Honourable the Governor will always have par-
" ticular gratification in reflecting that their
" conduct in garrison which has ever been as
" exemplary as in the field, has been latterly under
,, his own immediate observation.

" The cordiality with which the officers and men
" have at all times acted with the company's troops
" is deserving of his warmest acknowledgments,
" and although he is precluded from granting to
" H.M.'s 89th Regiment on its quitting India,
" a donation of Batta similar to that which has
" been conferred on other regiments whose con-
" duct has not been more meritorious, he will
" not fail to bring to notice of the directors,
" the high claims which the regiment has es-
" tablished to every mark of their favourable
" consideration.

"By order of the Right Honorable
" The Governor in Council,
"(Signed) ROBERT CLERK,
" *Sec. to Government.*

" By order of the Commander-in-Chief,
" (Signed) T. H. S. Conway,
" Adjt.-General of the Army."

1831.
CHATHAM.

On the 7th May, 1831, the head-quarter division came to anchor off Gravesend, and on the following day were disembarked, and marched to Chatham after an absence of twenty-five years from the United Kingdom, comprising service in South America, South Africa, Ceylon, India, and the Indian Archipellago, and including operations in the Carnatic in suppression of the dissatisfaction of the Madras Army of 1809, capture of Bourbon and the Isle of France, Capture of Java, Expedition to Sumatra, campaign in the Deccan and southern Concan in 1818, and in the Sawant-Warree States in 1819, and finally in the war with Ava from 1824 to 1826.

CANTERBURY.

On the 13th of May the regiment marched for Canterbury, arriving there on the 15th. On the 31st August and 1st September the 89th again changed quarters, and proceeding in two divisions to Ramsgate, were embarked on board His Majesty's 74 gun Ships "Tallavera" and "Wellesley" for conveyance to Plymouth, where they arrived on the 3rd September and occupied the Citadel.

PLYMOUTH.

DEVONPORT.

On the 22nd November the regiment moved to Devonport, and were quartered in George's Square, Cumberland Square, and the several adjoining barracks, giving detachments to Pendennis Castle and Drakes Island.

1832.
DEVONPORT.

The regiment remained at Devonport under command of Sir Edward Miles, C.B. and K.I.S.

1833.
DEVONPORT.

This year was marked by an event memorable in the annals of the regiment, by the high honor conferred upon it in the presentation of its new colours, by the hands of Her Royal Highness the Princess Victoria, Heiress Presumptive to the Throne.

The Princess and her august mother the Duchess of Kent, arrived at Plymouth on the 2nd of August, with the view of inspecting the

PRINCESS VICTORIA'S REGIMENT.

1833.
DEVONPORT.

dockyards and great national establishments at that station, and Their Royal Highnesses very readily and graciously consented to take the opportunity of presenting the colours to the 89th Regiment.

The ceremony took place on the Hoe, at noon, the 3rd August, in the presence of General Lord Hill, Commander-in-Chief (who had opportunely arrived at Plymouth to inspect the garrison), Sir John McDonald the Adjutant General, Sir John Cameron, Major-General Commanding the District, and a large concourse of spectators, naval, military, and civil.

The troops in garrison consisting of the Royal Artillery, the reserve companies of the 22nd, 87th, and 98th Regiments, and the 89th Regiment, were drawn up in line extending from one end of the Hoe to the other, the 89th being in the centre.

On arriving on the ground, Their Royal Highnesses were received by General Lord Hill, and Major-General Sir John Cameron, and by a guard of honor of the Royal Artillery.

The Royal Carriage having taken up a position in front of the saluting flag, and the Royal salute having been given, the 89th were formed in three sides of a square. The new colours borne by Colonel Birch, Royal Engineers, and Colonel Pym, Royal Artillery, were then brought in front of their Royal Highness' carriage and uncased, and the ceremony of consecration was performed by the Revd. Richard Hanna, Chaplain to the garrison, in a very impressive and appropriate prayer. Her Royal Highness the Duchess of Kent then standing in front of her carriage, and with her arm embracing the Princess, in her name read the following gracious address to Colonel Sir Edward Miles:—

" SIR,
" I accede to the wish expressed that the Princess
" should present to His Majesty's 89th Regiment

1833.
DEVONPORT.

"their new Colours; she will do so with all the feelings that should distinguish a British Princess.

"The Princess' feelings have already, in reading the history of her country, responded to the national pride every Briton must feel, in looking back on the splendid achievements of the military force of this country. They are proud memorials of the past, and the best guarantee to the nation, that, if to support our national honor it is necessary to unfurl these colours before an enemy, the 89th Regiment will not only recollect the deeds of their brother soldiers of former times, but those that have marked the gallant career of this regiment since their formation, in every quarter of the globe, more particularly at those places which are borne on the colours that the Princess now confides to the regiment, in the King's name."

The new colours were now handed in succession to the Princess by Colonels Birch and Pym, and were by Her Royal Highness delivered to the two senior ensigns, (Ensigns Robert Falconer Miles, and Caledon Richard Egerton,) who received them kneeling.

Colonel Sir Edward Miles then returned thanks in the following manner:—

"In the name of the officers and soldiers of the 89th regiment, I return most sincere and grateful thanks for the distinguished and exalted honor your Royal Highness has this day conferred on the 89th Regiment by the presentation of these colours."

The new colours having been trooped in front of the line, and received with due honor, the troops marched past their Royal Highnesses and the ceremony concluded.

CORK.

On the 8th of August, 1833, the regiment embarked on board H.M.S. "Romney" for conveyance to Cork, and having landed there on the

12th, marched into barracks, giving detachments to Mill Street and Macroom.

On the 8th of November, Major George Jones K.H., succeeded to the command of the regiment *vice* Colonel Sir Edward Miles.

At this period the new system of drill was introduced into the regiment. Major-General Sir Thomas Arbuthnot took frequent opportunities of examining the progress of it, and was pleased to express his satisfaction at the advancement made both in drill and discipline.

1833.
CORK.

In the month of August, 1834, the regiment marched to Fermoy, giving detachments to Mallow and Michelstown.

1834.
FERMOY.

On the 2nd of October the Commander-in-Chief of the Forces in Ireland, Lieutenant-General Sir Hussey Vivian, visited Fermoy and inspected the 89th regiment, on which occasion he intimated his highest approbation of the steadiness of the men under arms, as well as of their performances of the different movements, as appears by the following Regimental Order :—

" REGIMENTAL ORDER.

"Lieutenant-Colonel Jones has extreme gratifi-
" cation in announcing to the regiment the high
" encomium passed upon it by Lieutenant-General
" Sir Hussey Vivian, Commander-in-Chief to the
" Forces in Ireland, on his inspection and review of
" it this morning. He was pleased to remark
" to the Lieutenant-Colonel that he had scarcely
" ever seen so steady a regiment under arms,
" and the manner in which they performed the
" different evolutions they were put through, met
" his highest approbation.

" It is a source of additional gratification to the
" Commanding officer, that he has received the
" Commander-in-Chief's instructions to convey
" these sentiments to the officers and non-com-
" missioned officers and regiment at large."

1834.
FERMOY.

On the 27th October, 1834, the half-yearly inspection took place by Major-General Sir Thomas Arbuthnot, K.C.B., whose remarks upon the improvement which had taken place in the corps were of the most gratifying description, testifying his high approbation of the discipline and appearance of the officers and men, as well as the state of the interior economy. *Vide* regimental orders, as follows :—

"REGIMENTAL ORDERS.

" Lieutenant-Colonel Jones has much satisfac-
" tion in announcing to the regiment, that he has
" received the commands of the Major-General Sir
" Thomas Arbuthnot, to express his unqualified
" satisfaction at the masterly manner in which they
" performed the various evolutions at this morning's
" parade. The efficient state and cleanly appear-
" ance of the men, and their steadiness under
" arms was particularly remarked, as also the very
" clean state and neat appearance of the barrack-
" rooms; the state of the hospital, regimental
" schools, &c., drew forth the Major-General's praise
" and approbation, and the Lieutenant-Colonel
" offers his best thanks to the officers and non-
" commissioned officers &c., &c., for the assistance
" and co-operation they have given him on this
" as on former occasions."

During the sojourn of the regiment at Fermoy Colonel Stewart, formerly a field officer of the corps, and who served with it in Egypt, presented to the regiment a Turkish Gold Medal, which had been given by the Pacha of Egypt, for one of the Majors, but had remained unclaimed.*

In the month of October, additional detachments were furnished by the regiment to Charleville, Donerail, and Castletown Roche.

---

* *Note.*—No trace of this Medal can now be found, nor does it seem to have ever been in the Officers' Mess.

PRINCESS VICTORIA'S REGIMENT.

1834
FERMOY.

In the months of October, November, and December, the regiment was employed on several occasions of seizing and distraining for tithes, and for their steadiness and forbearance amidst most trying circumstances, received the thanks of Lord Hill, the General Commanding-in-Chief.

The want of standing orders in the 89th having been long felt, Lieutenant-Colonel Jones considered it necessary to revive the orders of the corps, and from those and the general regulations for the army, to complete a code for the use of the corps, which were printed and circulated to every officer and non-commissioned officer.

1835.
NAAS.

On the 7th January, two companies were detached to Youghall, and on the 9th, one company to Cappoquin in aid of civil power during the general election.

On the 21st January the regiment was ordered to be held in readiness to march to Naas, and to distribute detachments to Carlow, (two companies) Baltinglass, Gores Bridge, Graigne, Maryboro', Athy, Irim, and Navan, and on the 28th, 29th, and 30th, the corps quitted Fermoy in three divisions, the head-quarters reaching Naas on 9th February.

The company at Gores Bridge and Graigne, was shortly after removed to Kells, and the detachment at Navan was called in.

In the month of May a company was also stationed at Newbridge.

In the month of June a considerable part of the regiment was employed in aid of the civil power at Carlow, Athy, Hacketstown, Rathvilly, &c., &c., and their conduct during these services elicited the commendation of the Lieutenant-General Commanding in Ireland.

On the 17th July, Lieutenant-Colonel H. R. Hartley was appointed to the command of the regiment *vice* Lieutenant-Colonel G. Jones who exchanged with that officer to the 57th regiment.

1835.
DUBLIN.

On the 22nd of August the head-quarters marched to Dublin, and in a few days the whole regiment was assembled together and occupied Richmond Barracks.

The corps was at this time in the highest state of order and discipline, and looked forward to passing the usual year's service in Dublin garrison, but in this expectation was disappointed, for on the 27th August, orders were received from the depôt, to hold the service companies in readiness to proceed to Cork for embarkation to the West Indies.

On the 4th September Lieutenant-Colonel Richard Doherty of the 1st West India Regiment, was appointed to the command of the 89th Regiment *vice* Lieutenant-Colonel Hartley who retired on half-pay.

On the 10th of September the service and depôt companies were told off and inspected by Major-General Sir Edward Blakeney, commanding the eastern district, who expressed himself particularly pleased with the corps.

The 1st division of the service companies under the command of Major Pearse, embarked at the North Wall on the 18th September on board the "Innisfall" steamer, for Spike Island, where they were landed, and occupied barracks the following evening. The 2nd division followed on the 26th, detachments were given to Carlisle and Camden Forts, and Hawlbowline Islands.

After a home tour of only four years and one month, following on a service of 25 years in India, the head-quarters under the command of Major W. Pearse, embarked on the 19th October, on board the "Parmelia" Transport, to enter on another course of service within the tropics.

The second division embarked the following day on board the Transport "Prince Regent."

BARBADOES.

Both vessels sailed on 22nd for Barbadoes, where the head-quarters landed on the 3rd

1835.
BARBADOES.

December. The regiment occupied the brick barrack at St. Ann's.

Lieutenant-Colonel Doherty joined and assumed the command on the 23rd December.

On the 30th December the regiment was inspected in barracks by Major-General Sir Lionel Smith commanding the forces in the Windward and Leeward Islands, who was pleased to express his approbation of its general appearance both as to its health and cleanliness, and to the men's soldierlike demeanour and carriage.

The reserve companies under the command of Brevet Lieutenant-Colonel Basden, C.B., left Richmond Barracks, Dublin, on the 28th September, arriving at Drogheda on the 29th, where they were stationed, detaching one company to Navan.

1836.
TRINIDAD.

On the 1st of January, the regiment furnished detachments to Gun Hill, Moncrief, and Oistens.

On the 25th of March, the head quarter division of the regiment embarked at Barbadoes on board the "Columbia" steamer for Trinidad, touching at Tobago, and leaving there a detachment of two companies, under Captain Aplin.

The head-quarters landed at Trinidad, on the 27th, and marched to St. James's Barracks, giving a detachment to Naparima. The 2nd division followed the beginning of April.

During the month of April, the yellow fever broke out in the detachment at Tobago, causing a great mortality particularly in the Grenadier Company, but it happily subsided in the beginning of May.

On the 21st June, Lieutenant-Colonel Doherty, proceeded to England on leave of absence, and Major W. Pearse assumed the command of the regiment.

The following order was issued by the Lieutenant-Colonel on this occasion.

1836.

TRINIDAD.

"*St. James's Barracks,*
Trinidad,
21*st June*, 1836.

"REGIMENTAL MORNING ORDER.

"Lieutenant-Colonel Doherty, being on the eve of availing himself of leave of absence, the command of the regiment will be assumed by Major Pearse, to whom all reports will be accordingly addressed.

"Captain Thorp, being the Senior Captain present at head-quarters, will do duty as Major until further orders.

"The Lieutenant-Colonel takes this opportunity to return his best thanks to the officers and non-commissioned officers, for their efficient co-operation during the period of his command, and to the soldiers of the regiment generally for their exemplary conduct, particularly since their arrival in Trinidad, and to which must mainly be attributed the excellent health they enjoy.

"He trusts all will steadily persevere in a course so creditable and so conducive to their own advantage, and that he will be afforded the gratifying pleasure on his return to the corps, of being called on to congratulate officers and men, on the state of the battalion both as to health and discipline."

The few months during which the regiment had the advantage of serving under Lieutenant-Colonel Doherty's command, proved of the greatest benefit to the corps, from the admirable system of interior economy and arrangement adapted to the West Indian climate, established by that excellent officer, (the result of an experience of many years service in the country) and, if while unaccompanied by the improved barrack accommodation and other sanitary measures since adapted, it proved inefficient in warding off the ill effects of that unhealthy climate, it at least tended very considerably to mitigate the evil when it came.

During the autumn (the unhealthy season) the yellow fever visited both the islands of Trinidad and Tobago with great severity, and many valuable lives were lost to the regiment. The number of deaths during the year was ninety, upwards of eighteen per cent. on the strength.

The depôt left Drogheda, on the 26th July, 1836, for Omagh, and arrived there on the 1st August, giving a detachment to Lifford.—A draft consisting of 1 subaltern, 1 sergeant, 30 rank and file, embarked in the autumn to join the service companies.

The draft from the depôt under Ensign Pigott, joined head quarters on the 28th February.

In the issue of this year's clothing, the black and colored worm was omitted in the lace of the regiment, and the sergeants received double-breasted coatees without lace, in accordance with General Order, dated Horse Guards, 20th September, 1836.

On the 18th of June, intelligence having arrived at St. James' during the night, that a mutiny had broken out in the 1st West India Regiment at St. Joseph, the Light company made a forced march to that station, arriving there with extraordinary despatch, but the mutineers had already dispersed, and having fortunately broken into some casks of blank ammunition without knowing the difference, fewer lives had been lost than might have been expected. A subaltern's party was left in barracks, and the remainder of the company returned to their quarters.

On the 26th September, Lieutenant-General Sir Charles Bulkeley Egerton, G.C.M.G. & K.C.H., (who had served in and commanded the regiment) was appointed Colonel *vice* General Sir Robert Macfarlane, removed to 32nd Regiment.

1836.
TRINIDAD.

1837.

1837.
TRINIDAD.

In the month of December, the subaltern's detachments at St. Joseph and Naparima, were increased to companies, and Captain Kenny's company embarked for Tobago, to relieve the two companies stationed there under Captain Aplin, which joined head quarters.

The regiment was generally more healthy this year than during the past.

The depôt companies left Omagh, on the 19th May, 1837, for Londonderry, and arrived there on the 20th, from whence, on the 10th September following, they embarked for Warren Point, and marched to Newry. On the 14th October, they again embarked on board H.M.S. "Messenger," for England, and having landed at Gosport, on the 17th October, occupied quarters at Forton Barracks.

1838.

A draft, consisting of 1 captain, 2 subalterns, 2 sergeants, 1 drummer, and 100 rank and file, embarked this year for the service companies.

The regiment continued this year also at Trinidad and Tobago.

On the 26th March, the draft under Captain Pole joined head-quarters.

On the 7th July, Lieutenant-Colonel Badsen, C.B., succeeded to the command of the regiment, *vice* Lieutenant-Colonel Sir Richard Doherty, appointed Governor of Sierra Leone, and Colonel on the staff in West Africa.

The portion of the Regiment at Trinidad, suffered very severely this year. In July, yellow fever in its most virulent form attacked the light company at St. Joseph, where it had not appeared for 20 years, carrying off nearly one half of the detachment in the space of one fortnight, after which the company was withdrawn and a weekly guard furnished to take care of the barracks; many of the men on this duty, also fell victims to the fever.

In November and December, the head-quarters

suffered in like manner, the officers as per margin, and many non-commissioned officers and men died this year, and so many officers were invalided, that the regiment had no staff, and hardly one officer per company available. Major Pearse was invalided, and the command involved on Major Aplin. The detachment at Tobago, was very healthy at this period.

The depôt remained this year at Forton Barracks, Gosport.

A draft, consisting of — captain, — subaltern, 2 sergeants, 1 drummer, 80 rank and file, embarked for the service companies.

1838.
TRINIDAD.

Died of Yellow Fever:
Captain Pearson,
Lieuts. Blunt & Need,
Surgeon Orr.

On the 9th of February, the head-quarters and the right wing of the regiment, embarked at Trinidad, for Antigua, under the command of Lieutenant McCausland.

The left wing, under Major Aplin, proceeded to St. Kitts. The head-quarters arrived at Antigua, on the 17th February, on which day, Lieutenant-Colonel Basden assumed the command.

The head-quarter division gave a detachment to Montserrat, and the left wing one to Nevis.

The detachment from Tobago, joined on the 21st February.

Lieutenant-General Sir Samford Whittingham, commanding the forces, inspected the regiment on 8th April.

The draft arrived at head-quarters, the latter end of April.

The regiment was comparatively healthy during the year, though a good many deaths occurred from fever, in the detachment at St. Kitts.

The depôt remained this year also at Gosport. Two captains, 3 subalterns, 1 sergeant, 111 rank and file, embarked early in the year for the service companies, and a further draft of 1 captain, 1 subaltern, 3 sergeants, 137 rank and file, at the end of the year.

1839.
ANTIGUA.

Officers died during the year:
Captain Gray, Lieut. McCausland.

1840.
ANTIGUA.

On the 31st March, a company was despatched to St. John's.

On the 25th March, the draft under Captain Clarke, joined head quarters.

On the 19th May, the regiment was inspected by Lieutenant-General Maister, commanding the forces in the Windward and Leeward Islands, on which occasion, the following general order was issued.

"*Head-quarters, Antigua,*
"*19th May,* 1840.

"GENERAL ORDERS.

"The Lieutenant-General commanding has much "pleasure in expressing his satisfaction, with the "clean, healthy, and soldierlike appearance of both "wings of the 89th Regiment, at their recent in- "spection, as well as with their interior system "and arrangements; and he begs that Lieutenant- "Colonel Basden and Major Aplin, will convey to "the officers and non-commissioned officers and "privates, under their respective commands, the "Lieutenant-General's favourable opinion.

"By command,
"(Signed) T. H. TIDY,
"*Captain,* 14*th Regiment,*
"*For the Deputy Adjutant-General.*"

On the 28th June, the Grenadiers from Antigua, and Light Company from St. Kitts, were detached to Dominica, under the command of Captain Pole.

The regiment suffered a good deal during the year from fever, particularly that portion at St. Kitts. The head-quarters suffered chiefly from dysentery.

The depôt companies embarked on the 4th of August, at Gosport, on board H.M. Steamer, "Vesuvius" for Ireland, under command of Major Pearse, they landed at Ballinacurra, and marched to Fermoy, where they arrived on 7th August. On the 14th and 15th September, the depôt left Fermoy, in two divisions for Clonmel, and arrived on the 16th and 17th, giving a detachment of one company to Cashel.

1840.
ANTIGUA.

On the 1st April, the head-quarters embarked on board H.M.S "Sapphire" for Barbadoes, and arriving there on the 6th, were disembarked next day, and encamped at St. Ann's.

1841.
BARBADOES.

On the arrival of the 2nd Division on the 22nd of April, the commanding officer issued the following regimental orders.

"*St. Ann's, Barbadoes,*
"*22nd April*, 1841.

"REGIMENTAL ORDERS.

"The troop ship "Athol," having arrived with the "remainder of the regiment, Lieutenant-Colonel "Basden has much pleasure in congratulating "the corps on their re-union, after so many years "being separated. The trifling errors that have "been brought to the commanding officer's notice "since the arrival at head-quarters, justify his "saying there has been total absence of crime, "a character he confidently hopes the regiment "will sustain during its short stay in this island."

On the 1st May, the whole regiment embarked on board the troop ship "Abercromby Robinson," for Quebec, thus bringing to a close a service of five years and a half in the West Indies.

QUEBEC.

The "Abercromby Robinson" arrived off Quebec on the 5th June, and on the 6th, the regiment was transhipped to the steamer "Queen," and proceeded up the river to Montreal, *en route* to Amherstburg, on the Western frontier of the upper Province, where the head-quarters arrived on the 29th June.

AMHERSTBURG.

On the 8th July, the draft, under Captain Daly, joined head-quarters.

The regiment this year received one colour-

1841.
AMHERSTBURG.

sergeant, one drummer, 38 rank and file as volunteers from the 24th, and gave one sergeant, 12 rank and file, as volunteers to the Canadian rifles.

The depôt remained at Clonmel, detaching one company first to Cashel and afterwards to Carrick-on-Suir, until the 28th July, 1841, when it marched for Drogheda, arriving there on the 6th August. One company was detached to Cavan. A draft of 2 captains, 3 subalterns, 3 sergeants, 102 rank and file, embarked in the spring of this year for the service companies.

1842.
CHAMBLY.

On the 16th July, the 89th, under command of Major Thorp left Amherstburg and proceeded to Chambly, arriving there on the 24th July, and detaching one company to St. John's. In September, the detachment at St. John's was withdrawn, and two companies were sent to Sorrell for the winter.

The regiment received this year a strong reinforcement in volunteers from the 56th and 67th Regiments, in all 243 rank and file, and a remarkably fine body of men.

The depôt left Drogheda on the 7th June for Naas, and arrived there on the 9th, giving at different periods detachments to Newbridge, Carlow, and Rathangan, at the latter place in aid of civil power, for the purpose of escorting barges along the canal. A draft of 6 men only embarked for the service companies.

1843.
MONTREAL.

On the 5th May, 1843, the regiment moved from Chambly to Montreal.

In the month of July, Major A. S. H. Aplin succeeded to the Lieutenant-Colonelcy *vice* Lieutenant-Colonel J. L. Basden, C.B., who retired on full pay after a service of 37 years in the 89th Regiment, (which he joined as Captain), including much hard fighting in which his gallantry was always conspicuous.

PRINCESS VICTORIA'S REGIMENT. 97

1843.
MONTREAL.

Lieutenant-Colonel Aplin shortly after exchanged to the 86th, and Lieutenant-Colonel J. W. Bouverie was appointed to the command of the Regiment.

The regiment this year received 2 sergeants, 1 drummer, 22 rank and file volunteers from the 70th Regiment, and 1 sergeant, 10 rank and file from the 85th Light Infantry and 2nd battalion of the 1st Royals.

The depôt moved on the 3rd April from Naas to Kilkenny, detaching one company to Carlow.

On the 16th May, the depôt again left Kilkenny for Clonmel, where it arrived on the 18th, giving detachments at different periods to Carrick-on-Suir, Cahir Castle, and Windgap, the latter in aid of civil power. On the 23rd November, the same year, the depôt marched from Clonmel to Cork, arriving there on the 27th November, and detaching companies to Ballincollig and Dunmanway.

1844.
MONTREAL.

The regiment remained during the year at Montreal, Lieutenant-Colonel Bouverie in command.

The depôt remained at Cork until the 18th September, when they embarked on board H.M. steamer "Alban" for Dublin, *en route* for Newbridge, and arrived there on the 21st September: while at Cork, a draft of 2 subalterns and 10 rank and file embarked for the service companies, and 37 rank and file volunteered for the 61st Regiment, then under orders for India.

1845.
QUEBEC.

In the month of February, Major E. Thorpe succeeded to the Lieutenant-Colonelcy of the regiment, *vice* Lieutenant-Colonel Bouverie deceased.

On the 9th of May, 1845, the head-quarter division, consisting of 3 companies, band and staff proceeded from Montreal to Quebec.

1845.
QUEBEC.

The left wing joined head-quarters at Quebec on the 16th of the same month.

On the occasion of the two calamitous fires at Quebec on the 28th of May, and 28th June, 1845, whereby no less than 71 streets and nearly 3,000 houses were destroyed, the 89th Regiment rendered most efficient service; their conduct in conjunction with that of other troops in garrison, received the approbation of Her Majesty, as expressed in the general orders of the army, dated Horse Guards, 8th July, and 13th August, 1845—Nos. 574 and 575.

"*Horse Guards,*
"*8th July,* 1845

" GENERAL ORDERS.

" The Commander-in-Chief has received from "Major-General Sir James Hope, reports of the "circumstances of the late conflagration in the city "of Quebec, in the province of Canada, of the con-"duct of the officers and troops composing the "garrison at the time, and the copy of the general "order issued upon the occasion by the com-"mander of the forces in North America, the late "Lieutenant-General Sir Richard Jackson, K.C.B.

"The Commander-in-Chief having considered "it his duty to lay the documents before the "Queen, Her Majesty was graciously pleased to "notice the discretion, intelligence, and ability "manifested by the officers, the zeal, persevering "fortitude, energy, and activity of the troops "under their command.

"On the occasion of communicating to the troops "in North America, his approbation of the con-"duct of Major-General Sir James Hope, and of "the officers and troops under his command, and the "information of the gracious notice thereof taken "by Her Majesty, the Commander-in-Chief desires "to draw the attention of the army at large, to "the fresh instance thus brought to its knowledge "of the advantage afforded by its discipline, and

"good order, subordination, and habits of
"obedience upon all occasions on which its
"fortitude, its zeal, its active and energetic
"action, can be required.

1845.
QUEBEC.

"The perusal of these papers will demonstrate
"to the officers and troops, that even in times of
"profound peace, circumstances may occur which
"may enable them to display all their good quali-
"ties, to render the most important services, and
"thus to acquire for them the respect of their
"fellow subjects, the approbation of their super-
"iors, and above all the notice of their Most
"Gracious Sovereign.

"By command of Field Marshal,
"The DUKE OF WELLINGTON,
"*Commander-in-Chief.*
"(Signed) JOHN McDONALD,
"*Adjutant-General.*"

"*Horse Guards,*
"13*th August,* 1845.
"GENERAL ORDERS.

"The Commander-in-Chief has received from
"Lieutenant-General the Earl Cathcart, com-
"manding the forces in North America, reports of
"the conduct of Major-General Sir James Hope,
"and of the officers and troops at Quebec, upon
"the occasion of a second conflagration, which
"unfortunately occurred in that city on the night
"of 28th June. He has laid these reports before
"Her Majesty, and he is happy in having another
"opportunity of expressing his approbation of the
"conduct of Major-General Sir James Hope, and
"of the officers and troops at Quebec.

"He particularly notices the reports made of
"Captain Boxer, of the Royal Navy, Lieutenant-
"Colonel Walker, Captain Warburton, and
"Lieutenant Shakespear, of the Royal Artillery,
"Lieutenant-Colonel Ward, of the Royal Engineers,
"Lieutenant-Colonel Thorp, of the 89th Regiment,

1845.
QUÉBEC.

"Major Watson, of the 14th Regiment, Lieutenant-
"Colonel Pritchard, Assistant Adjutant General,
"Captain Ingall, Deputy Assistant Quarter-Master-
"General, and Captain Hope, Aide-de-camp to
"Major-General Hope, and he draws the attention
"of the army at large to the fresh display in this
"transaction, of the good qualities of British Offi-
"cers and soldiers, cool deliberation and judg-
"ment in the direction of the measures to be
"adopted, energy in the superintendence of their
"execution, and the zeal, intrepidity, activity, and
"persevering labor of all to attain the object
"in view—that of arresting the progress of the
"misfortune, and saving the lives and property of
"Her Majesty's subjects.

"By command of Field Marshal,
"The DUKE OF WELLINGTON,
"*Commander-in-Chief.*

"(Signed) JOHN MACDONALD,
"*Adjutant-General.*"

The depôt left Newbridge on the 22nd of May, and embarked at Kingston on the 23rd on board Her Majesty's Steamer "Rhadamantus," for Whitehaven *en route* for Carlisle, where they arrived on the 26th, and occupied barracks in the Castle.

1846.

The establishment of the regiment was increased from 1st of April this year, to 50 sergeants, 1000 rank and file. On the 16th of July the new Percussion Arms were issued to the regiment.

On the 18th of July, the service companies embarked at Quebec on board H.M.'s Ship "Bellisle" for Halifax; on which occasion the following addresses were presented to the Regiment, from "The Magistrates," "The Town Council," and from the "Grand Jury" of the city of Quebec.

PRINCESS VICTORIA'S REGIMENT.

1846.
QUEBEC.

" *H.M.S. " Bellisle.*"
" REGIMENTAL ORDERS BY LIEUT.-COLONEL THORP.

" Lieutenant-Colonel Thorp has great pleasure "in communicating to the officers, non-com- "missioned officers and men of the 89th Regi- "ment, the two following addresses presented by "the Magistrates and Council of the city of "Quebec, on the departure of the Regiment "from that Garrison. The Lieutenant-Colonel "has made suitable acknowledgments in reply "thereto, and he feels convinced that the "gratifying and flattering opinions thus recorded "will be duly appreciated by the 89th Regiment, "and be ever borne in mind as an incentive to "gain by good conduct, and every exertion when "called for, the good will and approval of our "fellow subjects, in whatever part of the Globe "the 89th Regiment may be stationed."

" SIR,
" The Magistrates of the city of Quebec, on the "approaching departure of the 89th Regiment, "feel much pleasure in bearing testimony to the "exemplary conduct, of both men and officers "during the time the 89th Regiment has been "stationed in this Garrison, and to the eminently "useful service rendered by them on the many "occasions when the public calamities have "afforded the regiment an opportunity of ren- "dering their zealous assistance, and particularly "at the two fires of the 28th of May, and "the 28th of June, 1845.

" The Magistrates avail themselves of the "opportunity to convey to yourself personally, "an expression of the highest sense they "entertain of your own zealous and successful "exertions in the public service, and in the main- "tenance of the best possible understanding "between the citizens and the military, and they "beg you will be pleased to convey to the

1846.
QUEBEC.

"officers, non-commissioned officers and men "under your command, their regret at the "approaching departure of the regiment, and "the gratification the magistrates feel in "acknowledging their good conduct and services "in garrison.

"In taking leave of you, sir, the magistrates "wish to yourself, your officers and men, all "health and happiness, and a speedy and "prosperous voyage to your destination.

(Signed) W. K. McCord,
        Inspr. & Sub. of Police.
      " F. O. Aylwin, J.P.
      " Noah Freer, J.P.
      " H. Gowan, J.P.
      " H. Le Mesurier, J.P.
      " A. J. Wolf, J.P.
      " J. K. Paradis, J.P.
      " R. J. Alleyn, J.P.
      " Joshua Hunt, J.P.
      " John McLeod, J.P.
      " W. Phillips, J.P.

(Signed) C. M. De Foy, J.P.
    " C. Henderson, J.P.
    " J. Painchand, J.P.
    " R. Symes, J.P.
    " E. Dugal, J.P.
    " W. Petry, J.P.
    " J. C. Lee, J.P.
    " W. H. A. Davies, J.P.
    " J. McKenzie, J.P.
    " J. Racey, J.P.
    " John Legore, J.P.

"To
  "Lieutenant-Colonel Thorp,
    "Commanding Her Majesty's
      "89th Regiment of Foot."

"*Quebec, July 18th,* 1846.
"SIR,
"I have the honor to enclose a resolution of "the Mayor and Councillors of the city of "Quebec, which was adopted yesterday evening, "upon the approaching departure of the 89th "Regiment under your command, being inti-"mated to the Council.

    "I have the honor to be,
      "(Signed) G. O'KILL STUART,
                    "*Mayor of Quebec.*"

      "*City Clerk's Office,*
        "*Quebec,* 18*th July,* 1846.
"At a meeting of the City Council, held on "17th July, it was unanimously resolved:—
  "That his worship the Mayor be requested to

PRINCESS VICTORIA'S REGIMENT.

1846.
QUEBEC.

" convey to Lieutenant-Colonel Thorp, the
" officers and men of the 89th Regiment, and
" to Major Watson, and the officers and men
" of the 14th Regiment, the regret of this
" Council and the citizens generally, at their
" approaching departure, the high sense they
" entertain of the many services rendered by
" their regiments on various occasions, and this
" Council willingly bears testimony of their high
" state of discipline, and their general excellent
" conduct in garrison.

> " Certified "
> " (Signed) F. X. GARNEAU,
> " *City Clerk.*"

The regiment disembarked at Halifax, Nova Scotia, on the 31st July, and occupied barracks, giving detachments to Sydney, Cape Breton, and to Prince Edward's Island.

The depôt was moved from Carlisle to Hull on the 20th March, arrived there by railway the same day, and occupied the Citadel, subsequently giving detachments to Leeds and Sheffield.

1847.
HALIFAX.

The service companies embarked at Halifax on their return to England on the 8th April, on board the Freight ship "Herefordshire."

The following highly gratifying general order was issued on the embarkation of the regiment.

> " *Head-quarters,*
> " *Halifax,*
> " *7th April,* 1847.

" GENERAL ORDER.
" Upon the occasion of embarkation for Europe
" of the 89th Regiment, Lieutenant-General Sir
" J. Harvey desires to assure Lieutenant-Colonel
" Thorp, the officers, non-commissioned officers
" and soldiers of that excellent corps, that it will
" afford him pleasure to bring to the knowledge
" of His Grace the Commander-in-Chief, the

1847.
HALIFAX.

"favourable opinion with which the conduct of that corps has impressed him, during the period of its having been under his command.

"The 89th Regiment carries with it His Excellency's best wishes for its honor and happiness."

CHICHESTER.

The "Herefordshire" arrived at Spithead on the 27th April, and the regiment was disembarked at Portsmouth on the 29th, and proceeded to Chichester.

While at Chichester, the regiment was inspected by Major-General Lord Frederick Fitzclarence, commanding the South Western district, who expressed himself highly pleased with the thoroughly soldier-like appearance of the corps.

DOVER.

The service companies moved from Chichester to Dover in two divisions, on the 6th and 7th of May. The depôt left Hull on the 27th April for Weedon, and moved from thence to Dover on 6th and 7th of May.

The whole regiment was thus re-united at Dover, after a tour of eleven years and nine months foreign service. The following order was issued by the commanding officer on the occasion:—

"*Dover,*
"11*th May,* 1847.

"Regimental order by Lieutenant-Colonel "Thorp:—

"The commanding officer takes this opportunity of congratulating the service companies on their return home, after an honourable service in the West Indies and British North America of nearly 12 years.

"The conduct of the non-commissioned officers and men during the time the Lieutenant-Colonel has been in command has been most satisfactory, and their meritorious conduct at the two calamitous fires at Quebec, stands recorded by His Grace the Commander-in-Chief.

"The embarkation of the regiment at Quebec and also at Halifax, was of a most soldier-like description, and their conduct during the voyage and since their disembarkation has been most praiseworthy.

"With a view to their present happiness, and also of ensuring to themselves all the advantages of which the service admits on discharge, Lieutenant-Colonel Thorp calls on the men of the service companies as well as the regiment at large, to persevere in that line of good conduct which has lately so strongly developed itself, assuring the well conducted soldier that nothing shall be wanting on his part to make his position whilst serving as happy and comfortable as circumstances will admit of, and of securing for him on discharge, every advantage which he is entitled to."

1847.
DOVER.

While the regiment remained at Dover, it detached 1 field officer and 4 companies to Sheerness. On the 9th and 10th November, the regiment left Dover in two divisions, the headquarters for "Ashton-under-lyne," giving field-officers' detachments at Burnley and Burslem, and companies to Colne, Wigan, and Bolton.

On the occasion of leaving Dover, the following address was presented to the regiment by the town council of Dover:—

"*Borough of Dover.*

"At a meeting of the Town Council of this Borough, held the 9th November, 1847, the following resolution was passed:—

RESOLVED:—"That the thanks of the corporation be given to Lieutenant-Colonel Thorp, and the officers of the 89th Regiment, for their great courtesy towards the inhabitants of this town, in allowing the band of the said regiment to perform for the amusement of the inhabitants and visitors, and that this council do also express

1847.
DOVER.

"its entire approbation of the exemplary good "conduct of the men of the 89th Regiment "during their stay in this garrison.

"(Signed) G. W. LEDGER,
"*Town Clerk.*"

1848.
ASHTON-UNDER-LYNE.

The head-quarters arrived at Ashton on the 12th November.

In the spring and summer of this year, the disaffection of the Chartists in England, and the attempted rebellion headed by Smith O'Brien in Ireland, both of them sympathetic results of the French Revolution of February, 1848, gave cause for many harassing moves to the troops, in which the 89th had full share.

Early in April, a portion of the regiment was moved into Manchester, and was soon after sent on from thence in aid of civil power to Liverpool. This detachment was afterwards ordered across the river to Birkenhead, where they occupied billets. On the 20th of April, the head-quarters left "Ashton-under-lyne" for Preston, and marched into Fulwood Barracks the same day.

On the 8th of May, the companies from Birkenhead rejoined head-quarters, and the whole regiment was concentrated into one barracks for the first time during thirteen years, and now for a very short period only.

The regiment was inspected by Major-General Sir William Warre, on the 29th of May, who passed the highest encomiums on the state of the corps. On the 31st of May, five companies were despatched before daylight by express to Manchester, in aid of civil power, and were employed under arms in the streets till mid-night, in preserving the peace. The party returned next day to Preston.

On the 10th of June, six companies were sent to Liverpool in aid of civil power. Three of these companies returned to Preston on the 19th of

June. On the 22nd of June, the head-quarters were removed from Preston, back to Ashton-under-lyne, giving detachments to Burnley, Stockport and Macclesfield, Sheffield and Barnsley. Three companies still remaining at Liverpool.

1848.
ASHTON-UNDER-LYNE.

On the 25th July the head-quarters and five companies sailed under sudden orders for Ireland, the left wing following the next day. Head-quarters and two companies proceeded to Birr, arriving there on the 27th, two companies were sent to Templemore, and the remaining six proceeded to Kilkenny, the immediate seat of the attempted rising, where they were encamped within the barrack enclosure.

BIRR.

In the month of September the detachments from Kilkenny and Templemore, joined head-quarters at Birr. Detachments were shortly afterwards sent out, and were continued with some slight changes at the following stations during the whole period the regiment remained at Birr,—Banagher, Portumna, Shannon Bridge, Loughrea, Roscrea, and during short periods at Gort and Templemore.

The head-quarters continued this year at Birr. In September Lieutenant-Colonel A. H. Ferryman from the 44th Regiment was appointed to command, *vice* Lieutenant-Colonel Thorp who exchanged.

1849.
BIRR.

On the 18th October the head-quarters left Birr for Dublin, arriving there on the 19th. The detachments joined soon after and the whole regiment was quartered in the Linen Hall Barracks.

1850.
DUBLIN.

On leaving Birr the following address was presented to the regiment by the Right Honourable the Earl of Rosse, and one hundred and twenty-two of the respectable inhabitants of Parsonstown :—

1850.
DUBLIN.

Address to Lieutenant-Colonel Ferryman, the officers, non-commissioned officers and men of the 89th Regiment:—

"We, the inhabitants of Parsonstown and its vicinity, feel bound on the departure of the regiment from this garrison to testify our sense of the excellent conduct which distinguished your corps while quartered at Parsonstown.

"It is a circumstance reflecting the highest credit on the regiment that during a period of two years, not one of the men was ever charged with any offence against the law, was ever engaged even in a dispute with the inhabitants, but the claims of the 89th Regiment on the kindly recollections of our people do not rest here. It will long be remembered amongst us that in the past year, during a period of great distress, the 89th Regiment was foremost in the work of charity and that by the exertion and contributions not less of the men than of the officers, upwards of eighty families of our distressed population were saved from want, and carried through that trying season."

(Signed) Rosse.
" Pearse Grome, J.P.
" W. McCausland,
 Curate of Birr.
" Thomas Maloney,
 Catholic Chaplain,
 Birr Barracks.
" Martin Cleary, C.C. Birr
" Bath Scanlan, C.C. Birr
 &c., &c., &c.

(Signed) Marcus McCausland.
 Rector of Birr.
" Thomas Hackett, J.P.
" Henry Fry, *Assistant*
 Curate.
" G. Waters, M.D.
" Jno. Warburton, J.P.
" H. Pollock, J.P.
" Thomas Woods, M.D.
 &c., &c., &c.

1851
CLONMEL.

In May, the regiment moved to Richmond Barracks. On the 20th September, the regiment left Dublin. The head-quarters for Clonmel detaching two companies to Carrick-on-Suir, to Ballinmult, Cappoquin, and Clogheen.

1852.
CLONMEL.

In June, a company was detached to Cashel.

In July, the head-quarters and several detachments of the corps were employed in aid of civil power at the general elections, a duty which

PRINCESS VICTORIA'S REGIMENT.

proved most harassing and unpleasant from the excitement which prevailed, and the violence displayed by the people.

The head-quarters marched from Clonmel *en route* for Templemore, on the 4th August, and arrived there on the 6th. While at Templemore the regiment gave detachments to Cashel, Thurles Callan, Maryboro', and Carlow.

On the 28th December, the head-quarters were moved to Buttevant, and a detachment of three companies under a field officer proceeded to Spike Island.

The Minie Rifle was this year introduced into the service, and 25 per company issued to the regiment.

On the 9th March, the head-quarters of the 89th proceeded into Cork, and in addition to the detachment at Spike Island, companies were sent to Camden Fort, Carlisle Fort, Haulbowline, and for a time to Bandon and Youghal.

Early in July the detachments were called in and the regiment concentrated in Cork, with the exception of one company stationed at Kinsale, for ball practice with the Minie Rifle. At the end of August a second company was detached to Buttevant.

The regiment received in the spring of this year, new accoutrements of the improved pattern, the waist belt being substituted for the side belt.

In this year the regiment received orders to embark for Gibraltar, the service and depôt companies were formed on the 1st January.

Depôt companies left Cork on the 9th January, 1854, for Fermoy, where they remained until April, 1854, when they removed to Waterford.

The 1st Division of the service companies' head-quarters consisting of 16 officers, 498 non-commissioned officers and men under command of Lieutenant-Colonel Ferryman, embarked on

1852.
CLONMEL.

TEMPLEMORE.

BUTTEVANT.

1853.
CORK.

1854.
Officers who embarked for Gibraltar:
Col. Ferryman, Major Egerton, Capt. Hon. C. Daly. (Bt.-Maj.) Capt Aylmer. (Bt.-Maj.) Capt MacDonald, Capt. Hill, Capt. Skynner, Capt. Phillips, Lieuts. Knipe, Darby, Mercer, Nixon, Selby, Pery, Conyers, Cresswell. Ensigns Longfield, Knatchbull, Pering, Gray. Pay-Mr.

1854.

Officers who embarked for Gibraltar:
Scott. Adjt. Cuppage. Qr.-Mr. Watson, Surg. Gilborne, Asst.-Surg. Wall.

Embarked at Gibraltar for the Crimea:
Field Officers, (2) Lieut.-Col. Ferryman, Major Egerton. *Capts.* (6) Bt.-Maj. Hon. Daly, Aylmer, Macdonald, Hill, Skynner, Phillips. *Subalterns.* (10) Lieuts. Darby, Mercer, Nixon, Selby, Pery, Conyers, Cresswell, Longfield, Knatchbull, Pering. *Staff* (6) Pay-Mr. Scott, Qr.-Mr. Watson, Adjt. Cuppage, Surg. Roberts, Asst.-Surgeon Wall.

Sergeants - - - 42
Corporals - - - 36
Drummers - - - 17
Privates - - - 593

N.B.—Surg. Gilborne joined the above at Scutari, and served through the siege of Sevastopol.

CRIMEA.

board the "Timandra" at Queenstown on the 20th April, and sailed the following day for Gibraltar, where they arrived on the 30th of the same month, and disembarked on the 1st of May. The second division consisting of 9 officers, 260 non-commissioned officers and men under command of Major Egerton, embarked at Queenstown on the 25th April sailed the following day, and arrived at Gibraltar on the 3rd May, and disembarked on the same day; the regiment served at Gibraltar until the 2nd December, on which day it embarked for service in the Crimea (on board the transport steam ship "Niagara") under the command of Colonel A. H. Ferryman, (strength as per margin), arrived in the harbour at Balaklava on the 15th of the same month, landed on the 17th, and marched to the camp of the 3rd division, which was under the command of Major-General Sir Richard England, K.C.B., and was attached to and did duty with the 3rd division in the trenches before Sebastopol until the end of the year.

At Scutari in the Bosphorus when on their way to the seat of the war, the regiment was armed with the Minie Rifle, for which however the Enfield Rifle, a lighter and even more effective weapon was substituted in the month of April following.

In June, 1854, the number of companies in regiments of the line was permanently fixed at 12 per battalion instead of 10. In December, 1854, each regiment of the line serving in the Crimea obtained a further augmentation of 4 captains and 8 subalterns, and a third major. This latter arrangement was changed in March, 1855, and 2 lieutenant-colonels and 2 majors, became the establishment of field officers for each battalion of the line serving in the Crimea.

The depôt companies after sending out a large draft to the service companies under Captain Hawley, which left Waterford after an unpre-

PRINCESS VICTORIA'S REGIMENT. 111

eedented manifestation of the good wishes of the principal citizens and inhabitants of Waterford and its vicinity, in the shape of a public dinner given to it, moved (from Waterford) to Limerick on the 23rd December, and shortly after became part of a depôt battalion there stationed.

1854.
CRIMEA.

During this year, the regiment served with the 3rd division of the army in the whole of the operations before Sebastopol, until its fall on the 8th of September, and was present at the assaults on the 18th of June and 8th of September. In this arduous siege, the regiment suffered greatly from disease and exposure, more especially during the latter part of the month of December, 1854, and in January, 1855. In the former month, the deaths from these causes were 43, and in the latter 35. The following officers are included in the above severe amount of casualties from disease alone, viz:—Major the Honourable Charles Daly, Brevet-Major Macdonald, Captain Darby, and Lieutenant Longfield, the two latter dying on their way home invalided.

On the night of the 26th of March, which was very dark, Captain A. E. Hill, a gallant and high-spirited officer, while engaged in posting his sentries in difficult ground in front of the advanced trenches, encountered a picquet of the enemy, fell wounded, and was taken prisoner; his death, a few hours after, was intimated under a flag of truce, by the Russian General Osten Sasken, next day.

The total number of deaths in the regiment from the time of landing in the Crimea until the fall of Sebastopol was of all ranks 218, and 137 were invalided.

Killed and wounded during the siege of Sebastopol.

Killed:
Captain A. E. Hill, 1 drummer, and 3 rank and file.

Annexed, is a statement of killed and wounded for the same period.

Wounded:
4 sergeants, 1 drummer, 68 rank and file, of whom 10 died of their wounds.

In May, a large draft from the depôt arrived at Malta, under command of Captain Thorp, and a reserve depôt of four companies was formed there, as in the case of all other regiments

1855.
CRIMEA.

of infantry serving in the Crimea. These depôts were formed into provisional battalions, which were kept up until the army in the East was broken up, after the conclusion of the treaty of Paris.

Major Egerton, Captains Tom and Pery; Lieuts. Hall and Barstow, Asst. Surgeon Wiles, 10 sergts., 3 drummers, 200 rank and file.

In the month of July, a party, (as per margin) under Major Egerton, marched from the heights before Sebastopol to the Baidar Valley, where they encamped for a month, during which they were employed in making gabions and collecting siege material. Their industry and good workmanship on this occasion were fully acknowledged by a most complimentary letter from the commanding Royal Engineer, Lieutenant-General Sir Harry Jones, K.C.B.

Captains Boyle, Hawley, White, Tom, Heycock; Lieuts: Morris, Holmes, Robinson, Hall, Beck, Breedon, Barstow, Harvest, Lloyd, Lamont, and Browning. Assistant Surgeons — Wiles and Roe. 11 sergeants, 1 drummer, and 391 rank and file.

Annexed is a list of the officers, who, in addition to those already mentioned as having landed in the Crimea with the service companies of the regiment, served with it during different periods of the siege, also a statement of the number of men who arrived to reinforce the regiment in the Crimea, up to the 8th of September.

The siege of Sebastopol having been ended by its fall on the 8th and 9th of September, the pressure of duty upon the troops (during the latter part of the siege excessive) was relaxed. The British army suspended active operations in that part of the Crimea.

On the 13th of September, the regiment marched from the camp of the 3rd division on the plateau above Sebastopol, to huts on the Marine Heights Balaklava, where it remained until the end of the year, employed chiefly in road-making and other duties of fatigue, in and about Balaklava.

By a circular letter dated 16th October, 1855, Her Majesty the Queen graciously accorded her permission that the regiment (and all others engaged in the siege) should bear on the regimental colour the distinction of the word "Sevastopol." A medal with clasp for Sebastopol was also most

PRINCESS VICTORIA'S REGIMENT.

graciously awarded to each officer and man, who had shared in the memorable struggle of the siege.

During the whole of this year the depôt remained at Limerick; recruiting was maintained with considerable success.

1855.
CRIMEA.

The commencement of 1856 found the regiment still in huts near Balaklava.

On the 9th of February, it was inspected on the Marine Heights, Balaklava, by Lieutenant-General Sir W. Eyre, K.C.B., who expressed himself much pleased with the discipline and appearance of the regiment, although it had labored under the disadvantage of having been almost exclusively employed on fatigue duties at Balaklava for the previous six months. The regiment received, while at Balaklava, further additions to the strength of the service companies, as per annexed detail, several officers and men however were from time to time invalided and sent to England during the same period.

1856.

Joined at Balaklava: Captain Thorp, Lieuts. Drage, Johnston, Dunn, Helme, Barron, Manners, and 123 non-commissioned officers and men.

In the winter of 1855-6, active operations being suspended on both sides, negotiations for peace were renewed between the belligerant powers, aided by the mediation of Austria. The result was that after an armstice had lasted some weeks, a treaty was signed at Paris, on or about the 29th of March, 1856. The evacuation of the Crimea by the allied armies shortly afterwards commenced, and was carried out by the 12th of July.

On the 24th of May, the regiment, under command of Lieutenant-Colonel Egerton, paraded on the Marine Heights, Balaklava, when the commander of the forces, General Sir William Codrington, K.C.B., performed the gratifying ceremony of fastening on the breasts of the men named in the annexed list, the French military war medal, conferred by His Majesty the Emperor

Sergeant J. Grant, Corporal J. Trenwith, Privates P. Kinnealy, D. Lenaghan, W. Heffernan.

1856.
CRIMEA.

Lieut.-Col. (Bt. Col.) Ferryman, who was also made C.B. Major (Bt. Lieut.-Col.) Aylmer, Captains (Bt. Major) Boyle, and Cuppage.

Lieut.-Col. Egerton, Major Skynner, Captain (Bt. Major) Hawley.

Lieut.-Col. (Bt. Col.) Ferryman, Lieut. - Col. Egerton, Majors Aylmer, (Bt.Lieut.-Col)Skynner, Captains (Bt. Majors) Boyle, Hawley, White, Cuppage, Captains Heycock, Pery, Lieuts. Robinson and Hall.

Officers who embarked from Crimea to Gibraltar:
Lieut.-Col. Ferryman. (Bt.-Col.)
Lieut.-Col. Egerton, Major Skynner, Capts. White,(Bt.Major)Thorp Tom, Cuppage. (Bt.Mjr.) Heycock, Pery, Morris.
Lieutenants Knatchbull, Robinson, Hall, Beck, Lloyd,Barstow,Lamont, Browning,Drage,Dunn, Helme, Manners, Barron.

Adjutant Holmes, Pay-Master Scott, Quarter-Mast. Sibbald, Assist. Surgeon Wiles, and Roe, with 51 sergts., 14 drummers, and 680 rank and file.

Officers who joined the ship at Malta:
Captains Nixon, and Conyers. Lieuts. Hobbs, Bowness, Dowdeswell, Warne. Ensign Brownrigg, with 7 sergeants, 5 drummers, and 70 rank and file.

of the French, for gallantry and good services in the trenches during the siege of Sebastopol.

It may here be stated that His Imperial Majesty subsequently decreed to four officers of the regiment, the decorations of the Legion of Honor 5th class, for their services during the siege, as well as to Private John Fisher, for distinguished conduct when one of a working party in the trenches under a heavy fire. This man's conduct was also praised and rewarded by the Field Marshal, Lord Raglan, G.C.B., commander of the forces at the time. The excellent services performed by 3 officers were also rewarded by the Sardinian medal, given by H.M. the King of Sardinia; Sergeant Patrick Scott who received a severe wound, also received this honourable distinction. His Majesty, the Sultan, was also pleased at a later period to recognize the services in the allied cause of 12 officers, by granting them the decoration of the order of the Medjidie 5th class.

After the parade on the 24th of May, already alluded to, the regiment marched down to Balaklava Harbour, where it embarked on board H.M.'s steam troop ship "Perseverance."

Colonel Ferryman, who had for some months been in command of the 1st Brigade of the Highland division, resumed the command of the regiment immediately on its embarkation. The "Perseverance" sailed next day, and having taken on board at Malta the reserve depot, arrived at Gibraltar on the 4th of June.

At Gibraltar, the regiment lost the services of several officers who had served with it during the siege of Sebastopol, in consequence of the reduction of the army at the termination of the war.

On the 7th August of this year, the regiment again embarked at short notice under command of Colonel Ferryman, for service at the Cape of Good Hope, where an immediate outbreak of the Kaffirs was expected.

The 13th Light Infantry also proceeded from Gibraltar to the Cape about the same time. The head-quarters of the 89th Regiment embarked on board the "Bahiana" steam transport, and the 2nd division under Major Skynner, in the steam transport "Cleopatra." The head-quarter division arrived at Cape Town on the 15th of September, and disembarked on the 16th with the exception of a detachment under Captain Heycock, which went on from Table Bay (Cape Town Harbour) to Algoa Bay, and landed at Port Elizabeth, whence it marched *viâ* Graham's town to King William's town, where it remained some months. The state of affairs in Kaffraria appearing very grave, the head-quarters of the regiment at once embarked at Cape Town on the 3rd of October in the "Cleopatra," (in which vessel the 2nd division had in the meantime arrived) leaving one strong company, the band and colours under Captain Thorp, at Cape Town. The regiment disembarked at the port of East London, (on the 9th of October,) on the frontiers of British Kaffraria, and were encamped on commanding ground about a mile from the town for the remainder of the year.

The 13th Light Infantry disembarked at Port Elizabeth, and marched to Grahamstown. The 86th Regiment had, a short time previous to the arrival of the 89th at East London, arrived in the colony from England, and at an earlier date the 85th Regiment had been suddenly withdrawn from the Mauritius and had arrived at the Cape.

These large reinforcements were followed about the beginning of 1857, by a very considerable number of military colonists, officers and men of the late British German Legion, which corps had been broken up after peace between the allied powers and Russia had been concluded.

The sudden pouring of so large a body of troops into the Cape Colony had the effect of preventing an open rupture with the Kaffirs, but

1856.

CRIMEA.

Officers awaiting the arrival of the ship at Gibraltar: Ensigns Dunn, Grier, Strong, Bishop, Newbigging.

THE CAPE.

Officers who arrived at the Cape of Good Hope from Gibraltar in September, 1856: Lieut.-Col. Ferryman, (Bt. Col.), Major Skynner, *Capts.* Thorp, Tom, Nixon, Heycock. *Lieutenants* Hall, Beck, Lloyd, Barstow, Lamont, Browning, Drage, Hobbs. *Ensigns*, Bishop, Grier, Dunn, Newbigging, Strong. Pay-Mr. Scott, Adjutant Holmes, Quarter-Master Sibbald, Surg. Gilborne, Assistant Surgeon Roe, with 55 sergeants, 18 drummers, and 718 rank and file.

1856.

THE CAPE.

the unsettled state of the country rendered escort and patrol duty constant and harassing throughout British Kaffraria, and parts of the eastern province of the colony.

The depôt remained at Limerick until the 21st of August, when "*viâ* Dublin" it proceeded to Chester, thence on 10th of December it was moved to camp at Colchester.

The tunic was this year substituted for the coatee.

1857.

The regiment remained under canvas at East London until the month of March, when a detachment of three companies under Major Skynner, crossed the Buffalo River, and established a line of posts on the left bank.

In April, the regiment was broken up into detachments, occupying a line of posts on each side of the Buffalo River, between East London on the sea, (where the head-quarters of the regiment remained encamped), and King William's town. These posts were as follows : on the right bank of the river, Fort Glamorgan, Fort Pato, Fort Grey, and Fort Murray ; on the left bank, Fort Blaney, (to which post the company from King William's town was moved), Fort Jackson, and the Amalinda Post.

The Kaffirs deceived by a false prophet, and over-awed by the strength of the British forces, instead of gaining lost territory and expelling "the white men," were about this time almost in a state of starvation. They had, on the strength of the prophet's confident assurances, destroyed the greater part of their live stock, and neglected the tilling of the soil. Their general rising did not take place, and they were reduced to a pitiable state of destitution and suffering, and many of them sought employment within the limits of the colony proper. The force on the frontiers could therefore safely be diminished.

PRINCESS VICTORIA'S REGIMENT.

1857.
THE CAPE.

The head-quarters of the regiment were ordered to Cape Town, and embarked under command of Colonel Ferryman, C.B., at East London, on the 11th of May, in Her Majesty's steam sloop "Geyser."

* Strength: 1 Field Officer, 1 Captain, 2 Subalterns, 3 Staff, and 123 'Non-commissioned Officers and men.

They disembarked at Cape Town on the 18th. Seven companies under Major Skynner remained distributed on the frontiers of British Kaffraria, as described above, Major Skynner himself being stationed at Fort Glamorgan, near East London.

In the beginning of June, the regiment was placed under orders for New Zealand, and the detachments on the frontier having been relieved, were concentrated at East London ready for embarkation.

But a much wider and more important field for the services of the regiment was in store for it.

A great crisis in the history of British Rule in India had occurred. The mutiny of the Bengal Sepoys had broken out. The strength of European troops in India owing to the Persian War and other causes was then small.

Lord Elphinstone, Governor of Bombay, had promptly despatched to Calcutta the only available regiments of H.M.'s service in the Bombay Presidency (the 64th and 78th) and the aspect of matters in that Presidency being threatening, he applied for assistance to the Governors of the Mauritius and the Cape Colony, from the former the 33rd Regiment was at once despatched.

Captain G. Jenkins, C.B., Indian Navy, the bearer of despatches from Lord Elphinstone to Sir George Gray the Governor of the Cape of Good Hope, arrived at Cape Town on the 6th of August. The Governor at once ordered the 89th to Bombay, he also ordered 2 companies of the Royal Artillery with guns, horses, and treasure to Calcutta, to the assistance of the Governor-General of India.

The head-quarters, under the command of Colonel Ferryman, C.B., embarked in H.M. Steam

Officers who embarked from the Cape for India:
Lt.-Col. Ferryman, C.B., (Brevet Col.)
Major Skynner.
Captains Boyle, (Brevet-Major) Thorp, Atkinson, Tom, Nixon, Heycock, Selby; *Lieuts.* Knatchbull, Pering, Beck, Lloyd, Barstow, Browning, Drage, Hobbs, Johnston, Dunn, Dowdeswell; *Ensigns,* Brownrigg, Baldwin, Bishop, Grier, Strong, Newbigging; Pay-Mr. Scott, Adjutant Holmes, Quarter-Master Sibbald, Surg. Gilborne, Assistant Surg. Roe and Bonnyman. with 41 sergeants, 18 drummers, and 635 rank and file.

1857.
THE CAPE.

Ship "Megrera" on the following day (7th August). On arriving at Algoa Bay they were transferred to the R.M. Screw Steamer "England," and anchoring off East London on the 16th, they received on board the whole of the frontier detachments, and put to sea the same evening. A second division under Captain Thorp (leaving Lieutenant Robinson in charge of the sick, families, and some heavy baggage), sailed from Cape Town (in ship "Ocean Wave,") on the 16th August also. After quick passages (the "England" coaling at Port Louis, Mauritius), the two divisions arrived at Bombay, the first on the 11th and the second on the 12th September.

The regiment was, without disembarking, immediately despatched from Bombay to Guzerat, leaving one company under Captain Thorp, to proceed to Cambay with heavy stores. The regiment sailed from Bombay Harbour on the 13th September, and having disembarked at Gogo, marched for Ahmedabad, a distance of about 150 miles, during the rains. The march was conducted under great difficulties, the country being much covered with water, and the soil a deep yielding mud; and as the baggage could not keep pace with the regiment, the men were more than once, for several successive days without covering from the sun or rain. Under these trying circumstances, the regiment went through this harassing march with the cheerfulness and alacrity which has always characterised it.

AHMEDABAD.

Colonel Ferryman, C.B. having been appointed a Brigadier of the 1st class, the regiment arrived at Ahmedabad under command of Major Skynner. The regiment was accompanied on the above march by a battery of Bombay European Artillery. The company under Captain Thorp, and one of the 86th Regiment had reached Ahmedabad before the arrival of the head-quarters of the regiment, which took place on the 14th October

The regiment was encamped at Ahmedabad,

and, a few days after arrival was present at an execution of a number of mutineers, Sepoys of the 2nd (Grenadier) Regiment of Bombay Native Infantry.

1857.
AHMEDABAD.

On the 29th of October, the right wing under Brevet-Major Boyle marched for Deesa, and arrived in cantonments there on the 7th November, furnishing a detachment at Mount Aboo Sanitarium.

The head-quarters and the left wing remained encamped at Ahmedabad until the end of the year.

The regiment was augmented, after being taken on the Indian strength by one Lieutenant-Colonel, Major Skynner, attaining that rank, and by one assistant Surgeon: the establishment of rank and file with the service companies was augmented to 1,000, in ten companies; while the depôt companies were fixed at two in number, to consist in all of 200 rank and file.

During this year General Sir Charles B. Egerton G.C.M.G., K.C.H., who had been Colonel of the 89th for nearly twenty years, and always shewn great interest in its welfare, died; he was succeeded by Major-General C. G. J. Arbuthnot, appointed Colonel of the regiment 9th July, 1857.

The depôt, forming part of the 3rd depôt battalion at camp, Colchester, remained there until September, when it was moved to Shorncliffe, and towards the end of the year it was transferred to a depôt battalion formed at Fermoy, Ireland. A considerable number of men were discharged during the year, and recruiting was not very successful till towards its close.

The regiment remained distributed by wings at Ahmedabad and Deesa, (head-quarters being at the former place, and a small detachment from the latter place being at Mount Aboo Sanitarium,) until April. Major Phillips having arrived from

1858

1858.
AHMEDABAD.

England took command of the Right Wing on 7th February.

Early in April two companies under command of Captain Thorp quitted Ahmedabad to form part of a Field force under Major Grimes, sent to Sadra to commence the disarmament of part of Guzerat, upon which measure the political resident at Baroda, Sir R. Shakespeare, who also commanded the northern division of the Bombay army at that time, had determined.

On the 23rd April head-quarters and the remaining companies of the left wing of the regiment, together with field detachments of artillery, irregular cavalry, &c., the whole under command of Captain Heycock of the 89th left Ahmedabad, and proceeded in a few days (during which the process of disarming the province was carried on) to join the force under Major Grimes. The junction of these field forces took place near a large village called Honoraria, (when Captain Thorp took command of the head-quarter wing of the 89th) the inhabitants of which were by no means disposed peaceably to give up their weapons. The imposing array of Major Grimes' force however, and a few rounds from a field battery soon caused them to succumb.

GUZERAT.

The force after leaving Honoraria visited the towns of Beejapoor, Ahmednuggur, and other places in that part of Guzerat. About the 23rd May, the head-quarters of the regiment were detached from the field force, leaving one company with it under Captain Heycock, and marched into Deesa station on the 28th joining the right wing.

The regiment was not accompanied on the above service by its commanding officer, Lieutenant-Colonel Skynner, he was detained at Ahmedabad by an attack of fever, which after hopes of his recovery had been confidently entertained, unhappily terminated fatally on the 8th May. He was succeeded in the Lieutenant-

Colonelcy and in the command of the regiment by Major Phillips.

The company under Captain Heycock (with Lieutenant Browning) which was detached from the head-quarter wing in May, as already stated, was present at a skirmish with some insurgent Bheels on the 30th May, at the village of Dubhora, and the Tarringa Hills, during which the efficacy of the Enfield Rifle was fully displayed, one of the enemy having fallen from a rifle shot at 800 yards distance as related in Major Grimes' despatch. A few days subsequently this company went into quarters at Ahmedabad.

About this time a draft from the depôt of 80 men under Captain Conyers, with Lieutenant Breedon reached Ahmedabad on its way to the head-quarters of the regiment. Shortly afterwards two small drafts numbering in all 50 men arrived from Bombay at Broach. The doubtful state of feeling on the part of the inhabitants of Guzerat caused these several drafts to be detained at Ahmedabad and Broach respectively, for several months including the rainy season. A small party of 5 men only who had arrived at Bombay overland from the depôt, reached head-quarters about this time, viz : on 1st June. On the same day, Assistant-Surgeon Price joined. In July the detachment at Mount Aboo was increased from Deesa, to two full companies.

In the month of July, the rebels having advanced after many defeats, from Gwalior, to threaten Rajpootana, and attempt to raise the numerous independent states in that region; several columns were put in motion, either in pursuit or to cover important points which the rebels might have attempted to seize. The principle column left Nusseerabad, under Major General Roberts. Being foiled in an advance on Jeypoor by this column, the rebels turned in a south-westerly direction, and after much delay had been experienced on both sides from the

1858.
GUZERAT.

Officers, Lieut. Bowness Ensigns, Warburton and Sealy, and 50 men.

OODEYPORE.

1858.

OODEYPORE.

rainy season being at its height, they entered Oodeypore State, apparently with the desperate resolve to seize that city (Oodeypore), the capital of Meywar, and then to push on to Guzerat. They were closely followed by General Roberts and Colonel Holmes. From the Oodeypore State, passes intersect the Aravulli Mountains, opening into Marwar or Jondpore, one, the Chutterbooj Pass, is narrow and difficult, but through it the rebels might have gained the Jondpore States, or might have turned southwards through Seerohee into Guzerat. To counteract this possible move on the part of the enemy, a small field force was quickly despatched from Deesa, towards Nusseerabad, leaving the former place on the 13th August. It comprised (including a company from Mount Aboo, which joined at Anadra), 200 of the 89th, under Captain Selby, half a battery of Artillery, a detachment 31st Native Infantry, and some Guzerat Horse, with other irregular Cavalry, the whole under command of Major Boyle, 89th.

These field detachments marched to Erinpoora, but before their arrival, the Chutterbooj Pass, had with others been secured, and Major-General Roberts, had inflicted two signal defeats on the rebels, causing them to leave Oodypore, and turn eastwards to re-cross the Chumbul. He thereafter dispensed with the further services of the field detachments, which accordingly returned to Deesa, except the company from Mount Aboo, which returned to the latter place and not to Deesa, until three weeks later, *i.e.*, about the 25th September.

In consequence of the above mentioned advance of the rebels into Rajpootana, the field force of Major Grimes which had remained near Edur, was moved on early in August to Oodeypore. It was found necessary, to avert disturbances among the Hill Tribes near Edur, to detach fresh troops from Ahmedabad to that district. A company of the 89th left Ahmedabad under Captain Conyers (with Lieutenant Browning), who was shortly after relieved by Captain Heycock, on whom the command of field detachments amounting to several hundred men, and comprising the three arms of the service devolved. The malcontents continuing troublesome, and resisting the reasonable demands made upon them, it was found necessary to attack the strongly situated and fortified village of Mondetti, which was in a short time carried. A few days after this vindication of the British Power, the greater part of the force returned to Ahmedabad.

1858.

OODEYPORE.

Casualties at Mondetti, 22nd August, 1858: Lieut. Browning, (Staff Officer to the Force), horse shot under him. Private T. Fallon, dangerously wounded, dying shortly afterwards.

Lieutenant-Colonel Phillips, a deservedly popular officer, being compelled by ill-health to give up command of the regiment, and proceed from Deesa to Bombay, with a view of thence sailing for England, unhappily died on his passage from Cambay to Bombay on the 12th of October. He was succeeded to the Lieutenant-Colonelcy, and in the immediate command of the regiment by Major Boyle.

In October, the regiment was ordered from Deesa to Neemuch in Rajpootana; and on the 4th of November a division of three companies under Major Thorp, commenced the march *viâ* Nusseerabad. The head-quarters were ordered to march by a shorter route, viz: by Edur, Dongerpoor, and the hilly tracks of Meywar. They were relieved at Deesa by a wing of H.M.'s 33rd Regiment, on the 6th of December. The same day also a draft from the depôt as per margin, reached Deesa.

About 110 rank and file, under Captain Pery, and Ensign Harrison.

At this date, the rebel forces under the Rao Sahib, and Tantia Topee, which had recently threatened Baroda the capital, were still believed to be on the point of entering the province of Guzerat. A small field force was ordered from Deesa to Edur, to counteract the rebel movements.

1858.
GUZERAT.

Accordingly, head-quarters and 200 effective men of the regiment, 150 of the 31st Bombay N.I., a troop of the 2nd Bombay Light Cavalry, and two 9 pounder guns, all under Lieutenant-Colonel Boyle 89th, left Deesa on the 7th and pushed rapidly on to Edur. The remainder of the regiment followed them by easy stages, under command of Major Atkinson.

From Edur, the 2nd Light Cavalry and guns from Deesa were sent to Morassa, but the 89th and N. I. advanced to the mouth of the Sumeyra Pass, where they were reinforced by two guns, (9 pounders,) under Major Hatch, and a hundred of the 89th under Captain Heycock, these reinforcements having come from Ahmedabad.

These troops moved by a forced march up the Sumeyra Pass to Khairwarrah, an isolated station (with a resident political officer, and head-quarters of the Meywar Bheel corps) which was supposed to be threatened by the rebels advancing by Banswarra. It appeared however that they had turned off and had gone to Saloomber a strong fortress, the Rajah of which was notoriously disaffected, though not in arms against the British power.

The instructions of the Bombay Government being that Oodeypore, the capital of Meywar and residence of the Maha Rana, a firm ally of the British power, should of all things be effectually protected by the force under Lieutenant-Colonel Boyle, it advanced up the narrow passes leading from Khairwarrah to Oodeypore, which from the steep and rocky nature of the road—as everywhere in the hilly tracks of Meywar—presented many difficulties to the passage of Artillery. Learning, however, that the rebels had moved southwards from Saloomber, closely pressed as they were by Brigadier Parke's pursuing column, Lieutenant-Colonel Boyle made a corresponding move with part of his force, to prevent the rebel egress from the hilly track in a southward direction. Sending on a hundred of the 89th under Captain Heycock to Oodeypore, and leaving the 31st N.I. to watch the Pursad or Pursole Ghat, a narrow gorge leading from Saloomber into the pass from Khairwarrah to Oodeypore, and also into Marwar by mountain tracks; the rest of the force reinforced temporarily by 100 of the Guzerat Irregular Horse, and 100 of the Meywar Bheel Corps, rapidly re-passed Khairwarrah and moved through Dongerpoor to Sangwarra. There, news having been received on the 27th of December of the defeat of the rebels at Pertabghur, by a small column from Neemuch under Major Rorke, and of the rebels having escaped towards Central India, the small force under Lieutenant-Colonel Boyle was broken up; the 89th returned to Khairwarrah on the 31st of December, and were joined on the 1st of January, 1859 by the remainder of the regiment from Deesa and Ahmedabad under Major Atkinson, which detachment had been for some days halted in observation at Tintoee in Guzerat.

1858.
GUZERAT.

The depôt remained at Fermoy during this year; a large number of recruits were raised.

In addition to the deaths of Lieutenant-Colonel Skynner and Phillips already alluded to, the regiment had in this year to lament those of Captain A. Nixon, Lieutenant H. Lamont, and Ensign F. Warburton, in India, and of Captain Morris, at the depôt. The mortality in the ranks was happily not remarkably great.

The regiment marched from Khairwarrah, *en route* to Oodeypore on the 5th of January, a detachment of a 100 men under Captain Browning being left at Khairwarrah, together with the detachment 31st N. I. as a temporary measure, on account of the turbulent demeanour of some of the Bheel Tribes. At Oodeypore, Captain Heycock's detachment rejoined the regiment which then marched to Neemuch, arriving on

1859.
OODEYPORE.

NEEMUCH.

1859.

NEEMUCH.

the 21st of January, Major Thorp's division had arrived there on the 16th of December. The detachments from Khairwarrah reached Neemuch on the 27th of January, and the company from Mount Aboo (upwards of 100 strong) under Captain Knatchbull, which had been detained at Nusseerabad about a month from the want of European troops there at a critical period, on the 15th of February. All the companies of the regiment in India were thus brought together once more. On his arrival at Neemuch, Lieutenant-Colonel Boyle, the senior officer, took command of the station, and Major Thorp consequently that of the regiment.

The regiment was only a few hours altogether, for in consequence of the third entry about this time of the rebel forces into Meywar, (this time from the Jondpore territory, led by the Rao Sahib and Prince Feroze Shah) it became necessary at once to send out troops from Neemuch to confront and head them. With this intention field detachments were at once put in motion in several directions. The 89th furnished three separate detachments, the first 250 strong commanded by Captain Holmes, accompanied a field force under Major Simpson, which effected a junction near Oodeypoor, with some guns and detachments of European troops, which happened to be marching *en route* for Neemuch. Major Simpson's force pressed hard on the flying rebels, who at this period exhausted and dispirited, were attempting by enormous forced marches to elude the many avenging British columns which were then in the field in Rajpootana.

A second detachment of 100 men of the 89th under Captain Heycock, in conjunction with 100 of the 13th Bombay N.I., did good service near Burra Sadree, in closely watching the enemy, then estimated at 1000 strong (mostly cavalry), and preventing their turning into the Durriawud Jungles. A third detachment of the 89th under

Captain Pery (100 strong), formed part of a small column commanded by Major Atkinson, 89th, which moved from Neemuch on the night of the 19th February to cover Mundesore and Pertabghur.

1859.
NEEMUCH.

The rebels evincing a disposition under the severe pressure of pursuit to treat for surrender, and Major-General Sir J. Michel having himself joined the flying column of Brigadier Somerset, which had become the force nearest to the enemy who re-crossed the Chumbull about the 24th February, the further services of the columns of which the 89th formed part were dispensed with, and on the 2nd March the whole of the companies of the regiment were re-united at Neemuch.

The families of the regiment, and a detail of men under Captain Robinson, which had been left at the Cape of Good Hope on the sudden embarkation of the regiment for service in India in August, 1857, arrived at Neemuch in February; also a draft of about 60 recruits under Ensign Pott.

On the 6th April another draft from the depot of nearly 80 recruits joined the regiment at Neemuch, together with 9 men volunteers from H.M's 86th Regiment.

The success of the British campaign in Oude, in the cold season of 1858-9 enabling the supreme Government to send home to England a few battalions, the transfer from the Bombay to the Bengal Presidency of two of H.M.'s regiments and a battery of R.A., was ordered. The 89th was named as one of the regiments to be transferred.

It was at first ordered to march from Neemuch to Agra, direct, but subsequently to Goonah, a station on the grand trunk road between Indore and Gwalior.

Being relieved by a detachment of H.M.'s 95th Regiment, and leaving a detachment of 60 men under Captain Browning, with the families, until the hot season should have passed by, the regi-

1859.
NEEMUCH.

ment left Neemuch on 10th April, and marching through Jalra, Patun, and Chuppa, reached Goonah on 1st May. There another draft of about 40 recruits under Ensign Atthill joined from Bombay.

At Goonah instructions were received for head-quarters and 600 men to march on Seronge, near which town ground had been selected as suitable for encampment during the rainy season of a body of European troops. Seronge, moreover, having been fixed on as a centre place for the presence of a field force to keep down disaffection in the surrounding districts, and to overawe and disperse detached bodies of rebels, who had chosen the surrounding jungles and difficult country as secure haunts whence to carry on a desultory and marauding style of warfare.

SERONGE.

Head-quarters and the left wing accordingly left Goonah on the 4th, and arrived near Seronge on the 7th May, on the latter day the right wing under Major Thorp left Goonah *en route* for Agra.

A considerable force was at this time assembled near Seronge under Brigadier-General Sir R. Napier, K.C.B., but was on the point of breaking up. Sir R. Napier left for Gwalior with a part of the force, and another part went to cantonments in Rajpootana. Lieutenant-Colonel Boyle of the 89th then assumed command of the troops remaining in camp near Seronge, but in a few days resigned it, and that of the regiment (which he had resumed on leaving Neemuch) to Colonel Ferryman, C.B., who rejoined the regiment from brigade command at Deesa, Bombay, on the corps being transferred to the Bengal Presidency. Colonel Ferryman however shortly obtained the command of a brigade in the Bengal Presidency, and on his setting off to assume it Lieutenant-Colonel Boyle again took command of the regiment and of the Seronge field force.

PRINCESS VICTORIA'S REGIMENT.

The head-quarters and a strong wing (5 companies) were hutted at camp Deopore, near Seronge, by the beginning of the rainy season. The huts were simply their tents placed under sheds with verandahs. During June and part of July, a company 100 strong, under Captain Robinson, occupied the fort of Agra-Burkhaira, about 15 miles from Seronge, from which they made several expeditions in pursuit of bands of rebels. On the 1st of August, intelligence having reached camp Deopore, that a considerable body of rebels had established themselves in a strong position in dense jungles, near the old fort of Vasseeghur, between Lehteri and Muxoodunghur, a small force was dispatched to dislodge them. It comprised a company of the 89th, a detachment of the Bombay N.I., and a party of Her Majesty's Irregular Horse, all under command of Captain Holmes of the 89th Regiment. They succeeded on the 3rd of August in surprising the rebel camp, and in driving them from their position with a loss of upwards 40 killed; two casualties only occurred in the 89th.

1859.
SERONGE.

Captain Robinson,
Lieutenant Atthill,
100 N.C.O's and men.

Captain Holmes,
Lieutenant Sealy,
Ensign Burton,
75 N.C.O's and men.

2 Privates wounded.

This service met with the "cordial acknowledgement of the government of India." A few days after the return of Captain Holmes' force, a fresh column was put in motion from Camp Deopore, in consequence of the proximity of a body of rebels, headed by Adil Mahommed Khan. This column was under Captain Richards, of the 10th Bombay N. I., and including a detachment of the 89th. Most of the jungles between Seronge and Nursingur, as far at least as the river Parbuttee, were effectively scoured by this small column under very great difficulties, arising from the wetness of the weather and the density of the vegetation in the jungles. An immediate result was the surrender of a local rebel of some influence in the district, named Chutter Sal.

Lieutenant Lloyd,
Ensign Burton,
Assistant-Surgeon Price
and one Company 80 strong.

A portion of the Seronge field force had been detached under Captain Roome, of the 10th

1859.
SERONGE.

Bombay N.I., to Basoda, beyond the river Betwa, and from that post had performed good service and inflicted severe chastisement on bodies of rebels on several occasions.

The effect of the operations—extending over several months—here imperfectly detailed, of the Seronge Field Force, added to the moral effect of the presence in the lawless districts round Seronge, of so large a body of efficient troops belonging to the British Government, and combined with the contemporaneous re-establishment of British authority throughout India, was the gradual disappearance in the Seronge Districts of all but small fugitive parties of rebels, including mutinied sepoys, and desperadoes of all classes and castes, whose life was one of hardships and constant alarms, and who were without organization, or any plan of united armed resistance. Some of the leaders indeed, still remained at large, including the Rao-Sahib, Prince Feroze Shah, and Adil Mahommed Khan, but even their persistence failed to give cohesion to the rebel cause, and they themselves generally traversed the country in disguise. About the commencement of the cold season, the task of tracing out and crushing these remnants of the rebel forces, was confided to officers specially selected and invested with certain political powers, and small flying columns were placed at their disposal consisting of native troops, chiefly irregulars.

The right wing of the 89th which had reached Agra at the end of May, remained there until the end of October, when it was moved to the Gwalior Division, replacing the 3rd Regiment of Bengal Europeans. After remaining a few days at Morar Cantonments, Gwalior, it moved southwards, and was divided between Sepree and Goonah. The detachment from Neemuch under Captain Browning, with the families, having reached Goonah by the beginning of December. Some minor changes took place, and **at Christmas**

PRINCESS VICTORIA'S REGIMENT.   131

day the regiment was thus divided, viz : at Camp near Seronge, head-quarters and 5 companies, at Sepree, 2 companies under Major Thorp, and at Goonah, 3 companies under Major Atkinson; the two last named stations being on the great road from Agra to Mhow.

1859.
SERONGE.

The officers named in the margin joined the service companies from the regimental depôt in the last quarter of the year; also Assistant Surgeon Walsh from the staff. Ensign Burton also joined on appointment late in the year, having previously done duty with the regiment as interpreter, while a local Lieutenant in the Bombay army unattached. A draft of 40 recruits also joined from the depôt in November, and a few volunteers from the 61st in July.

Lieutenant Helme, Instructor of M., Ensign Hay, Hubbersty, Rudall, Price, and Ostler.

There was considerable sickness in the regiment during the latter half of this year up to the month of December, but the mortality throughout the whole year was not greater than 3 per cent. At one period of the year the total strength was upwards of 1100, the establishment being 1077. Lieutenant Harrison died in March at Mhow, *en route* to England on medical certificate, and Ensign Dickson *en route* to join, met with his death by an accidental fall at Calcutta in September. About 30 men were invalided to England this year, and a considerable number availed themselves of permission to be discharged: the regiment also furnished 24 volunteers to the Bengal Artillery.

During the year the regiment was completed with new equipments, of the improved pattern with two pouches and frog bayonet belts; and the sergeants were furnished with the short Enfield Rifle. Instead of cloth shell jackets, red serge frocks were for the first time issued as annual clothing, and khakee coloured light clothing was substituted for white. The regiment was also (partially) completed with wicker helmets, covered with khakee coloured cloth, in

1859.
SERONGE.

lieu of the shako. New and improved pioneer appointments were also received, and taken into use. About the end of the year the Turkish medals accorded by His Imperial Highness the Sultan, to the officers and men who had been engaged in the Crimean war, were received

In this year too, the "Field Exercise," and "Evolutions of Infantry" edition of 1859, were learnt and adopted in the regiment.

The depôt remained at Fermoy during 1859.

1860.
JHANSI.

Lieutenant-Colonel Boyle having obtained leave of absence to England, Major Thorp took over command of the regiment on the 19th February 1860 at Seronge, and on the 28th February the head-quarter wing (5 companies) left that place, arriving at Jhansi on the 13th March,—giving the following detachments during the hot seasons and rains, 2 companies at Goonah, 2 companies at Lullutpoor, 1 company at Sepree.

Colonel Ferryman, C.B. having exchanged into the 75th Regiment with Lieutenant-Colonel Bouchier, the latter officer arrived at Jhansi, on the 20th May and commanded the 89th from that date. The two companies at Goonah left that station and arrived at Sepree in the month of July, joining the other companies quartered there, and the three companies marched for the fortress of Gwalior in the month of October, and were in garrison there, under Major Thorp, until the end of the year.

The regiment was very unhealthy and suffered much from sickness this year, more particularly the head-quarter wing at Jhansi, 81 deaths occurred, out of which 70 took place at Jhansi; 51 men were invalided to England for change of climate, or discharge from the service.

The depôt remained at Fermoy in 1863.

1861.
UMBALLA.

On being relieved by the 52nd Light Infantry, the head-quarters of the regiment, joined by the two companies from Tullutpoor, left Jhansi on 26th of January, reaching Gwalior where there were three companies on detachment, on the last day of the month, and the whole regiment under command of Lieutenant-Colonel Bouchier then proceeded to Umballa, where it arrived on the 8th of March. A draft of 112 recruits with Lieutenants Hobbs and Sewell, joined the regiment on its arrival at Umballa, also Surgeon Smith * and Brevet-Major Cuppage about the same time.

1861.

UMBALLA.

Draft under Lieutenant Hobbs arrived, 112 strong.

* The appointment of this officer to the regiment, was ultimately cancelled.

Lieutenant-Colonel Boyle resumed command of the regiment from leave of absence on 28th May.

Fever was prevalent in the regiment during the hot season of 1861, and nearly 150 men were sent to the convalescent depôt, Kussowlie, in the lower range of the Himalaya mountains.

During the rains, epidemic cholera of a malignant type appeared in many of the principal cities and stations of India, especially in the N.W. Provinces and the Punjaub, and it broke out in the regiment in the end of July. Leaving necessary details (to carry on duty) and the sick in hospital, the regiment was promptly moved out of Umballa into camp, and remained under canvas for nearly a month in the vicinity of a village called Jallroo, about eleven miles from the cantonments; this change was beneficial to the general health of the corps. The loss by this afflicting scourge, amounted to 45 men, 2 women, and 8 children.

The establishment of the service companies was this year altered as follows:—

	Sergts.	Corpls.	Drs.	Pts.
from	57	50	21	950
to	47	40	21	810

and that of the depôt companies:—

	Sergts.	Corpls.	Drs.	Pts.
from	10	10	4	190
to	10	10	4	90

1861.
UMBALLA.

These reductions were consequent on the entire re-establishment of tranquillity in India, and in furtherance of State economy. Some volunteers from the 5th Fusiliers and the 64th Regiment were received this year.

On the 9th November, the regiment was inspected by H.E. General Sir Hugh Rose, G.C.B., Commander-in-Chief in India, who at the close of the day's proceedings addressed the battalion in a highly complimentary speech. In this year Major Atkinson, and Lieutenant Sewell died at Umballa, the latter from the effects of a fall from horseback. Brevet-Major Gibson joined on exchange from the 87th Royal Irish Fusiliers. Lieutenant Baldwin joined from the depôt, and Ensign Campbell on appointment.

The depôt companies remained as part of the 19th Depôt Battalion at Fermoy, during the whole of the year, 1861.

1862.

The regiment remained at Umballa until the 6th November, when it marched for Mooltan, *viâ* Ferozepore; it reached it destination on 11th December.

The regiment was more healthy this year than in 1861, only 2 deaths occurred from cholera (in May), the total number of deaths in the year was eight.

His Excellency Sir H. Rose, Commander-in-Chief, was encamped at Umballa with the head-quarter staff of the army, during the greater part of the month of March, the regiment took part in a series of Reviews and Field days, under his personal command, and was again minutely inspected by him.

Draft of 50 rank and file, under Captain Pery, with Ensigns Hayward and Hassall.

A draft as per margin joined from the depôt this year (in February). The following officers also joined the service companies, viz: Surgeon Bacot, from the staff, Lieutenant Fraser, from the 22nd Foot, Ensigns King, Jones, and Grenville from the depôt.

The depôt remained at Fermoy during the year, 1862.

1862.
UMBALLA.

The regiment was quartered at Mooltan during the whole of 1863, and the depôt companies at Fermoy, as part of the 19th depôt battalion.

Captain R. Selby died at Mooltan, on the 17th August.

1863.
MOOLTAN.

During the whole of 1864, the regiment remained at Mooltan. In March, a strong company under Captain Heycock was embarked to Dehra Ismail Khan, an important outpost on the Indus.

1864.
MOOLTAN.

A draft from the depôt joined the service companies in February.

Draft of 50 rank and file, under Bvt-Maj. Holmes'

The depôt companies remained at Fermoy,

On the 4th July Major-General C. Gascoyne was appointed Colonel of the regiment, *vice* Lieutenant-General Arbuthnot, transferred to the 91st Highlanders.

The regiment was prepared to march from Mooltan to Subathoe, on relief by the 35th Regiment in January of this year, but received an unexpected order to embark for England. The supreme Government had resolved to reduce the number of battalions of British Infantry in India by sending two of them home. After giving 228 volunteers to various regiments stationed in the Bengal Presidency, the regiment, including the detachments that had been recalled from Dehra Ismail Khan, embarked at Mooltan in two divisions, and proceeded in steamers down the Chenab and Indus to Kurrachee, which place was reached by head-quarters on the 8th March.

1865.
MOOLTAN.

Head-quarters and seven (7) companies of the regiment embarked at Kurrachee, in the ship "Walmer Castle," for England on the 8th April; Major Thorp commanded the regiment on its voyage home, Colonel Boyle having obtained

L

1865. MOOLTAN.	permission to proceed by overland route. The 2nd division (3 companies) left Kurrachee on the 8th May, in the ship "Salamanca," under the command of Major Cuppage. The two ships reached Spithead within a few hours of each other. They were sent on to Dover, where both divisions of the regiment disembarked on the 8th August, in a most efficient and creditable condition, and proceeded at once by rail to Shorncliffe Camp, where the depôt companies, which had left Fermoy in June, and had been meanwhile stationed at Dover, rejoined headquarters the same day, and the entire regiment thus became once more re-assembled together.
SHORNCLIFFE.	Ensign Luke Henry Jones died on the homeward voyage. Colonel Boyle resumed command of the regiment on its landing at Dover.

The established strength of the regiment on landing from India was twelve companies, comprising—57 sergeants, 50 corporals, 25 drummers, and 650 privates; the effective strength was in all, 723—50 sergeants, 43 corporals, 20 drummers, 610 privates—total 723, which was soon further reduced by many discharges taking place.

New rifles of the Enfield pattern, on the interchangeable principle, were issued to the regiment at Shorncliffe Camp, and the accoutrements were improved by new pouches and ball bags.

The regiment was present on the 4th October, at a field day of all the troops in the Dover division, under Major-General Sir R. Garrett, K.C.B. before H.R.H. the F.M. Commanding-in-Chief, who the next day specially inspected the Shorncliffe brigade. On both occasions he praised the regiment.

1866. ALDERSHOT.	The regiment was moved by rail from Shorncliffe to Aldershot camp on the 29th March, and attached to the 3rd Brigade of Infantry in huts in the North Camp under command of Brigadier-General Sir Alfred Horsford, K.C.B.

On the 5th April an honour rarely conferred in modern times was bestowed upon the regiment, eclipsing all former distinctions, and calling forth the most devoted feelings of loyalty and gratitude.

1866.
ALDERSHOT.

It having been humbly represented to the Queen by the commanding officer through H.R.H. the F.M. Commanding-in-Chief that the colours which she herself had presented to the regiment in 1833 were completely worn out and required to be replaced, Her Majesty was graciously pleased to intimate her intention of presenting new colours in person, and appointed the 5th April for the occasion.

Her Majesty arrived in camp Aldershot from Windsor Castle early in the afternoon of the day in question, drove through the camp where she was received with acclamations by the soldiers, visited the Prince Consort's library and the Gymnasium, and spent some time at the Royal Pavilion.

At 3 p.m., the Queen, accompanied by their Royal Highnesses the Princesses Helena and Louise, Prince Arthur, and by the Field Marshal Commanding-in-Chief H.R.H. the Duke of Cambridge, attended by her suite and preceded by the Adjutant General Lord W. Paulet, the Quarter-Master-General, Sir J. Hope Grant, and a numerous and brilliant staff, arrived with an escort of the 17th Lancers at the Queen's Parade, North Camp. Her Majesty was received with a royal salute from the whole of the troops comprising the Aldershot division, under the command of Lieutenant-General Sir James Yorke Scarlett, K.C.B.

The force was formed in three sides of a square as follows:—A battery of the Royal Horse Artillery and the 3rd K.O. Hussars formed the right face; two field batteries of the Royal Artillery the left; in the centre, the 17th Lancers were on the right next the 1st Infantry

1866.
ALDERSHOT.

Brigade: (the 1st Bn. 17th, the 81st, and 52nd Light Infantry), then the 3rd Infantry Brigade (the 69th, 89th, and 71st H.L.I.), next the 2nd Infantry Brigade (the 1st Bn. 13th Prince Albert's L.I., 63rd, and 28th), and next the 8th Hussars; the Artillery being in column of batteries at full intervals, the cavalry in close columns of squadrons, the infantry in line of contiguous columns at quarter distance. The Royal Engineers, Royal Engineers train, and the military train, formed a second line in rear of the infantry. The 89th, the centre regiment of the division was in advance of the line of infantry columns, and had been deployed into line.

After the Royal salute, Her Majesty's carriage having been drawn up close to the saluting point, the ceremony of trooping the old colours of the regiment for the last time immediately commenced, which being concluded, these cherished but tattered banners, which had been borne in all the four quarters of the globe, were cased and removed from the field. The regiment having then been formed into three sides of an oblong (two deep) the new colors were brought forward, and placed on a pile of drums hastily formed near Her Majesty's carriage. The Chaplain-General the Rev. G. R. Gleig, who was assisted by the Rev. E. J. Rogers and the Rev. F. I. Abbott, military chaplains, then solemnly consecrated the colours, which were afterwards handed to the Queen by Majors E. B. Thorp and J. B. Kirk kneeling. Her Majesty then standing on the step of her carriage handed the Queen's colour to Ensign D. Campbell and the regimental colour to Ensign H. K. I. Grenville, who both knelt to receive them; Her Majesty at the same time said:—" I have "much pleasure in renewing the colours I gave "you many years ago, relying confidently on the "loyal devotion to my service by which you and "all my troops have ever been distinguished."

His Royal Highness the Duke of Cambridge, by Her Majesty's command, then advanced on foot towards the regiment, and read out to them the gracious words just uttered by the Sovereign.

1866.
ALDERSHOT.

Colonel Boyle, commanding the regiment, then endeavoured to express his sense of the honour conferred on the regiment, and their unanimous feeling, in the following words to H.R. Highness :—" I beg to assure Her Majesty "in the name of the regiment, and in my own "name, that Her Gracious confidence in us will "never be misplaced."

After the new colours had been received by the corps with the prescribed honours, Colonel Boyle called on them for " three cheers for Her Majesty the Queen," which were given with tremendous effect.

Line being then reformed, the regiment broke into open column and marched past the Queen in slow time, after which they rejoined their brigade. The whole force afterwards marched past, the cavalry and artillery at a walk in open column of squadrons, and by batteries, and the infantry by grand divisions in quick time. The review concluded with another Royal salute ; and subsequently the whole of the commanding officers of corps were presented on horseback to Her Majesty as she sat in her carriage on the parade. The Royal cortège then drove back to Windsor. The Colonel of the regiment, Lieut.-General C. Gascoyne, was present on the occasion, and there were many other distinguished spectators.

On the following day the officers gave a grand entertainment to a large party of friends and guests at the Club house, Aldershot, and three days later a bountiful dinner to the men of the regiment, their wives, and families.

The sergeants also celebrated the occasion by a spirited ball and supper to which the officers contributed. Much enthusiasm and good-feeling

1866.
ALDERSHOT.

was evinced at this happy time by all ranks in the regiment. On the day of the ceremony the commanding officer released all men under regimental punishment.

Shortly afterwards the regiment received a distinguished title under the authority conveyed in the following letter:—

"*Horse Guards,*
"*23rd April,* 1866.

"SIR,

"I have the pleasure by direction of the Field-"Marshal Commanding-in-Chief, to intimate "to you that the Queen has been graciously "pleased to command that the 89th Foot may "henceforth bear the title of " Princess Victoria's "Regiment," in commemoration of the recent "presentation of new colours, to replace those "presented 33 years ago by Her Majesty when "Princess Victoria.

"I have the honor to be, &c.,
"W. PAULET,
"*A.G.*

"The Officer Commanding,
"89th Regiment,
"Aldershot."

This information duly appeared in the *London Gazette* of the 22nd May, 1866.

Her Majesty was further pleased to permit the officers of the 89th "Princess Victoria's" Regiment to wear on their forage caps, above the regulation numbers 89, the badge of a Princess's coronet, (this was announced in Regimental orders of the 4th of February, 1867), and an additional proof of Royal kindness and consideration was afforded by Her Majesty presenting to the regiment, a water-colour drawing of the ceremony of presenting the colours at Aldershot, executed by her command by Mr. G. W. Thomas.

With Her Majesty's sanction, the old colours of the regiment were finally deposited in the Military Church of All Saints, Aldershot, on the 13th of September, after an interesting special religious ceremony, and an appropriate sermon by the Rev. E. J. Rogers, Chaplain; Colonel C. R. Egerton, Deputy-Adjutant General at the Horse Guards, who had as Ensign, received the regimental colour from the Princess Victoria in 1833, and had served in the regiment until the reduction in 1856, being present. In this church at Aldershot early in the following year, a stained glass window was erected.—" In memory " of those who had died while serving under the " old colours of the regiment, by the united " subscription of all ranks serving in the regi- " ment, and of many of the officers who had " formerly served in it."

1866.
ALDERSHOT.

The establishment of the regiment for the financial year from 1st April, 1866, to 31st March, 1867, was fixed at 10 companies, comprising 49 sergeants, 40 corporals, 21 drummers, and 640 privates, and during that period, 200 recruits joined the regiment, about three-quarters of whom were raised in the South of England. The regiment remained in camp during the remainder of this year, taking part in all the field days and reviews of the season. On the 7th of June, Their Royal Highnesses, The Prince and Princess of Wales, with other Royal and illustrious personages, attended a review at the camp. On the 1st of October the Field Marshal Commanding-in-Chief inspected and manœuvred the division, and he expressed himself as much pleased with the regiment on the occasion.

In the month of January, the regiment was armed with the new breech-loading rifle, (snider pattern) in lieu of muzzle loaders.

1867.
ALDERSHOT.

On the night of the 11th March, the regiment received sudden orders by telegram to proceed

1867.
ALDERSHOT.

from Aldershot to Ireland, where a fenian outbreak had taken place. Accordingly, they marched out of camp in a heavy snow storm at half-past 9 o'clock on the morning of the 12th, and were forwarded by special railway train from Farnborough station direct to Holyhead, and thence by steamer at once to Dublin, where they landed about 11 o'clock in the forenoon of the 13th. They proceeded by rail the same day to Curragh Camp.

THE CURRAGH.

With reference to the hurried departure of the regiment from Aldershot, Lieutenant-General Sir J. Y. Scarlett reported that "the 89th had left "in the most satisfactory manner, which was in "unison with their conduct during their stay at "Aldershot; the sudden order had been met with "the least possible inconvenience from the excel- "lent discipline of the corps." The Field Marshal Commanding-in-Chief thereupon notified through the Quarter-Master General of the forces, in a letter dated 16th March, His Royal Highness's satisfaction at receiving so favourable a report of the conduct of the battalion on leaving camp.

The regiment was at this time more than complete in numbers, and fully equipped. Two companies under a field officer proceeded to Naas on the 17th March, and a company to Carlow, a few days later. The companies at Naas were relieved by 2 other companies, on the 26th June.

DUBLIN.

Early in July, the regiment was ordered to Dublin, on the 10th one company, and on the 11th two more companies were sent to Dungannon, Portadown, and Downpatrick, for the preservation of the public peace, but they all rejoined head-quarters on the 16th, on which day the whole regiment was concentrated into the Royal Barracks, Dublin, except the company from Carlow, which, after a course of musketry at the Curragh, arrived in Dublin on the 31st of July.

The Oxford grey tartan trousers which were issued in 1866, in place of blue serge, were not

PRINCESS VICTORIA'S REGIMENT.   143

found to wear well, and summer trousers (Oxford mixture) of a somewhat improved material were issued this year to the regiment.

Early in November, 2 companies under a field officer were despatched to Mullingar.

1867.
DUBLIN.

The distribution of the regiment continued as at the end of 1867, until the month of July.

During the memorable visit to Ireland of their Royal Highnesses the Prince and Princess of Wales, in the month of April, the regiment took part in the military pageant, on the occasion of the installation of the Prince as a Knight of St. Patrick. It furnished a guard of honour at the national Ball at the Great Exhibition Building, and formed part of the force at the grand review and field day in the Phœnix Park, under the command of General Lord Strathnairn, commander of the forces in Ireland. The Marquis, (afterwards Duke) of Abercorn, held the Vice Royalty of Ireland at this period.

1868.
DUBLIN.

On the 7th of July, head-quarters and two companies from Dublin, and the two companies from Mullingar, proceeded by rail to Athlone, a highly important strategical post, nearly in the centre of Ireland, situated on the river Shannon. Two companies were about the same date sent to Galway, two more to Castlebar, and one to Sligo, and Boyle respectively. The two latter companies were withdrawn to Athlone in November, towards the end of which month, after some temporary moves of companies on account of the general election, two other companies proceeded to Ballina, where a part of the union workhouse was set apart for their accommodation during the winter.

1868.
ATHLONE.

In the month of January, the regiment was once more placed under orders for India, to embark in February, 1870, and the establishment of the regiment was fixed for the years 1870 and

1869.
ATHLONE.

1869.

ATHLONE.

2nd Bn. 4th, 2nd Bn. 15th, 2nd Bn. 16th, 1st Bn. 18th, 1st Bn. 24th, 48th, 54th, 64th, 70th, 71st, 95th, and 97th Regts.

1871, at the augmented strength of 59 sergeants, 25 drummers, and 850 rank and file.

Upwards of a 100 volunteers from different corps as per margin, joined the regiment at Athlone in March, and many recruits were received up to the end of this year, from a recruiting party from the regiment stationed at York, and from the various recruiting districts in England. A few Irish recruits also joined during the year.

A company was detached to Mullingar in the month of March, and in April the two companies at Ballina were removed to Sligo and Boyle respectively. In the course of the summer, the detachments at Castlebar and Galway were reduced by one company each, and the company at Boyle was withdrawn, the Mullingar party was increased to two companies.

On the 25th of August, three companies under command of Brevet Lieutenant-Colonel Thorp, proceeded, two from Athlone, and one from Mullingar, to Enniskillen.

Towards the end of October, the whole regiment was moved by rail in several divisions from the West and North West of Ireland, to Fermoy, Co. Cork, where an 11th company destined to be one of the depôt companies, was formed from 1st November and detached to Mitchelstown.

Some alterations in the shape and ornamentation of the tunics took place in this year.

1870.

FERMOY.

In the month of January, 1870, intimation was received that the embarkation of the regiment for India, previously fixed for the end of February, was postponed until at soonest the following autumn. The 11th company was relieved and broken up accordingly.

Early in the Spring, in consequence of the political state of the country, two companies were detached to Kanturk, Co. Cork, where temporary quarters in the Union Workhouse were provided for them; a company was also detached to Killarney, and similarly accommodated. Another company was sent to occupy barracks at Tralee.

1870.
FERMOY.

Later in the year, for a few weeks, two companies were detached to Ballincolig, one of these companies under the command of Captain Barstow, was on duty in the city of Cork during a contested election, and received the thanks of the authorities for their good services and excellent conduct on the occasion.

By the middle of July, all the detachments were recalled to Fermoy, except one company at Mitchelstown.

The regiment, this summer, received a large number of volunteers from other corps (as marginly detailed) to complete the establishment for India. This was ordered to be as follows:—

EIGHT SERVICE COMPANIES

F.Os.	Capts.	Subs.	Staff.	Sergts.	Drs.	Corpls.	Pts.
3	8	16	6	48	17	40	760

TWO DEPÔT COMPANIES

—	2	2	—	8	4	8	92

Volunteers from
S.F. Gds. - - - 2
2nd Bn. 15th - - 9
1st. Bn. 16th - - 8
1st & 2nd Bn. 18th - 23
1st Bn. 20th - - 7
31st Foot - - 3
43rd L.I. - - 3
47th - - 13
52nd L.I. - - 3
64th - - 12
68th L.I. - - 11
69th - - 6
80th - - 3
96th L.I. - - 24
95th - - 9
98th - - 15
100th - - 19
———
Total 170

Eventually, before embarkation, the number of privates for the service companies was ordered to be 780, and 5 per cent. in addition.

On the 1st of August, orders were unexpectedly received by telegram for the regiment to move from Fermoy to Limerick, strong detachments averaging about 120 men each, to be furnished at Clare Castle, Gort, Neuagh and Tipperary—the company at Mitchelstown to be withdrawn. These moves took place accordingly, the head-quarters of the regiment arriving at Limerick on the 6th of August.

The great war between France and Prussia now for a time clouded the political atmosphere of England, and it seemed doubtful whether any troops could be spared from home

LIMERICK.

1870.
LIMERICK.

service in the United Kingdom. After a short pause, however, the regimental preparations for embarkation for India were actively resumed.

On the 2nd of September, Major-General Campbell, commanding the Cork (or S.W. of Ireland) District, inspected the head-quarters of the service companies, and also the depôt companies. Nearly thirty eligible recruits joined from England later in the month, and were taken on the strength of the service companies.

Officers who embarked for India:
Lt.-Col. (Bt.-Col.) Boyle
Maj.(Bt. Lt.-Col.) Thorp
,, Penton.
Capts. Knatchbull, Dunn, Harvest, Grier, Hubbersty, Hassall, Murray
Lieuts. Fawkes, Daubeny (I. of M.), Campbell, Godwin, Austen, Caddell, Cuthbert, Ribton, Barker, Brereton, McMurray, Cox.
Ensigns: Vipan, Gordon, Brown, Ellis, Boyle, Anton.
Adjutant Sealy.
Quarter-Master Osborne.
Surgeon Sparrow.
Assistant Surgeons Long and Ward.

Strength of N.C.O.'s and men embarked for India, 30th Sept., 1870:
914, with 106 women, and nearly as many children.

Part of the regiment embarked at Queenstown on the 29th of September, in H.M.'s Indian steam troopship "Crocodile," the head-quarters of the regiment leaving Limerick early on the morning of the 30th, proceeded by rail to Cork, thence by river steamer to Queenstown, and also embarked in the "Crocodile" with the remainder of the service companies; the vessel sailed the same afternoon.

The regiment reached Alexandria after a quick passage in very fine weather, on the 14th of October, and having traversed Egypt by rail, sailed again from Suez on the 16th, in H.M's. Indian steam Troopship "Jumna." The voyage to Bombay was also very prosperous, and the "Jumna" anchored at Bombay Harbour on the 30th October.

On the 1st of November, the regiment having been ordered to the Madras Presidency, embarked and sailed from Bombay in the sailing ships "Calcutta," and "Queen of Australia," and the Indian Government steamer "Dalhousie" for Cannanore, on the Malabar coast, where the corps had formerly been quartered in 1815-16, and 1823-24. The regiment landed at Cannanore on the 6th and 7th November. A few days later, one company was detached to Calicut, and another to Malliapooram.

The depôt companies remained a few weeks at Limerick, after separation from the service companies, and then crossed the channel to Bristol,

PRINCESS VICTORIA'S REGIMENT.   147

and were attached there to the 50th (Queen's Own) Regiment.

Major-General Garvock, K.C.B., was gazetted Colonel of the 89th Regiment from the 22nd of October, *vice* Lieutenant-General C. Gascoyne transferred to 72nd Highlanders, which corps he had commanded as Lieutenant-Colonel.

1870.
LIMERICK.

The regiment remained at Cannanore, and was fairly healthy during this year. The companies at Calicut, and Malliapooram, were relieved by others from head-quarters in the month of December.

Ensign C. N. Jones, joined on appointment.

Some volunteers from 1st Bn. 19th, 38th, 3rd Bn. 60th Rifles, and 104th Bengal Fusiliers, joined towards the end of the year.

About 30 invalids were sent home from the service companies.

The depôt companies remained attached to the 50th Queen's Own Regiment, which corps, in the course of the summer moved from Bristol to Aldershot Camp.

The rank of Ensign was done away with in this year by the act of Parliament which also abolished purchase. The total number of Subalterns in the regiment remained at eighteen.

1871.
CANNANORE.

The regiment remained at Cannanore until the 4th of November, on which date, having been relieved by the 43rd Light Infantry from Ireland direct, through the Suez Canal to Cannanore, the head-quarters and 6 companies commanded by Colonel Boyle, C.B., marched for Bangalore, passing through part of Coorg into Mysore, and halting for one night at Seringapatam; they reached Bangalore in relief of the 1st Bn. 21st Fusiliers on the 26th November. The companies from Calicut and Malliapooram, rejoined head-quarters on the 6th December.

1872.
CANNANORE.

1872.
BANGALORE.
2 Sergeants and 34 Privates.

A draft, strength as per margin, from the depôt joined in December, and about the same time a considerable number of volunteers from the 2nd Bn. 10th, and the 2nd Bn. 21st Fusiliers, the 2nd Bn. 24th, and the 105th Light Infantry, were added to the strength of the regiment, raising it to 109 above the establishment.

The regiment lost ten (10) men by death during the year, and about 38 men were invalided to England.

The depôt companies remained with the 50th Regiment at Aldershot, when they became attached to the 2nd Bn. 22nd Foot, and once more were sent to Ireland, taking up quarters with the 2nd Bn. 22nd at Fermoy, this being the fourth occasion since 1853, that a portion of the 89th Regiment had been sent to that station, viz., the depôt three times, and head-quarters once (see 1869).

1873.
BANGALORE.

Colonel Boyle, C.B., proceeded on sick leave to England in the month of May, and Lieutenant-Colonel Thorp assumed command of the regiment on the 2nd of June, on his arrival from Wellington, where he had been nearly two years in command of a convalescent depôt.

At the meeting of the Southern India Rifle Association, held at Bangalore, in September, the regiment was very successful, carrying off the Bangalore Cup, and the non-commissioned officers' plate, with a higher score in each case than had been achieved on any previous occasion.

Quarter-Master F. Osborne died at Bangalore on the 2nd of October.

Lieutenant Welsh, and Sub-Lieutenants Fasken, M. Meade, and J. de C. Meade, joined the service companies. Captain Dunn, and Lieutenant Campbell left India for duty at the depôt, and Captain Sealy went on sick leave to England this year.

The regiment remained at Bangalore the whole

PRINCESS VICTORIA'S REGIMENT. 149

year, and was very healthy; nine deaths occurred and forty-one men were invalided during this period.

The depôt left Fermoy for Mullingar, where it was attached to the 94th Regiment, the battalion with which it was to be connected for the future.

The regiment marched on the 5th of January under command of Lieutenant-Colonel Thorp to the Camp of Exercise, which was composed exclusively of troops belonging to the Madras Presidency, and was situated about eight miles east of Bangalore, it there formed part of the 2nd Infantry Brigade (1st Division) under command of Colonel W. G. Owen.

The men paraded every morning for brigade drill; on one occasion part of the brigade was opposed to the other, and another time the first brigade was opposed to the 2nd brigade of the same division. After remaining a fortnight at Neckondy, the two brigades of the 1st Division changed their camping ground, and took up an extended position in line with cavalry and artillery, under command of Major-General A. Borton, C.B., at Jinkinpally, north of the railway and the Madras road, about 7 miles from Bangalore, and near the village of Kristuaveram.

During the next fortnight, divisional field days frequently took place, the brigades were again opposed to one another, and afterwards the two divisions.

The camp was under immediate command of Lieutenant-General Sir F. K. Haines, K.C.B., General Lord Napier of Magdala, G.C.B. & G.C.S.I. Commander-in-Chief in India, was present at some of the principle manœuvres, and the whole force marched past before him on the 22nd of January.

On the 30th of January, the day before the camp broke up, all the troops again marched past, before Sir F. K. Haines, K.C.B., the Com-

1873.
BANGALORE.

1874.
BANGALORE.

1874.

BANGALORE.

mander-in-Chief of the Madras Army, at the conclusion of which he cordially thanked the superior officers for the able and hearty manner in which they had each and all endeavoured to produce the best results from the various proceedings that had taken place in camp, and further requested them to inform their men that nothing could have been better than the conduct of the troops.

Colonel W. Boyle, C.B. who had commanded the regiment for many years, died in London, in February, much regretted by all.

In March, a small draft (19 men) arrived, and Major Knatchbull left for England on leave.

Major-General C. R. Egerton, who had recently been appointed Colonel of the regiment, and who had previously served in it for a great many years, died in London in May, and was succeeded by Lieutenant-General Lord Henry Percy, K.C. B., V.C.

Officers left for England:
Captain Harvest, *(For Depot)*.
Captain Murray, *(Staff College)*;
Lieutenant Caddell, *(Sick leave)*.

Officers arrived from England:
Lieutenant Barrow, Sub-Lieutenant Tufnell.

The Bangalore cup was again won by the 89th, with a score of 328 points, the highest yet made. The regiment remained at Bangalore the whole year, and was very healthy, 5 deaths occurred, about 50 men were invalided, and 29 volunteered for other corps.

The depôt companies were quartered at Mullingar, and at the Curragh Camp, and were armed with the Martini-Henry Rifle.

1875.

MADRAS.

The regiment having been inspected by Major-General Borton, C.B., on the 27th January, and most favourably reported upon by him, moved into camp on the Arab Lines on the 1st February, and left Bangalore the following day, *en-route* to Madras, under command of Lieutenant-Colonel Thorp.

The regiment marched into Fort St. George, on the 26th February, two companies (D & F) being sent on detachment to Trichinopoly.

A strong company of 4 officers and 135 men,

PRINCESS VICTORIA'S REGIMENT.

embarked on the 20th April, for Port Blair, Andaman Islands, in relief of a detachment 21st Fusiliers.

The regiment attended the funeral of the late Lord Hobart, Governor of Madras, on the 28th April; he was succeeded by the Duke of Buckingham and Chandos, who entered on the duties of his appointment, in time to welcome His Royal Highness the Prince of Wales, who arrived in Madras, on the 13th December, and remained there a week.

The festivities on this occasion were shared by all classes, and also participated in by the soldiers and school children. Frequent guards of honour were furnished by the regiment.

His Excellency Sir Frederick Haines, K.C.B., the Commander-in-Chief of the Madras Army, left Madras on resigning his command, on the 24th December, and as his last official military act, complimented the men of the regiment, on their clean and smart appearance, and the admirable way in which they turned out on all occasions.

Lieut. (and local Captain) Ormsby Cox, died on the 9th December.

The regiment continued healthy during the year, thirteen deaths occurred, and about 36 men were invalided.

The depôt companies left the Curragh for Belfast.

The regiment was inspected by Brigadier-General Raikes, C.B., on the 11th of January, and favourably reported upon. Orders were received to move to British Burmah, to be quartered, the head quarters and right-half battalion under Lieutenant-Colonel Penton, at Thayetmyo, the left-half battalion at Tonghoo, under Major Grantham. The 1st party as per margin, sailed from Madras, in the Government Transport "Tennasserim," on the 21st January.

1875.
MADRAS.

Officers left for England:
Surg.-Major Sparrow.
Lieut. Boyle.
Major Anderson, (Pay-Master).
Capt. Daubeny.
 ,, Godwin Austin.
Lieut. Jones, and
 ,, Brereton
 (*To Depot*).

Officers arrived from England:
Major Grantham.
Capts. Sealy.
 ,, Collins.
 ,, Richmond.
Lieut. Vipan.
Sub-Lieut. Harman.
Major Forster,(Pay-Mr.)
Capt. Cave.

1876.
MADRAS.

Companies A, D, E, & F:
Major Grantham.
Captain Collins.
Lieuts. Smith, Boyle, Barrow.

M

1876.

MADRAS.

Lieut.-Colonel Penton, Commanding.
Brevet-Major Robinson.
Captain Cave.
Lieutenants Vipan, McMurray, J. de C. D. Meade.
Sub-Lieut. Harman.
Adjutant Cuthbert.
Pay-Mr. Major Forster.
Quarter-Master Archer.
Surgeon Barrow, with B, G, & H, Companies.

To England:
Lieut.-Colonel Thorp.
Major Hubbersty (*to Depot*).
Major Sealy.
Lieutenant Anton.
Lieut. Vipan (to Depôt).

Joined from England:
Brevet-Major Dunn.
Captain Caddell.
Lieut. Boyle, Brown, Jones.
Sub-Lieut. Standen.
Surg.-Major Sparrow.

On the 8th February, the head quarters and three companies as per margin, sailed in the same steamer for Rangoon. "C" Company under Captain Richmond, rejoined head quarters at Thayetmyo, from Port Blair. Lieutenant-Colonel Thorp, proceeded on leave of absence to England, Brevet Lieutenant-Colonel Penton, assuming the command of the regiment.

The changes as per margin took place amongst the officers during the year. Lieutenant-Colonel Thorp, retired on full-pay, on the 12th August. The promotion being given in the regiment to Brevet Lieutenant-Colonel Penton, Brevet-Major Robinson, and Lieutenant Cuthbert, the seniors in each rank. 23 non-commissioned officers and men were invalided, and 31 time expired men left for England. A draft, consisting of 2 corporals and 63 privates, under Brevet-Major Dunn, arrived at Thayetmyo, on 20th April, 1876.

The depôt companies of the regiment, proceeded from Belfast to Armagh, to join the 65th Brigade depôt, under the new system of linked battalions and brigade depots.

Deaths during the year, 11.

1877.

THAYETMYO.

To England:
Capt. Richmond, (*to Depôt*).
Lieut. Vipan, (*to Depôt*).
Sub-Lieut. Standen, (*Sick*).
Qr.-Mr. Archer, (*on leave*).

From England:
Bt.-Major Harvest, (*from Depôt*).
2nd Lieut. Davidson (*on appointment from Militia*).
Lieut. Anton (*from leave*).
Capt. Barker, (*on promotion*).
Sub-Lieuts. Maxwell and Rogers (*on appointment.*)

The head-quarters and right-half battalion were inspected by Major-General Knox Gore Commanding British Burmah Division, on the 19th January, and the left-half battalion at Tonghoo, on the 9th of March; both were favourably reported upon.

The changes as per margin occurred amongst the officers during the year.

Thirty-seven men were sent home "time expired," 21 men were invalided from Thayetmyo and 48 from Tonghoo, and there were during the year fourteen (14) deaths.

A draft of 25 men under Captain Barker, arrived from the Brigade Depôt at Armagh, and 23 volunteers were received from other corps.

The head quarters remained at Thayetmyo till 20th December, when on being relieved by the 44th Regiment, they embarked on board H.M.S. "Irrawaddy" for conveyance to Prome, thence by rail to Rangoon on 21st December, having remained one night at Prome.

The Tonghoo detachment under Major Grantham, joined head quarters at Rangoon on the 22nd January 1878, except "G." Company, under Captain Cave, which having been made up to 4 officers and 135 rank and file, proceeded on detachment to Port Blair, Andaman Islands

A silver medal was sent to each regiment in India, this year, to be presented to the most deserving soldier, to commemorate the assumption of the title of Empress of India by Her Majesty. The commanding officer selected Sergeant-Major Murray for this decoration, the medal was accordingly presented by Lieutenant-Colonel Penton to the Sergeant-Major, at a full-dress parade.

Martini-Henry rifles were issued to the regiment this year, in lieu of the snider pattern.

Her Majesty was pleased to sanction the "Princess Victoria's Coronet," the regimental badge, to be worn on the collars of the tunics, instead of the universal crown, hitherto worn by the men of the regiment. *Vide* Horse Guards letter dated 22nd August, 1877, No. C, 7846.

The rank of Sub-Lieutenant was abolished and that of 2nd Lieutenant substituted.

The regiment was inspected on the 25th of March, by Major-General Knox Gore, commanding Burmah Division, and was most favourably reported upon.

The changes as per margin, took place during the year.

A draft of 150 rank and file, made up from the brigade depôt and 94th Regiment (connected battalion) under Captain Brereton, arrived from

1877.
THAYETMYO.

RANGOON.

1878.
RANGOON.

From England:
Captain Brereton, (*for Depot*).
Lieutenant Cahusac, (*appointed*).
Quarter-Master Archer (*from leave*).
2nd Lieutenant Dobbie, (*on appointment*).

1878.

RANGOON.

To England:
Lieut.-Colonel Penton, *(sick certificate).*
Lieut. Anton, *(sick).*
Major Dunn, *(leave).*

England 15th January, and 23 volunteers from other corps, also joined.

Lieutenant-Colonel Penton, proceeded to England in April on sick certificate, and was succeeded in the temporary command of the regiment by Major Grantham the next senior officer.

The move of the regiment (to Secunderabad) was countermanded for another year, owing to the war in Afghanistan.

There were 16 time expired, and 39 invalids sent home. Captain Richmond joined the Army Pay Department, and his step given in the regiment to Lieutenant and Adjutant McMurray, the latter being succeeded in the Adjutancy by Lieutenant C. E. Harman. Pay-Master Major Forster, was appointed to the department, under the new system.

An attack of cholera broke out in "A" Company, which was moved into camp at once, and remained so for 11 days, 4 cases out of 6, proved fatal.

"G" Company remained on detachment at Port Blair, the whole year.

1879.

RANGOON.

Death:
Qr.-Master J. Archer.

From England:
Lieut.-Col. Penton, *(sick).*
Lieutenants Ellis and Standen, *(sick).*
Cpt. Hubbersty, *(Depot).*
Lieut. Vipan, *(Depot).*
2nd Lieutenant Fry, *(on appointment sent out from R.M.C., Sandhurst).*
2nd Lieutenant Moore, *(on appointment from militia).*
Bt.-Major Dunn, *(leave).*

To Staff Corps.
Lieut. E. G. Barrow, Bengal S.C.

2nd Lieut. Davidson, to 94th Regiment, on promotion.

The regiment was again inspected this year by Major General Knox Gore (5th February) who expressed himself well satisfied with the efficiency, steadiness under arms, and general bearing of the battalion.

The changes that took place among the officers during the year (as per margin) were as follows: Quarter-Master Archer died at Rangoon, 21st January. Lieutenant Vipan joined from the regimental depot bringing a draft chiefly consisting of transfers from the different sub-district brigades in Ireland, whose strength was 2 sergeants, 2 corporals, 120 privates. These men were detained at Fort St. George, Madras, for the whole year awaiting the arrival of the regiment from Burmah.

Lieutenant-Colonel Penton who was promoted Colonel on the 28th March resumed command of the regiment from leave of absence on the 19th April.

Lieutenant-Colonel C. C. Grantham placed on half-pay proceeded to England. Brevet-Major Dunn was promoted to the vacant majority. Lieutenant Vipan promoted Captain, and 2nd Lieutenant Davidson promoted to a Lieutenancy in the linked battalion (94th Regiment) on active service at Natal.

Sergeant-Major John Watkins promoted Quarter-Master *vice* Quarter-Master James Archer, deceased.

The changes in the distribution of the regiment were as follows:—"E" company consisting of 3 sergeants, 7 corporals, 123 privates proceeded to Fort Blair, Andaman, to relieve "G" company.

The head-quarters of the regiment A, B, C, & G companies under command of local Colonel Grantham made up to a total strength of 12 officers (as per margin), 12 sergeants, 14 corporals, 11 drummers, and 312 privates, embarked on 23rd March to proceed to Tayrangoon, situated on the left bank of the river Irrawaddy, and about 7 miles south of the Frontier between upper and British Burmah. The avowed object being to suppress any aggressive movement on the part of King Theebaw (King of Burmah) which at that time appeared to be extremely imminent. These companies remained at Tayrangoon, quartered in bamboo huts, and the health of both officers and men during that period was very good.

On the arrival of Colonel Penton from England, head-quarters were transferred to Rangoon. Major Robinson from Rangoon succeeded to the command of the above half-battalion on the departure of Colonel Grantham.

During the latter part of this year the men of the head-quarters at Rangoon suffered severely

---

1879.

RANGOON.

To England;
Col. Grantham, *(half-pay).*
Capt. McMurray, *(leave)*
„ Brereton, *(sick leave)*
„ Cave, *(regtl depot)*
Lieut. Munn, *(sick leave)*

Colonel Grantham.
Brevet-Major Harvest.
Captains Cave, Cuthbert
McMurray.
Lieutenants Jones, Ellis, Rogers.
2nd Lieut. Davidson.
Lieut. & Adjt. Harman.
Surg.-Mj. Healy, A.M.D
Surg. Fogherty, A.M.D.

TAYRANGOON.

1879.
TAYRANGOON.

from repeated attacks of fever of an intermittent type.

1880.
RANGOON.

Officers from England:
Captain Boyle.
Lieutenant Brown.
2nd Lieutenants Campbell and Hill, (*on appointment*).

The head-quarters of the regiment were inspected for the fourth time by Major-General Knox Gore commanding British Burmah Division, at Rangoon on the 24th and 26th of February.

The Major-General expressed himself very well satisfied with the regiment in all respects. The half-battalion at Tayrangoon, which was inspected by him a little later also met with his approval in every way.

This half-battalion under command of Major Robinson rejoined head-quarters during the latter end of March having been absent from Rangoon for 12 months, during which period the health and discipline of the wing was exceptionally good.

S.S. "Tennasserim:"
Colonel Penton Comdg.
Major Harvest.
Captains Hubbersty, Fawkes & Boyle.
Lieutenant Dobbie.
2nd Lieuts. Fry & Hill.
Adjutant Harman
Qr.-Mr. Watkins.
Staff Pay-Mr. Forster.
Surg.-Maj. Waters, A.M.D.
Surgeon Routh, and 366 N.C.O.'s and men.

S.S. "Czarewitch:"
Major Dunn, Comdg.
Captain Smith
Lieuts. Brown, Rogers, Standen, & Cahusac.
Surg. Kirkwood, A.M.D
297 N.C.O.'s and men.

A draft of 35 rank and file under command of Captain Boyle joined 26th February, 1881.

General J. A. Lambert was appointed Colonel of the regiment *vice* Sir H. de Bathe transferred to 85th Foot.

The regiment had to lament the death of Captain John Cuthbert who died in London, September 9th.

The regiment embarked at Rangoon, 27th December in the Transports "Tennasserim" and "Czarewitch" for Vingorla *en route* to Belgaum, calling at Port Blair Andaman Islands for the detachment there.

During the year the regiment suffered from intermittent fever, and numbers of the men including nearly the whole of the band, had to be sent to Wellington for a change of air. 5 deaths occurred, and 117 men were discharged or invalided.

1881.
BELGAUM.

The regiment disembarked at Vingorla, January 8th, and marched for Belgaum on the 11th, arriving there on the 17th. Seven

PRINCESS VICTORIA'S REGIMENT.

1881.
BELGAUM.

companies occupied the barracks, and one company the fort about 1½ miles distant.

January 26th Lieutenant F. H. Munn was appointed Instructor of Musketry. Colonel Penton having been appointed to command a brigade of the Kandahar field force, handed over command of the battalion to Major Dunn on February 5th. The regiment was inspected on March 5th and 7th by Brigadier-General C. M. Govan in temporary command Belgaum District, who was thoroughly satisfied.

On May 23rd a company was sent on detachment under Captain Smith to Kolapore, 70 miles north of Belgaum, there to be stationed.

Lieutenant C. R. Rogers was appointed Adjutant *vice* Harman promoted to a company in the 94th Regiment.

By Horse Guards, G.O. No. 41 specially issued 11th April, 1881, Her Gracious Majesty was pleased to make the following changes in the organization, title, and uniform:—

The 89th Princess Victoria's Regiment to be localized with the 87th Royal Irish Fusiliers, and to become the 2nd Battalion Royal Irish Fusiliers (Princess Victoria's). The facings to be *blue*, the pattern of the lace *shamrock*. The number of the regimental district to be 87th. By a subsequent G.O. No. 70, dated June 30th, 1881, the name of the regiment was changed to Princess Victoria's (Royal Irish Fusiliers).

July 1st the rank of 2nd lieutenant was abolished and the following was fixed as the establishment of the battalion:—

	Lieut.-Col.	Maj.	Capts.	Lieuts.	Adjt.	Qr.-Mr.
India	2	4	4	16	1	1
Depôt			1	1		

	Sergt.-Major.	Qr.-Mr.-Sergt.	Band Master.	Sergt. Dr.	Pay-Mr. Sergt.	Arm. Sergt.	Hospital Sergt.	Ord.-room Srgt.	Color Sergts.	Sergeants.	Sergt. I. of M.	Sergt. Pioneer.	Drummers.	Corporals.	Privates.
India	1	1	1	1	1	1	1	1	8	32	1	1	16	40	780

1881.

BELGAUM.

Colonel Penton rejoined the regiment June 2nd from brigade command but immediately proceeded on privilege leave. He again rejoined on August 2nd and took over command, but handed it over on August 12th to Major Dunn by order received by telegram, he having completed five years as Lieutenant-Colonel commanding on that date.

Six officers joined the head-quarters during the year, on appointment, viz: 2nd Lieutenants Davison and Hext, January 25th; 2nd Lieutenants Nurse, Brinckman, Angell, and Williams, April 2nd. 8 men died, and 203 were sent home, or discharged.

1882.

BELGAUM.

Lieutenants Plomer, Cartwright, Laing, Harrison.

Lieutenant-Colonel Robinson having rejoined from sick leave took over command of the battalion on February 6th, when the officers named in the margin also joined from England on appointment.

February 1st "F" company under command of Captain Brown marched for Kolapore in relief of "A" company, the latter rejoining head-quarters on the 12th February under command of Captain Smith.

Five companies of the battalion were encamped at Batchie, five miles from Belgaum on the Vingorla road, under the command of Lieutenant-Colonel Robinson, from the 16th to 28th of February for the purpose of field firing. Captain Caddell was promoted Major on the 9th January, and joined the depôt companies from service with the auxiliary forces, and rejoined the battalion on the 20th January, 1883.

Brigadier-General G. T. Brice, commanding the Belgaum District inspected the battalion on the 8th March and expressed himself much satisfied with the efficiency and smart appearance of the men.

A team of men under Lieutenant Munn (Instructor of Musketry) went to Poona in September to compete at the annual rifle

PRINCESS VICTORIA'S REGIMENT. 159

meeting, and carried off a large number of prizes including the "Deccan Cup."

On the 11th December "B" company made up to 100 rank and file under command of Captain Gordon with Lieutenant Hill and Davison, proceeded to Kolapore to relieve "F" company under Captain Brown.

1882.
BELGAUM.

On the 22nd and 23rd of January, Brigadier-General G. T. Brice commanding Belgaum District made the annual inspection of the battalion which was in all respects most satisfactory.

1883.
BELGAUM.

Captain Brown died at Malta on 10th of April, on his passage to England on medical certificate.

The officers named in the margin joined the Indian Staff Corps during the year.

Lieuts. Fry, Cartwright, Shakespear, Laing.

On the 12th of November, 231 non-commissioned officers and men proceeded to Rawul Pindi to join the 1st battalion on their arrival in India; these men were compulsory transfers, not having completed six years service in India.

His Excellency the Commander-in-Chief of the Bombay Presidency, General the Hon. A. E. Hardinge, C. B., Equerry to the Queen, inspected the barracks on the 28th December, and on the following day the battalion was brigaded for field movements under his supervision.

Brigadier-General G. T. Brice, commanding the Belgaum District made his annual inspection of the battalion on the 8th and 9th January, and spoke most favourably of them, and regretted their departure after serving in his command for the last three years.

1884.
BELGAUM.

The battalion left Belgaum on the 19th of January *en route* to England after a tour of foreign service of nearly 14 years, during which period they served six years in the Madras Presidency, five years in British Burmah, and the remaining three in Belgaum in the Bombay

1884.

BELGAUM.

Officers, 18.
Rank and file, 340.
Women, 26.
Children, 62.

1884.

THE SOUDAN.

Officers present at El Teb:

Lieut.-Col. Robinson.
Major Caddell.
Capts. Smith, Gordon, Reeves, and Munn.
Lieuts. Moore, Hill, Davison, Hext, Nurse, Brinckman, Angell, Williams, and Plomer.
Capt. and Adjt. Rogers.
Qr.-Master. Watkins.

Presidency, to which station they were sent to recruit the health of the men after so prolonged a service in Burmah, where latterly they had suffered from fever and dysentery.

On the march to Vingorla for embarkation, owing to a slight outbreak of small pox, the battalion was detained at the Amboli Ghauts for 11 days, but subsequently embarked on board H.M. Indian troopship "Jumna" on the 7th February for conveyance to England, strength as per margin.

On arrival off Aden the battalion was detained, and received orders to proceed to Suakim on the coast of Nubia, to join an expeditionary force organized under command of Sir Gerald Graham V.C., K.C.B., to operate against fanatical Arabs in the Soudan, led by Osman Digna a lieutenant of the Mahdi's. The "Jumna" arrived there on the 19th of February; on the 23rd February the battalion proceeded round the coast to Trinkitat, disembarked and formed a part of the 1st Brigade under command of Sir Redvers Buller, V.C., K.C.M.G., and advanced a few days afterwards to Fort Baker, which they occupied until sufficient supplies were collected for a general advance. On the morning of the 29th February, the whole division being then concentrated, an advance towards Tokar was ordered, the object being to relieve the town which was supposed to be in the hands of the arabs. On arriving at El Teb about 4 miles distant from Fort Baker the arabs were discovered to be strongly entrenched, and had several guns in position which they had previously taken from Baker Pasha's Egyptian force, and whose troops they had totally defeated. The division advanced in a hollow square, guns manned by sailors from the fleet placed at each angle, the 2nd battalion Royal Irish Fusiliers forming the right face of the square. The division moved steadily on by the left flank of the enemy at a distance of about 600 yards, General Graham intending to attack them on their reverse flank. During this movement the square was subjected to a smart rifle fire, but no casualties occurred in the Fusiliers at this time. On reaching the reverse flank of the enemy's position, the square moved to its left, the Fusiliers thus became its rear face. The attack then became general and lasted for four hours, the enemy were finally driven from their position, their guns taken, besides suffering a very heavy loss of killed and wounded, estimated at about 2000. In this action the Regiment was peculiarly fortunate, only one officer and seven rank and file being wounded. During the ensuing night the battalion bivouacked in the enemy's entrenchments sending "A" company under Captain Gordon on outlying picquet.

The division continued its march towards Tokar the following morning at 8 o'clock, and reached the town about 4 o'clock in the afternoon, after a dreary and tedious march of 12 miles, through the desert in the same formation as the day before with the exception of the Fusiliers being placed in the front face of the square. The town offered no resistance; on the march the men suffered much from want of water, and also the excessive heat. A banner of the Mahdi's was captured, and sent as a trophy home to Her Majesty the Queen. The division returned to Trinkitat on the 4th March, after a long and toilsome march of seventeen miles over sand and brushwood.

Osman Digna having collected a large force of Arabs, many of them refugees from "El Teb" and "Tokar," among the hills about fourteen miles from Suakim, Sir G. Graham determined to dislodge them, as it would not have been advisable to withdraw from the country whilst the safety of Suakim was menaced. The regiment accordingly re-embarked on the 6th of March, on board H.M.S. "Humber" for Suakim, and landed the same day, where they remained in camp till all arrangements were made for a second advance.

1884.
THE SOUDAN.

Wounded:
Qr.-Mr. John Watkins, Sergt. Stubbington, and 7 rank and file.

1884
THE SOUDAN.

Officers present at "Tamai":
Lieut.-Col. Robinson.
Capts. Smith, Gordon, Reeves, Munn.
Lieuts. Moore, Hill, Davison, Hext, Nurse, Brinckman, Williams, Plomer.
Capt. & Adjt. Rogers.
Qr.-Master Watkins.

On the evening of the 11th March, the Division again started, and proceeded seven miles inland, halted some hours, and then continued the march on the afternoon of the 12th to the foot of the hills, where the Arabs showed themselves in small parties, but not in any force. The General then decided on bivouacking for the night, and accordingly threw up a Zereba (an abattis formed with the prickly bushes growing in the desert) sufficiently large in the form of a square to contain the whole division; nothing occurred to disturb the camp in any way till a short time after midnight, when a volley was fired by the Arabs into the Zereba, fortunately to no effect. A desultory fire was kept up by them till day-break, orders were given to the men to remain perfectly quiet and not return the fire; in this way the night was passed and only one man of the York and Lancaster Regiment killed.

On the morning of the 13th March the Division formed up at eight o'clock in two brigades. The Royal Irish Fusiliers was in the 1st Brigade under command of Sir Redvers Buller, V.C., K.C.M.G., which advanced towards Tamai in square formation (two companies of the regiment in the front and two on the left faces) to attack the enemy who were not above one thousand yards distant concealed in a deep ravine. The 2nd Brigade had advanced a short time before the first, and were hotly engaged, the Arabs attacking them with great determination, so much so as to compel them to retire and abandon some guns. At this juncture the 1st Brigade came up, opened a heavy fire on the advancing Arabs, which considerably relieved the position of the 2nd Brigade and enabled the guns to be retaken. The Arabs fought with the greatest bravery, but were completely vanquished by the fire brought to bear on them. The action lasted for 3 hours, and the Fusiliers were again most fortunate in having only one sergeant and

Wounded:
Lt.-Col. Robinson, Sergt. Clark and 5 rank and file.

five men wounded, though the whole British Force lost about 112 killed and 150 wounded; the Arabs about 2000 killed. After the action the 1st Brigade followed up the retreating Arabs some distance in the hills, and burned Osman Digna's camp, and then returned to the Zereba where they had bivouacked the previous night.

On the following morning Sir G. Graham again advanced over the battle field of Tamai, and further into the hills, and succeeded in destroying an immense quantity of ammunition, but no enemy being visible the Brigade returned to a Zereba about seven miles from Suakim, bivouacked for the night, and returned to that place next morning.

After remaining in camp for 10 days Sir G. Graham determined to make a third attempt to capture Osman Digna, and accordingly the force proceeded to the wells of Tamanieb, a distance of 17 miles from Suakim among the hills, but without success. "A" Company, under command of Captain Gordon, had been sent out previously with a convoy of water to a Zereba half way, held by the Gordon Highlanders. The three senior officers being on the sick list, Captain Gordon commanded on this third expedition.

The short but decisive campaign being now ended, the regiment embarked on the 29th March at Suakim on H.M. Indian troopship "Jumna" for England, and arrived at Portsmouth on the 21st April (at which town they were ordered to be stationed), after an absence of nearly 14 years on foreign service.

After the arrival of the battalion in England Lieutenant-Colonel Robinson received a very complimentary letter from Sir Redvers Buller, V.C., K.C.M.G., in whose brigade they served during the Soudan campaign, speaking in high terms "of the steadiness in action, discipline during the marches, and willingness on fatigue."

A large draft of 369 non-commissioned officers

1884.
PORTSMOUTH.

and men joined the battalion after their arrival in England, being transfers from the 1st battalion on their embarking for India.

The battalion was inspected on the 8th of September, by Lieutenant-General Sir George Willis, K.C.B., commanding the Southern district, and Lieutenant-Governor of Portsmouth, who expressed himself pleased with the battalion and with its interior economy.

On the 13th November, His Royal Highness the Field Marshal Commanding-in-Chief, presented to the officers and men of the battalion, on Southsea common, the Egyptian War Medal, for their services in Eastern Soudan, in presence of the whole of the troops. His Royal Highness took the opportunity of addressing the battalion, and speaking most favourably of them. His Highness the Khedive of Egypt, also conferred a bronze star on the officers, non-commissioned officers and men, in recognition of their services. Her Majesty the Queen, was graciously pleased to approve of the word and date, "*Egypt, 1884,*" being borne on the colours of the battalion.

On Appointment:
Lts. H. A. Coddington, W. E. Cairnes.
Transfer from 1st Batt.:
Lieut. A. F. Terry.

During the year, 3 drafts, amounting to 113 non-commissioned officers and men, joined headquarters from the depôt. The battalion remained stationed at Portsmouth, where the officers named in the margin joined it.

1885.
PORTSMOUTH.
Officers 25, Sergts. 39, Rank and File, 607.

The regiment strength as per margin, was inspected on the 14th July, at Portsmouth, by Lieutenant-General Sir George Willis, K.C.B., and favourably reported upon.

On the 12th August Colonel Robinson, C.B., having completed 4 years in command, was placed on half-pay, and handed over command to Lieutenant-Colonel Dunn.

On Appointment:
Lieut. R. W. Leeper.
Transfer from 1st Batt.:
Colonel Geo. Cox.
Lieut. Hon. E. B. L. Stopford.
Lieut. Banbury.

A draft of 1 sergeant and 74 rank and file, embarked on the 19th September, to join the 1st Battalion in India. In November, the strength of the regiment, was raised to 600 rank and file, and 682 of all ranks.

PRINCESS VICTORIA'S REGIMENT.

The officers named in the margin joined during the year, and 165 recruits also joined from the regimental depôt, Armagh.

1884.
PORTSMOUTH.

On the 3rd of February the battalion moved from Clarence Barracks, Portsmouth, to C. & D. lines, South Camp, Aldershot, and joined the 1st Brigade.

1886.
ALDERSHOT.

Lieutenant R. Brinckman, was appointed Adjutant (May 27th), *vice* Rogers, who had completed five years in that appointment.

In June, the authorised strength of the battalion was increased to :—

O.	W.O.	Sergts.	Corpls.	Drs.	Pvts.
24	2	40	40	16	710

No less than 482 recruits joined head-quarters from the regimental depôt during the year. Two drafts also proceeded to the 1st battalion, stationed at Nowshera, India, amounting to 254 rank and file.

The annual inspection was made by Major-General W. S. Cooper, commanding the 1st Infantry Brigade, on 5th and 6th August.

In the *London Gazette*, November 6th, Quarter-Master J. Watkins, was specially promoted to the rank of Honorary Captain, for his services during the Soudan Campaign, 1884.

Five officers joined head quarters on appointment, namely, Lieutenants Parker, Gray, Silver, Higginson, and Swettenham.

On the 9th July, the battalion under command of Colonel J. Dunn, took part in the Royal Jubilee Review at Aldershot, before Her Majesty Queen Victoria. It formed part of a Fusilier Brigade, the other battalions being 2nd Northumberland Fusiliers, 2nd Royal Inniskilling Fusiliers, and 1st Royal Munster Fusiliers—total strength of the brigade, 2,510. Grand total of all arms at this Review, was 57,169. The march past took place in the Long Valley, and occupied about three hours.

1887.
ALDERSHOT.

1887.
ALDERSHOT.

On the 26th July, the battalion under command of Colonel G. Cox, took part in a "flying column" consisting of the 1st Aldershot Infantry Brigade, a Regiment of Cavalry and a Battery of Artillery, the whole commanded by Major-General W. S. Cooper. The column after being daily occupied in marches or field manœuvres, returned to camp on 4th August.

Colonel G. Cox, on the 12th August, assumed command of the battalion, *vice* Colonel J. Dunn, retired. On the 18th September, General Ferryman, C.B., was appointed colonel of the regiment, *vice* General Lambert, deceased.

In November, regimental transport was introduced in the battalion, and the following were received:—

Draft Horses.	Riding Horses.	Mules.	Waggon.	Cart.
2	1	2	1	1

2nd Lieutenant F. L. V. Jenkins.
2nd Lieutenant H. de V. Harvest.

The rank of 2nd lieutenant which was abolished by the Royal Warrant of 1st July, 1881, was this year again created and two officers were posted to the battalion as 2nd lieutenants.

Recruiting was still briskly carried on at the depôt, Armagh, 221 recruits being sent to join the battalion during the year. A draft of 125 rank and file was sent to the 1st battalion at Peshawur, in December.

1888.
DOVER.

The battalion moved on the 14th April, from Aldershot to Dover, with head quarters in the South Front Barracks.

The Standing Orders for the regiment compiled by Lieutenant-Colonel Jones, in 1834, having been out of print for many years, the issue of new ones was much needed. New Standing Orders were therefore very carefully and fully compiled by Colonel G. Cox commanding the battalion, and issued for use.

APPENDIX.

ROLL OF STATIONS.

Roll of Stations in which the 89th Regiment has been Quartered since it was raised in 1793.

Year	Country.	Station.	Date.
1793	Ireland	Raised by General Crosbie	3 December, 1793
1794	England	Southampton Camp	Early in 1794
1794	Holland	Campaign under Duke of York	26 June, 1794
1795	England	Scarborough } Whitby }	April, 1795
		Whitburn Camp	Middle of 1795
1795	Ireland	Arklow	End of 1795
		Wexford	A few weeks later
		Loughlinstown Camp	Beginning of 1796
		Clonmel	During 1796
		Fermoy	During 1797
		Suppressing Irish Rebellion	1798
		Battle of Vinegar Hill	21 June, 1798
1799	Sicily	Messina	3 January, 1799
1800	Malta	Blockade of La Valetta	During 1800
1801	Egypt	Active Service	2 March, 1801
1802	Ireland	Youghal	28 January, 1802
		Enniskillen	Latter half of 1802
		Athlone	1803
		Loughrea	1803
		Donerail	1804
		Cork	1804
		Kinsale	13 July, 1804
1805	Holland	Active Service	7 December, 1805
1806	England	Margate	February, 1806
		Ospringe	2 April, 1806
		Gosport	14 September, 1806
1807	South America	Monte Video	23 February, 1807
1807	South Africa	Cape Town	October, 1807
1808	Ceylon	Trincomalee	27 September, 1808
		Colombo	11 March, 1809

APPENDIX.

Year	Country.	Station.	Date.
1809	India	Madras (Fort St. George)	December, 1809
		Half-Battalion to Java and Sumatra, Active Service	February, 1811 to October, 1812
		Poonamallee	12 October, 1812
		Madras (Fort St. George)	4 January, 1813
		Bangalore	7 March, 1814
		Cannanore	3 June, 1815
		Quilon	6 November, 1816
		Half-Battalion on Active Service in the Mahratta War	14 January, 1818 to 11 May, 1819
		Cannanore	5 February, 1823
1824	Burmah	Active Service, Ava	April, 1824
1826	India	Madras (Fort St. George)	27 April, 1826
		,, St. Thomas' Mount	15 October, 1826
		,, Fort St. George	3 August, 1827
		Trichinopoly	24 October, 1828
		Madras	30 August, 1830
1831	England	Canterbury	15 May, 1831
		Plymouth (The Citadel)	3 September, 1831
		Devonport	22 November, 1831
1833	Ireland	Cork	12 August, 1833
		Fermoy	August, 1834
		Naas	9 February, 1835
		Dublin (Richmond Barracks)	22 August, 1835
1835	West Indies	Barbadoes (St. Anns)	3 December, 1835
		Trinidad	27 March, 1836
		Antigua	17 February, 1839
1841	Canada	Amherstburg	29 June, 1841
1842	Canada	Chambly	24 July, 1842
		Montreal	5 May, 1843
		Quebec	9 May, 1845
		Halifax (Nova Scotia)	31 July, 1846
1847	England	Chichester	29 April, 1847
		Ashton-under-Lyne	9 November, 1847
		Preston	20 April, 1848
		Ashton-under-Lyne	22 June, 1848
1848	Ireland	Birr	27 July, 1848
		Dublin (Linen Hall Barracks)	19 October, 1850
		,, (Richmond Barracks)	May, 1851
		Clonmel	20 September, 1851
		Templemore	6 August, 1852
		Buttevant	28 December, 1852
		Cork	9 March, 1853
1854	Gibraltar	Gibraltar	30 April, 1854
1854	The Crimea	Sevastopol	15 December, 1854
		Balaklava	13 September, 1855

APPENDIX.

Year	Country.	Station.	Date.
1856	Gibraltar	Gibraltar	4 June, 1856
1856	South Africa	Cape Town	16 September, 1856
		East London	9 October, 1856
		Cape Town	18 May, 1857
1857	India	Ahmedabad } Deesa }	14 October, 1857
		Guzerat, Neemuch, The Seronge Field Force, and innumerable Detachments and Expeditions, quelling the native rebels after the Mutiny	1858 & 1859
		Jhansi	13 March, 1860
1861	India	Umballa	8 March, 1861
		Mooltan	11 December, 1862
1865	England	Shorncliffe	8 August, 1865
		Aldershot (North Camp)	29 March, 1866
1867	Ireland	Curragh Camp	13 March, 1867
		Dublin (Royal Barracks)	July, 1867
		Athlone (Hd.-qrs. of Regt.)	7 July, 1868
		Fermoy (Head-quarters)	October, 1869
		Limerick (Head-quarters)	6 August, 1870
		During 1868, 1869, and 1870, the Regiment furnished innumerable Detachments all over the country on account of its very disturbed state.	
1870	India	Cannanore	6 November, 1870
		Bangalore	26 November, 1872
		Madras (Fort St. George)	26 February, 1875
		Detachments — Trichinopoly, Port Blair, Andaman Isles until 1880	
1876	British Burmah	Tonghoo } Thayetmyo }	January, 1876
		Rangoon	21 December, 1877
		Allanmyo	23 March, 1879
		Rangoon	End of 1879
1881	India	Belgaum	17 January, 1881
		Detachment, Kolapore	
1884	Egypt	Suakim Campaign	19 February, 1884
1884	England	Portsmouth (Clarence Bks.)	21 April, 1884
		Aldershot (South Camp)	3 February, 1886
		Dover	14 April, 1888

APPENDIX.

Year	Country.	Station.	Date.

THE COLOURS.

The "Colours" of the 89th Princess Victoria's Regiment bear on them the following honourable distinctions:—

"EGYPT."   "JAVA."   "NIAGARA."
"AVA."   "SEVASTOPOL."
"EGYPT, 1884."

The following is a short record of the various "Colours" which have from time to time been presented to the regiment.

Number.	Date of being Presented.	History.
1	1793.	Colours were presumably presented to the regiment on its being raised, and embodied as the 89th, in December, 1793. These were lost on December 13th, 1805, when the ship conveying the head-quarters of the regiment from England to Holland, was wrecked off the Dutch Coast, with the loss of many lives together with the Band, Officers' mess plate, regimental books, &c., in addition to the Colours. (Page 8).
2	1806.	In the summer of this year, new Colours were given to the regiment, at Ospringe, to replace those lost as above mentioned. There is no record to shew by whom they were presented. These were borne by the regiment for 14 years, entirely spent on foreign service in South Africa, Ceylon, and India.
3	1820. May 17th.	The third pair of Colours were given to the regiment at Quilon, on the 17th May, 1820, and were the loadstar of the 89th for 13 years, of which 11 were spent on foreign service, (9 in India and 2 on active service in Burmah and Ava).

APPENDIX.

Number.	Date of being Presented.	History.
4	1833. August 3rd.	On August 3rd, 1833, a rare honour was conferred on the regiment by H.R.H. the Princess Victoria, then Heiress Presumptive to the Throne (now H.M. Queen Victoria). The ceremony took place at noon, on the Hoe at Plymouth, the regiment being at the time quartered at Devonport. The address of the young Princess was read to the regiment by her mother, H.R.H. the Duchess of Kent, after which the Princess presented the Colours to the two Senior Ensigns (Ensign R. F. Miles and Ensign Caledon R. Egerton). (Page 83). These served for 33 years with the head-quarters of the regiment in all parts of the world, including 20 years foreign service in the "West Indies," "Canada," "The Crimea," "South Africa," and "India." They finally, when replaced by new ones, found a last resting place in the Garrison Church (All Saints), at Aldershot. (Page 141).
5	1866. April 5th.	On the 5th April, 1866, Her Most Gracious Majesty Queen Victoria for a second time most highly honoured the regiment by again presenting it with new Colours, to replace those she herself had given it 33 years before. The presentation ceremony took place on the Queen's Parade Ground at Aldershot. The Queen's Colour was received by Ensign Duncan Campbell, and the Regimental Colour by Ensign H. K. Grenville. It was in commemoration of this most gracious act, that Her Majesty was pleased to command that the 89th Foot should henceforth bear the title of "Princess Victoria's Regiment." Her Royal kindness was further shown by her presenting to the officers of the regiment a "Watercolor Drawing" of the ceremony, executed at her command, by Mr. G. W. Thomas, and which now hangs, a valued memento, in the officers' mess. These Colours are now themselves almost worn out, and have been borne by the Regiment for over 22 years, 14 years on foreign service in India and Burmah, and 8 years at home. (Page 137).

ACTIVE SERVICE

On which the 89th Regiment has been engaged, with the Actions in which it has taken part.

Campaign.	Actions, Casualites, &c.

HOLLAND. 1794.	Served with the Expeditionary Force under Major-General the Earl of Moira. Took part in the memorable retreat through Holland in the winter of 1794. The casualties appear to have been very great, though no record of them has been kept.
	Engaged in action at—
	    "Alost."
	    "Boxtel." (Suffered Severely).
	    "Tiet."
	    "Schener."
	(Page 1).

IRISH REBELLION. 1798.	Served in General Lake's force, in suppressing the Rebellion, and was present at— "Vinegar Hill," June 21st. (Page 3).
MALTA. 1800.	The 89th and 30th Regiments, with some Marines and Natives formed the Blockade of La Valetta, the capital of Malta, then in possession of the French. The Blockade commenced at the beginning of the year, and continued until General Pigott having arrived with reinforcements, reduced the garrison to such extremity that it surrendered on the 4th September. (Page 4).
EGYPT. 1801.	With the Army, under Lieutenant-General Sir Ralph Abercrombie. Was engaged at the Battle of Alexandria, when he was killed, and on several other occasions was opposed to the enemy. Also present at the "Capitulation of Cairo." (Page 4).

Campaign.	Actions, Casualties, &c.
HOLLAND. 1805.	In this unfortunate expedition, the head-quarter ship of the 89th was wrecked off the Dutch Coast, with the loss of many lives, those who escaped being made prisoners by the Dutch. The expedition lasted only a few weeks. (Page 8).
IN THE CARNATIC. 1809.	A portion of the regiment was employed in suppressing the mutiny in the Madras Army during this year. (Page 9).
BOURBON, ISLE OF FRANCE. 1810.	With the expedition under Major-General the Honourable John Abercrombie at the capture of these Islands. (Page 10).
JAVA. 1811.	Half the battalion engaged in the capture of Java, and the following actions:— "Bantam." "Weltervreeden." 8 killed, 39 wounded. "Fort Cornelius." 4 ,, 31 ,, (Page 10).
SUMATRA. 1812.	Half the battalion took part in the expedition to this Island. (Page 11).
CANADA. 1813.	The 2nd Battalion of the 89th took a very prominent part in this war against the United States, and fought in the following actions:— Killed. Wounded. "Christlers Farm." ... 5 62 "Blackrock." ... 3 5 "Delaware." ... 19 30 "Niagara." ... Casualties unknown. "Assault on Fort Erie." 4 8 "Action near Fort Erie." 1 23 (Pages 16 to 41).
MAHRATTA WAR. 1818–19.	This was principally a warfare against stockades and fortresses, built on isolated hills, and almost inaccessible. The 89th was present at the capture of— "Loghur." "Issapoor." "Teeconah."

Campaign.	Actions, Casaulties, &c.
MAHRATTA WAR. 1818–19.	"Toomgee." "Koaree." After 8 days investment. "Gunghur." "Goosella." "Tella." "Stockades of Indapore." "Ryghur." After 16 days bombardment, 8 men wounded. And in 1819, in the Sawant Warree States, was present at the capture of— "Fort Newtee." "Fort Waree." "Fort Raree." 2 killed, 5 wounded. This latter was carried by assault, although considered to be impregnable, it was called the "Gibraltar" of India. (Pages 42 to 48).

BURMESE WAR. 1824–26.	The regiment underwent great hardships in this campaign, owing to being badly equipped, having no native followers, and serving in a detestable climate. The majority of the fighting was in forcing stockades, behind which the Burmans fought well.
	
	 Engaged in action at—
	                                      Killed. Wounded.
	 Stockades of "Kymendine." 1 6
	 Surrender of "Tavoy."
	 Capture of "Fort Mergui." 6 24
	 Action near "Rangoon." 2 34
	 Stockades of "Cockain." 2 18
	      ,, "Donabew." 12 65
	      ,, "Prome."
	 Action near "Pergamew." (Pages 52 to 78).

THE CRIMEA. 1854–56.	The regiment landed in the Crimea in December, 1854, and immediately did duty with the 3rd Division in the trenches before "Sevastopol," and it continued to thus take part in the memorable Siege, until its surrender on the 8th September, 1855, including the assaults on the 18th June, and 8th September. The casualties in the regiment from the date of landing until the fall of Sevastopol, where no less than 218 of all ranks, chiefly from disease and exposure.

Campaign.	Actions, Casaulties, &c.
THE CRIMEA. 1854–56.	From the Fall of Sevastopol, until the regiment left the Crimea, in May 1856, it was principally occupied in fatigue work at Balaklava. (Pages 110 to 114).
KAFFRARIA. 1856–57.	Suddenly ordered to the Cape, in consequence of an expected rising of the Kaffirs, was engaged around " East London " in establishing a line of " Posts" on the Frontier, and in pacifying the Kaffirs. No fighting occurred. (Pages 115 to 117).
INDIAN MUTINY. 1857–59.	The regiment was employed for nearly two years in hunting the rebels after the mutiny, particularly in the country round Deesa, Neemuch, and Gwalior. Innumerable detachments and small expeditions were sent into the hills in pursuit, and several skirmishes took place. Took part in the Sudra Field Force, under Major Grimes, and the Seronge Field Force, under Colonel Boyle. (Pages 118 to 130).
THE SOUDAN. 1884.	The regiment, on its way from India to England, was stopped at Aden and sent to join the force under Sir General Graham, at Suakim, on the Red Sea Coast. Was present at— Battle of " El-Teb." Relief of " Tokar." Battle of " Tamai." Action of " Tamanieb." The campaign being for the time ended, the regiment after being six weeks only in the Soudan, resumed its voyage to England. (Pages 160 to 163).

SUCCESSION ROLLS
OF THE
COLONELS,
LIEUTENANT-COLONELS COMMANDING,
ADJUTANTS, QUARTER-MASTERS,
INSTRUCTORS OF MUSKETRY,
AND PAY-MASTERS,
FROM THE RAISING
OF THE 89TH
IN 1793.

Also a **SUCCESSION ROLL OF OFFICERS** who have
SERVED IN THE REGIMENT SINCE IT
WAS RAISED IN DECEMBER, 1793,
WITH THE DATES OF THEIR
VARIOUS COMMISSIONS,
AND
OF THEIR JOINING
AND LEAVING
H.M. 89TH
REGT.

I am indebted to Major-General G. T. Brice (late 17th Foot) for the use of the majority of the old Army Lists, from which the following Rolls have been compiled; and to the Prince Consort's Library, Aldershot, for the remainder.

Dover,
Aug. 1888.

R. BRINCKMAN, Capt. & Adjt.
2nd Batt. Princess Victoria's
(Irish Fusiliers).

A SUCCESSION ROLL OF COLONELS OF THE 89th REGIMENT.

Succession Number.	Rank and Name.	Date.
1	Major-General Willlam Crosbie	3 December, 1793
2	Major-General Andrew Gordon	23 December, 1795
3	Major-General Henry Bowyer	2 March, 1797
4	Major-General Alexander Ross	22 December, 1797
5	Lieutenant-General James Ogilvie	28 March, 1801
6	Lieutenant-General Sir Eyre Coote, K.B.	4 September, 1802
7	Lieutenant-General J. Whitelocke	26 May, 1806
8	General Albemarle, Earl of Lindsay	25 March, 1808
9	Major-General Sir George Beckwith, G.C.B.	21 September, 1818
10	Major-General Sir R. Macfarlane, K.C.B., G.C.H.	24 March, 1823
11	Lieutenant-General Sir Charles Bulkeley Egerton, G.C.M.G., K.C.H.	26 September, 1837
12	Lieut.-General C. George James Arbuthnot	9 July, 1857
13	Major-General Charles Gascoigne	4 July, 1864
14	Major-General Sir John Garvock, K.C.B.	22 October, 1870
15	Major-General Caledon Richard Egerton	20 February, 1874
16	Lieutenant-General Lord Henry H. M. Percy, V.C., K.C.B.	28 May, 1874
17	General Sir Perceval de Bathe, K.C.B.	4 December, 1877
18	General John Arthur Lambert	25 April, 1880
19	General A. H. Ferryman, C.B.	18 September, 1887

APPENDIX. 179

A SUCCESSION ROLL OF THE LIEUTENANT-COLONELS COMMANDING OF THE 89th REGIMENT.

Succession Number.	Rank and Name.	Date.
1	Lieutenant-Colonel Charles Handfield	3 December, 1793
2	Lieutenant-Colonel William Stewart	1795
3	Lieutenant-Colonel Lord Andrew Blayney	1802
4	Lieutenant-Colonel Robert Garden	1809
5	Lieutenant-Colonel Robert Sewell	1812
6	Lieutenant-Colonel W. A. Rainsford	1817
7	Lieutenant-Colonel Sir Edward Miles, C.B.	October, 1820
	Lt.-Col. Miller Clifford	April, 1824
	Major Basden — Sir E. Miles being given a Brigade in Burmah, these officers commanded the 89th until his return in 1831.	July, 1824
	Lt.-Col. J. M'Caskell	1828
8	Lieutenant-Colonel George Jones, K.H.	8 November, 1833
9	Lieutenant-Colonel H. Hartley	17 July, 1835
10	Lieutenant-Colonel Sir Richard Doherty	4 September, 1835
11	Lieutenant-Colonel James Lewis Basden	7 July, 1838
12	Lieut.-Colonel Andrew Snape Hammond Aplin	July, 1843
13	Lieutenant-Colonel Bouverie	1843
14	Lieutenant-Colonel Edward Thorp	26 February, 1845
15	Lieutenant-Colonel A. H. Ferryman	September, 1849
	Lt.-Col. Leslie Skynner	September, 1857
	Lieut.-Col. John Lewis Phillips — Lt.-Col. Ferryman was appointed Brigadier in 1857. These officers commanded until Colonel Ferryman left the regt. in 1860, never having returned.	May, 1858
	Lt.-Col. Wm. Boyle	October, 1858
16	Lieutenant-Colonel William Boyle	May, 1860
17	Lieutenant-Colonel Edward Buller Thorp	February, 1874
18	Lieutenant-Colonel John Penton	12 August, 1876
19	Lieutenant-Colonel Barnes Slyfield Robinson	12 August, 1881
20	Colonel Josias Dunn	12 August, 1885
21	Colonel George Cox	12 August, 1887

A SUCCESSION ROLL OF ADJUTANTS.

Succession Number.	Rank and Name.	Date.
1	Lieutenant Thomas Walker	3 December, 1793
2	,, William Perry	1 October, 1796
3	,, Patrick Agnew	1802
4	,, J. Armstrong	1803
5	,, Laurence Oakes	June 1804
6	,, H. Selway	7 March, 1805
7	,, Patrick Agnew	23 February, 1809
8	,, Charles Cannon	8 July, 1812
9	,, C. S. Naylor	1 October, 1820
10	,, Edward Kenny	26 June, 1823
11	,, C. S. Naylor	11 June, 1830
12	,, Christopher Lee	6 January, 1832
13	,, Charles Robert Bozzi Granville	10 April, 1835
14	,, Caledon Richard Egerton	23 September 1836
15	,, Henry Edmunds	12 May, 1839
16	,, Robert B. Hawley	27 October, 1846
17	,, John Macdonald Cuppage	17 January, 1851
18	,, Richard Francis Holmes	13 February, 1855
19	,, Robert G. Newbigging	10 December, 1858
20	,, William Sealy	6 April 1870
21	,, John Cuthbert	10 December, 1872
22	,, Joseph Robert McMurray	1 November, 1876
23	,, Charles Edward Harman	30 November, 1878
24	,, Claude Rainier Rogers	27 May, 1881
25	,, Rowland Brinckman	27 May, 1886

A SUCCESSION ROLL OF QUARTER-MASTERS.

Succession Number.	Name.	Date.
1	John Grant	3 December, 1793
2	Charles Pakenham Roddy	1 May, 1797
3	Thomas Toln	21 November, 1805
4	H. Selway	5 January, 1809
5	Thomas Sheridan	1816
6	T. W. Edwards	1822
7	James Dukes	1832
8	W. Watson	25 April, 1848
9	William Sibbald	14 September 1855
10	Francis W. Osborne	19 July, 1864
11	James Edward Bell	24 January, 1874
12	James Archer	3 November, 1875
13	John Watkins	30 April, 1879

A SUCCESSION ROLL OF PAY-MASTERS.

Succession Number.	Rank and Name.	Date.
1	Lieutenant John Grant	1 June, 1798
2	,, M. William Wilson	23 October, 1800
3	,, J. White	19 March, 1803
4	,, James Grant	22 June, 1820
5	Captain J. Anderson	1825
6	,, C. Dowson	1 March, 1827
7	,, William Bell	9 May, 1834
8	Lieutenant Robert Browne Thomas Boyd	26 March, 1841
9	Captain Lawrence Luke Esmond White	1 February, 1850
10	Lieutenant Edward Jonathan Head	17 January, 1851
11	,, Robert Scott	17 January, 1853
12	,, Arthur Gore Anderson	2 October. 1863
13	Major Archibald C. Forster	6 October, 1875
14	Captain Richard Meredith	24 November, 1884
15	Major Thomas Prince Lloyd	3 September, 1886

A SUCCESSION ROLL OF INSTRUCTORS OF MUSKETRY.

Succession Number.	Rank and Name.	Date.
1	Lieutenant George Harmer Pering	6 April, 1857
2	,, Burchall Helme	20 April, 1859
3	,, James Shaw Hay	15 October, 1863
4	,, Augustus William Price	4 October, 1867
5	,, Albert James H. Daubeny	23 June, 1869
6	,, Henry Caddell	16 May, 1873
7	,, George Osborne Smith	14 June, 1876
8	,, Frederick Henry Munn	26 January, 1881

In 1883, the appointment of "Instructor of Musketry" was abolished, but was revived again in 1887 under the name of "Assistant Adjutant."

The following is a Roll of Officers who have been

ASSISTANT ADJUTANTS.

Succession Number.	Rank and Name.	Date.
1	Lieutenant William H. Percival Plomer	1887

2nd BATTALION 89th REGIMENT.

LIEUTENANT-COLONELS COMMANDING.

Succession Number.	Name.	Date.
	No record of who was in command from the raising of the 2nd Battalion in 1803, until 1809. Lieutenant-Colonel Joseph Morrison	9 September, 1809

ADJUTANTS.

1	Nathaniel Goodall	21 February, 1805
2	J. M. Shand	20 March, 1806
3	Watson A. Steel	19 March, 1812
4	George Hopper	14 July, 1814
5	Francis Miles	3 July, 1815

QUARTER-MASTERS.

1	Alexander Campbell	18 April, 1805
2	Thomas Sheridan	20 March, 1806

PAY-MASTERS.

1	Charles Pakenham Roddy	18 April, 1805

ROLL OF ALL OFFICERS

WHO HAVE SERVED IN THE 89TH REGIMENT

FROM THE RAISING IN DEC., 1793,

UNTIL THE PRESENT DATE,

AUGUST, 1888.

The following Roll of Officers having been compiled from "Annual" Army Lists (mostly dated January), the names of those officers who joined the regiment and left it again in the same year, are probably in many cases omitted. Their names have, however, been inserted as far as possible.

> R. BRINCKMAN, Capt. & Adjt.,
> 2nd Bn. Princess Victoria's
> (Irish Fusiliers).

The dates in "italics" is service not passed in the 89th.

SUCCESSION ROLL OF OFFICERS SINCE 1793.

Succession Number	Name	Date of Joining	Ensign.	Lieutenant.	Captain.	Major.	Lieut.-Col.	Colonel.	Date of Leaving.	Remarks.
1	William Crosbie	1793	16 *July* 1757	8 *Sept.* 1759	6 *May* 1769	20 *Sep.* 1778	3 *May* 1780	3 *Dec.* 1793	1795	To be Com.-General of Stores in Ireland
2	Charles Handfield	1793	1 *Oct.* 1769	30 *Sept.* 1772	15 *Oct.* 1780	18 *Nov.* 1780	3 *Dec.* 1793	26 *Jan.* 1797	1798	
3	Lord Andrew Biayney	1793			28 *Feb.* 1792	3 *Dec.* 1793	3 *May* 1796	1 *Jan.* 1805	1814	
4	John Napier	1793			24 *Apl.* 1793	31 *Mar.* 1784			1795	To Royal Garrison Batt.
5	Robert King	1793		9 *Jan.* 1782	3 *Dec.* 1793				1795	To Royal Artillery
6	Henry Vennel	1793	14 *Oct.* 1789	30 *Sept.* 1793	3 *Dec.* 1793	11 *Nov.* 1795			1796	Retired on half pay
7	William Benson	1793		5 *Apl.* 1790	16 *Sept.* 1795				1802	Retired on half pay
8	James McDowall	1793		26 *Dec.* 1770					1800	
9	Mark Magrath	1793		20 *Jan.* 1781	16 *Sept.* 1795				1800	
10	George Power	1793		12 *Nov.* 1778	15 *Apl.* 1795				1799	
11	Gustavius Moore	1793		23 *Oct.* 1782					1798	
12	George Anderson	1793	3 *Dec.* 1793	1 *Apl.* 1795					1798	
13	Thomas Walker	1793	Adjutant 3 *Dec.* 1793						1797	To 91st Regt.
14	John Grant	1793	Qr.-Master 3 *Dec.* 1793						1800	
15	Joshua Meredith	1794	29 *Sept.* 1792	31 *Jan.* 1794					1796	
16	Richard Christie	1794	28 *Feb.* 1794	31 *Jan.* 1794					1802	
17	Lancelot Simpson	1794	28 *Feb.* 1794	15 *Apl.* 1795	30 *Apl.* 1796				1808	
18	John Burchell	1794	19 *Feb.* 1794	19 *Aug.* 1795					1800	
19	Arthur Hunt	1794	28 *Feb.* 1794						1795	
20	John Beatty	1794		26 *Mar.* 1794	9 *May* 1794				1795	
21	Bernard Stawell	1794		5 *Nov.* 1782					1801	
22	William Sherwin	1794							1795	To Loyal Cheshire Regt. of Foot.
23	Samuel Hall	1794		9 *May* 1794	3 *Sept.* 1801	8 *Mar.* 1810	12 *Aug.* 1819		1822	Exchanged to 65th Regt.
24	T. Lowther Allen	1794		9 *May* 1794					1795	To 88th Foot as Captain
25	William Hilliard	1794		30 *Sept.* 1793	28 *May* 1794	25 *Sep.* 1803			1810	Died January 1810
26	John Aylmer	1794		13 *Aug.* 1794	28 *May* 1794				1800	
27	George Gledstanes	1794		11 *Aug.* 1794	25 *June* 1803				1795	Exchanged to 62nd Foot
28	E. Kilby Matthews	1794	15 *Apl.* 1795	19 *Sept.* 1795					1807	To 6th W.I. Regt.
29	Christian Francois	1795		21 *Mar.* 1794					1798	Retired on half pay
30	W. Nethersole Long	1795	24 *June* 1795	28 *May* 1796	14 *Mar.* 1802				1801	
31	Archibald McDonald	1795	24 *June* 1795	28 *May* 1796	14 *Mar.* 1802				1808	Exchanged to 45th Foot

APPENDIX. 187

Succession Number.	Names	Date of Joining.	Ensign.	Lieutenant.	Captain.	Major.	Lieut.-Col.	Colonel.	Date of Leaving.	Remarks.
32	James McDonall	1795	5 Aug. 1795						1796	
33	William Vennell	1795	19 Aug. 1795	30 June 1796					1798	
34	William Stewart	1795					17 May 1794	1 Jan. 1800	1803	Retired.
35	Chas. Carr Carmichael	1795	16 Sept. 1795						1797	To 22nd Foot as Lieut.
36	Charles John Poshall	1795	22 Dec. 1795						1796	To 22nd Foot as Lieut.
37	Andrew Gordon	1795					29 July 1784	23 Dec. 1795	1797	To Colonelcy of 59th, and Lt.-Governor of Jersey
38	F. R. Broadbelt	1795		27 Aug. 1794					1797	
39	Hugh McKay	1795		27 Aug. 1794					1797	To half pay
40	John Cameron	1795		27 Aug. 1794					1796	
41	Gerard Radcliffe	1795		27 Aug. 1794					1796	
42	Patrick Agnew	1795		27 Aug. 1794					1796	
43	L. Legge	1795		28 Aug. 1794					1803	
44	John Le Mesnirer	1795		28 Aug. 1794	31 Aug. 1796				1796	To half pay
45	James McDowall	1795		10 Dec. 1795	30 June 1804				1805	To half pay
46	Robert McKeand	1795	20 Sept. 1795	1 Dec. 1796					1810	Died 14th Dec., 1810
47	James Graham	1795	30 Dec. 1795						1799	
48	— Emright	1795							1796	
49	James Kay	1795		6 Apl. 1795					1796	
50	William Perry	1796		21 Oct. 1795					1802	
51	Nathaniel Downie	1796		21 Oct. 1795					1801	
52	Hugh Gray	1796		4 Oct. 1790					1800	
53	Quintin McMillan	1796	3 Jan. 1796						1797	
54	Richard O'Connell	1796		6 Jan. 1796					1803	
55	Wm. E. M. Bayley	1796		30 May 1794					1798	
56	John McDonald	1796		2 Feb. 1796	22 Oct. 1802				1805	
57	Charles Handfield	1796	2 Feb. 1796	1 May 1797					1802	
58	John Taylor Perry	1796		3 Sept. 1795	29 Feb. 1796				1801	
59	John Sinclair	1796		17 Jan. 1793					1801	
60	John Chaplin	1796		31 Mar. 1796					1803	
61	William Thornton	1796	31 Mar. 1796		13 June 1794	30 June 1796			1797	To 46th Foot
62	Chas. Plenderleath	1796	29 May 1796						1797	To 46th Foot
63	Hon. Charles Boyle	1796		1 Dec. 1795	5 Aug. 1804				1799	
64	Robert McClure	1796	30 June 1796	31 Aug. 1796	17 May 1798				1806	
65	Dennis John Blake	1796		31 Aug. 1796					1802	
66	Richard Butler	1796		31 Aug. 1797	7 Mar. 1800	1 May 1809			1815	

APPENDIX.

Succession Number.	Name.	Date of Joining.	Ensign.	Lieutenant.	Captain.	Major.	Lieut.-Col.	Colonel.	Date of Leaving.	Remarks.
67	Hamilton Magrath	1796		18 Sept. 1796	5 Sept. 1901				1810	Died 18th Sept, 1810
68	Richard J. Wingfield	1796	1 Dec. 1796	1 Dec. 1797					1798	
69	Samuel Courtney	1796	1 Dec. 1796	1 Jan. 1797	24 July 1800				1902	
70	William Percival	1797							1903	
71	Charles Pakenham Roddy	1797	1 Apl. 1797 Qr.-Mr.	28 Apl. 1798					1816	On reduction of 2nd Batt.
72	Henry Bowyer	1797	1 May 1797				12 Mar. 1789	2 Mar. 1797 Major-Gen. 26 Feb. 1795	1797	To Colonelcy of 16th Foot
73	William Cowell	1797	1 Apl. 1797						1801	To 2nd Foot as Lieut.
74	Robert Dixon	1797	1 June 1797						1798	To 83rd Foot
75	Henry Eyre Evans	1797	1 Dec. 1797						1799	
76	Alexander Ross	1797					1 Sept. 1795	22 Dec. 1797 Major-Gen. 26 Feb. 1795	1801	To Colonelcy of 59th Regiment.
77	Thos. Hastings Irwin	1798	1 Mar. 1798	1 Jan. 1799					1902	
78	Christopher Atkin	1798	1 Mar. 1798	21 Aug. 1800					1803	
79	Charles Bulkeley Egerton	1798			22 Apl. 1795	1 June 1798	14 Nov. 1802		1809	To 44th Foot in exchange with Lt.-Col. Garden
80	James Brickell	1798	4 Aug. 1798	1 Sept. 1798	27 Aug. 1804	4 June 1814			1801	To 1st Foot as Lieut.
81	Laurence Oakes	1798	10 Nov. 1798						1817	Retired on half pay
82	James Arthur Rice	1798	10 Nov. 1798						1805	
83	James Tynte King	1798	1 Dec. 1798	1800	20 Sep. 1804				1804	
84	Richard Egerton	1798							1808	Promoted Lieut. in 29th Foot in 1800, and back to the 89th as Capt., in 1804. Exchanged to the 34th Foot in 1808
85	Lorenzo Nunn	1798	15 Dec. 1798	19 Nov. 1800	15 Dec. 1804	4 June 1814			1816	Retired
86	William Raymond	1799							1801	To 46th Foot
87	Robert Ongley Hilden	1800	7 Mar. 1800	3 Sept. 1801	6 Mar. 1806				1817	
88	Johnston St.Leger	1800	11 Apl. 1800	11 June 1801	18 July 1805		29 July 1799		1819	Died 1819
89	Richard French	1800	14 Mar. 1800	20 Dec. 1800	14 Nov. 1802	13 June 1811			1817	Retired on half pay

APPENDIX. 189

Succession Number	Name	Date of Joining	Ensign	Lieutenant	Captain	Major	Lieut.-Col.	Colonel	Date of Leaving	Remarks
90	James Ogilvie	1801						28 Mar. 1801 Major-Gen. 12 Oct. 1803 Lt.-Gen. 1 Jan. 1808	1802	To Colonelcy of 32nd Foot
91	Thos. Gage Montresor	1801	1 June 1801		17 June 1794	12 Apl. 1799	27 June 1801		1802	
92	Edwd. Colthard Smith	1801	11 June 1801	23 May 1802					1806	To 22nd Foot
93	Samuel Wilson	1801		27 Aug. 1804					1812	
94	Phillip Hay	1801		31 Oct. 1793	4 Sept. 1801				1806	To 66th Ft. in 1802, but returned to 89th in '03. To 66th Ft. again in 1806.
95	Henry Craig	1801		4 Sept. 1801					1803	
96	George McBeath	1801		5 Sept. 1801					1802	
97	Hugh Bullock	1801	3 Sept. 1801						1803	
98	Joseph Payne	1801	3 Sept. 1801						1802	
99	Sir Eyre Coote	1802						4 Sept. 1802 Major-Gen. 1 Jan. 1798	1806	To Colonelcy of 62nd Foot
100	Benjamin D'Urban	1802			2 July 1794	21 Nov. 1794	1 Jan. 1805		1807	To 1st W. India Regt.
101	James Boyd	1802	28 Mar. 1801	22 Oct. 1802	31 July 1808				1810	To 1st Dragoon Guards
102	Adam Dunscomb	1802	8 Sept. 1802	14 May 1804	19 Dec. 1810				1812	
103	J. M. Shand	1802	22 Oct. 1802	28 Aug. 1804	5 Mar. 1812				1817	
104	James Scott	1803		19 Oct. 1799					1804	
105	Henry Ross Gore	1803		18 Mar. 1803	4 Dec. 1806	12 Aug. 1819			1835	Retired on half pay
106	Hugh Fleming	1803		19 Feb. 1803					1804	
107	H. Cox	1803		23 Mar. 1801					1804	
108	Richard Croker Rose	1803		15 Oct. 1803	1 May 1809				1825	Killed at stockades of Donabew, Mar. 7, 1825
109	Samuel Reed	1803		24 Apl. 1803					1804	To 36th Foot
110	J. Armstrong	1803	21 Nov. 1805 Acting Adjt. 1803	23 Oct. 1806					1818	
111	Thomas Daniel	1803	20 Jan. 1803	31 Jan. 1805	18 Jan. 1812				1830	
112	Donald McBean	1804			7 Sept. 1804	1 July, 1810			1818	Retired on half pay
113	Alexander Leith	1804		9 July 1803					1812	Died August 1812

APPENDIX.

Succession Number	Name	Date of Joining	Ensign	Lieutenant	Captain	Major	Lieut.-Col.	Colonel	Date of Leaving	Remarks
114	Richard Armstrong	1804			9 July 1803				1805	To 9th R. Veteran Batt.
115	Daniel O'Donoghue	1804			27 Aug. 1803				1806	To 5th Garrison Batt.
116	Cadwallader Waddy	1804			24 June 1802				1807	
117	Henry Worsley	1804			7 Sept. 1804				1807	To 86th Foot
118	Thomas Ramsay	1804		10 Mar. 1804	18 Dec. 1810				1817	
119	Thomas Browne	1804		4 Aug. 1804	25 Dec. 1804				1815	
120	William Patterson	1804		17 Oct. 1799					1807	
121	James McCrohan	1804		22 Dec. 1803					1807	
122	George O'Kelly	1804		21 Apl. 1804					1814	To 4th Veteran Batt.
123	William Jervoise	1804		8 Aug. 1804	14 July 1806				1806	Exchanged to 57th Foot
124	Patrick Colley	1804	28 Apl. 1804						1813	Retired on half pay
125	Edward Lawrenson	1804	9 Aug. 1804	1 May 1805					1808	Died September 1808
126	Charles Croker	1804	13 Aug. 1804	9 May 1805	9 June 1813				1820	
127	Vesian Pick	1804	15 Aug. 1804	27 June 1805	10 June 1813				1818	
128	W. Moore Burchall	1804	16 Aug. 1804	9 Apl. 1806					1807	To 9th Garrison Batt.
129	John M. Dillon	1804	25 Sept. 1804						1805	To 98th Foot
130	William Sherlock	1804	26 Sept. 1804	10 Apl. 1806					1807	
131	Charles Coates	1804	27 Sept. 1804	16 June 1806	8 July 1813				1824	Died at Madras 1824 of disease contracted in Burmah
132	Phillip Bass	1804	28 Sept. 1804						1805	To 27th Foot
133	Abraham Low	1804	3 Oct. 1804	17 June 1806	24 Feb. 1814				1816	On reduction of 2nd Batt.
134	Henry Stanton	1804	4 Oct. 1804						1805	
135	George Percy	1804	5 Oct. 1804						1805	
136	Francis Savage	1804	19 Oct. 1804	18 June 1806	11 Aug. 1814	24 Sept. 1802	30 Nov. 1809		1816	On reduction of 2nd Batt.
137	Joseph Morrison	1805							1815	Retired on half pay
138	W. Bartelot Smith	1805			4 Apl. 1805				1908	Retired August 1808
139	George O'Malley	1805			25 Aug. 1805				1906	To 101st Foot
140	H. Selway	1805		4 Feb. 1805 Qr.-Mr.					1816	On reduction of 2nd Batt.
141	Stephen Grier	1805		5 Jan. 1809					1807	To 9th Garrison Batt.
142	Francis Richard Rowe	1805	21 Feb. 1805	20 Mar. 1805					1813	Died 28th March 1813
143	Nathaniel Goodall	1805		21 Mar. 1805					1806	
144	Peter Le Mesurier	1805	15 Dec. 1804	19 June 1806	23 Mar. 1810				1810	
145	Thomas Tuckey	1805	28 Feb. 1805	31 July 1806					1807	

APPENDIX.

Succession Number	Name	Date of Joining	Ensign	Lieutenant	Captain	Major	Lieut.-Col.	Colonel	Date of Leaving	Remarks
146	Richard French	1805	14 Mar. 1805	1 Sept. 1806	4 Apl. 1811				1813	On reduction of 2nd Batt.
147	John Cunningham	1805	11 Apl. 1805	2 Sept. 1806	27 Oct. 1814				1816	Promoted Lieut. in 101st Foot
148	Walter Scully	1805	12 Apl. 1805						1806	
149	Piomer Young	1805	8 May 1805	3 Sept. 1806	20 Apl. 1815				1828	
150	Ralph Allen	1805	9 May 1805						1806	
151	William Hilliard	1805	6 Jun. 1805	4 Sept. 1806					1811	Died 3rd April 1811
152	John Maguire	1805	27 Jun. 1805	9 Oct. 1806					1810	
153	Alexander Campbell	1805	Qr.-Master						1806	
154	Thomas Toln	1805	18 Apl. 1805 Qr.-Master						1809	
155	John Whitelooke	1806	21 Nov. 1805					26 May 1806 Major-Gen. 18 June 1798 Lieut.-Gen. 30 Oct. 1805	1808	
156	Thomas Sheridan	1806	Qr.-Master 29 Mar. 1806						1822	
157	James Lewis Basden	1806			4 Sept. 1806	30 Dec. 1813	22 July 1830		1843	Retired on Full Pay
158	William L. Fortescue	1806			9 Feb. 1804				1810	Died 23rd Sept. 1810
159	Henry Annesley	1806			13 Oct. 1804				1813	Killed in a Skirmish in North America, 24th August 1813
160	Hugh Lynch	1806	23 Nov. 1804	10 Oct. 1805					1808	
161	Roger Sheehy	1806	1 Dec. 1804	22 Oct. 1806					1824	
162	John Gilchrist	1806		29 Oct. 1806					1812	
163	John Boyton	1806		30 Oct. 1806					1807	
164	Henry R. Selway	1806	30 Jan. 1806	18 Dec. 1806					1812	
165	Charles Gardiner	1806	9 Apl. 1806						1807	
166	John Dillon Croker	1806	10 Apl. 1806						1809	
167	George E. Jones	1806	16 Jun. 1806	16 Apl. 1807	3 Oct. 1812	22 July 1830	8 Nov. 1833		1835	Exchanged to 57th Foot
168	Oliver Brush	1806	17 Jun. 1806	16 Jun. 1808					1819	
169	Charles Cannon	1806	18 Jun. 1806	21 Jun. 1808	12 Sept. 1822				1825	Killed at Stockades of Donabew 7 Mar., 1825
170	Alexander Dalgetty	1806	19 Jun. 1806	28 July 1808					1816	On reduction of 2nd Batt.

APPENDIX.

Succession Number.	Name.	Date of Joining.	Ensign.	Lieutenant.	Captain.	Major.	Lieut.-Col.	Colonel.	Date of Leaving.	Remarks.
171	Charles Eeles	1806	31 July 1806						1806	
172	Richard Wall	1807	7 Nov. 1806	3 May 1810					1813	
173	— Daniel	1806	3 Sept. 1806						1808	
174	John Thompson	1806	4 Sept. 1806						1810	Retired August 1808
175	Richard P. Maloney	1806	11 Sept. 1806						1808	
176	— Keatley	1806	11 Sept. 1806						1808	
177	Robert Simpson	1806	9 Oct. 1806						1808	
178	H. Malone	1806	23 Oct. 1806						1811	
179	Watson A. Steel	1806			4 Dec. 1806	13 Dec. 1821			1821	
180	Walter Pearse	1806	22 Aug. 1805	9 Dec. 1806	27 May 1819	24 Dec. 1833			1841	
181	Robert Sanderson	1806		11 Dec. 1806	27 Nov. 1817				1821	
182	James Blagrave	1806	18 Dec. 1806	8 May 1811					1819	
183	Phillip Ricketts	1806	19 Feb. 1807						1808	
184	Thomas Podmore	1807	12 Mar. 1807	20 Apl. 1809					1811	
185	John Cooper	1807	16 Apl. 1807						1808	
186	Charles Redmond	1807	9 Oct. 1806	7 May 1807	28 May 1819				1825	
187	Henry Torrens	1807				3 Nov. 1799	1 Jan. 1805		1811	To 3rd Foot Guards and Mil. Sec. to H.R.H. Comdg.-in-Chief
188	John Allen Bell	1807	20 June 1805	18 June 1807					1810	Exchanged to 104th Foot
189	Thomas Joseph Baines	1807		4 Sept. 1800	10 Sep. 1807				1808	To 2nd Foot
190	James Lowrey	1807		14 Sept. 1804					1808	
191	William Gibbs	1807		5 Aug. 1804					1810	
192	Bertie Albemarle *Earl of Lindsay*	1808						1818	1818	
193	Robert Garden	1808					5 Jan. 1808	25 Mar. 1808 General	1810	
194	Francis Maule	1808			25 Oct. 1799			26 Sept. 1808	1810	Retired on half pay June 1810
195	George Frederick Ord	1808			14 Feb. 1805				1812	
196	John James	1808			21 Jan. 1808				1811	
197	Hugh Bowen	1808		17 Feb. 1797					1812	
198	William Bell	1808	3 Mar. 1808	9 May 1811	25 Mar. 1824				1834	To Pay Department
199	William Watt	1808	25 Mar. 1808						1809	
200	David Chambers	1808	14 Apl. 1808	5 Apl. 1810					1821	
201	Francis Dunscomb	1808	26 May 1808						1810	

APPENDIX. 193

Succession Number	Name	Date of Joining	Ensign	Lieutenant	Captain	Major	Lieut.-Col.	Colonel	Date of Leaving	Remarks
202	John Crawford	1808	6 June 1808	18 July 1811					1819	
203	Daniel Browne	1808	16 June 1808	5 Mar. 1812					1820	
204	Osman Charles Watts	1808	23 June 1808	19 Mar. 1812					1820	
205	Thomas Taylor	1808	14 July 1808	19 Mar. 1812					1825	
206	Matthew Powell	1808	21 July 1808						1810	
207	Richard Gordon	1808	27 Oct. 1808						1810	
208	Edward Moulson	1808	22 Dec. 1808	24 Jan. 1812					1820	
209	George Hopper	1809	22 Feb. 1809	26 June 1812					1815	
210	Patrick Agnew	1809	23 Feb. 1809	1 Sept. 1812					1825	
211	Colin Mackenzie	1809	10 Aug. 1809						1811	
212	J. H. Peel	1810							1810	Retired April 1810
213	Robert Sewell	1810			8 Dec. 1803		26 Oct. 1804	4 Jun. 1813 Major-Gen. 12 Aug. 1819	1825	
214	William Gwyn	1810					27 Dec. 1810		1811	Appointed Inspecting Field Officer Recruiting Districts
215	Miller Clifford	1810				29 Nov. 1810	11 Nov. 1818		1826	On half pay unattached till 1827, when appointed Lieut.-Colonel 68th Foot
216	George West Barnes	1810			27 May 1806				1815	Cashiered Aug. 1811, but reinstated end of 1812
217	William Lancaster	1810			20 Dec. 1810				1815	
218	Ralph Wilde	1810			8 Dec. 1808				1814	Died Sept. 1814
219	John Hewson	1810		20 May 1781					1820	
220	Michael Gould Tyrry	1810		13 July 1809					1813	Died Feb. 1813.
221	John Sewell	1811	3 Jan. 1811						1811	
222	William Henry Clarke	1811	10 Jan. 1811	25 Apl. 1811					1811	
223	Patrick Graeme	1811							1814	Killed 4 March 1814 in a skirmish with a strong Patrol of the enemy in North America.
224	Joshua Gillespie	1811	1 May 1811	7 Mar. 1811					1812	
225	J. Smith Reynolds	1811	2 May 1811	2 Sept. 1812					1819	
226	Allen Stuart	1811	8 May 1811	3 Sept. 1812	8 Mar. 1825				1829	

APPENDIX.

Succession Number.	Name.	Date of Joining.	Ensign.	Lieutenant.	Captain.	Major.	Lieut.-Col.	Colonel.	Date of Leaving.	Remarks.
227	Robert Chapman	1811	6 June 1811	4 Sept. 1812					1820	
228	John Caulfield	1811	4 July 1811	23 Dec. 1812					1815	
229	Francis Hutchinson M. Johnston	1811	18 July 1811						1815	
230	John Henry Latham	1811	25 July 1811	8 Oct. 1812					1814	Killed in Canada, 25th July 1814
231	Robert Lloyd	1811	13 June 1811	3 Aug. 1813					1816	On reduction of 2nd Batt.
232	Hector Munro	1811	5 Sept. 1811						1813	
233	Robert Spunner	1812		13 Dec. 1810					1814	Killed in Canada, 25th July 1814
234	William Hill	1812			2 Sept. 1812				1817	
235	Andrew R. Charleton	1812		13 Aug. 1812					1813	Exchanged to 85th Foot
236	William Gray	1812		30 Jan. 1805					1818	Retired on half pay
237	Andrew Snape Hammond Aplin	1812								
238	Mortimer Jones	1812	5 Mar. 1812	24 Sept. 1812	9 Mar. 1825	7 July 1838			1843	Exchanged to 66th Regt.
239	Emmannel T. Poe	1812	19 Mar. 1812	4 Aug. 1813					1816	On reduction of 2nd Batt.
240	Henry Ogle Lewis	1812	28 Mar. 1812	5 Aug. 1813					1815	
241	Francis Miles	1812	4 June 1812	3 Feb. 1814					1816	On reduction of 2nd Batt.
242	George W. Thompson	1812	18 June 1812	5 Feb. 1814					1816	On reduction of 2nd Batt.
243	J. Petry	1812	23 July 1812	6 Feb. 1814					1816	On reduction of 2nd Batt.
244	William Leader	1812	20 Aug. 1812	27 Oct. 1814					1816	On reduction of 2nd Batt.
245	J. Milliquet Hewson	1812	2 Sept. 1812	22 May 1815	18 Mar. 1835				1843	
246	William Saunders	1812	3 Sept. 1812	23 May 1815					1816	On reduction of 2nd Batt.
247	W. Windham Philan	1812	4 Sept. 1812	24 May 1815					1816	On reduction of 2nd Batt.
248	Matthew Handcock	1812	24 Sept. 1812	25 May 1815					1816	On reduction of 2nd Batt.
249	G. F. Greaves	1813	14 Jan. 1813						1813	Exchanged to 3rd Foot.
250	J. H. Rvatt	1813			19 June 1811				1814	Exchanged to 3rd Ceylon Regt.
251	Abraham B. Taylor	1813		24 Dec. 1812	22 Apl. 1825				1833	
252	John Orr	1813		13 Oct. 1808					1817	On reduction of 2nd Batt.
253	James Davidson	1813		26 Sept. 1811					1818	Retired on half pay
254	John Robert Baker	1813		1 Apl. 1812					1815	Superseded
255	John William Leslie	1813	21 Jan. 1813						1815	
256	James Oughton	1813	20 Feb. 1812						1816	On reduction of 2nd Batt.
257	John Coventry	1813	6 May 1813						1817	

APPENDIX. 195

Succession Number	Name	Date of Joining	Ensign	Lieutenant	Captain	Major	Lieut.-Col.	Colonel	Date of Leaving	Remarks
258	Aylmer Dowdall	1813	20 May 1813	27 Nov. 1817	2 May 1829				1832	
259	John Goodwin	1813	5 Aug. 1813	20 Aug. 1817					1820	
260	*Hon. Ferdinand Curzon*	1813	16 Aug. 1813						1814	Exchanged to 9th Foot
261	William Barney	1814							1816	On reduction of 2nd Batt.
262	George Madden	1814		22 July 1813					1818	Exchanged to 65th Regt.
263	George Birtles	1814		7 Feb. 1814					1815	
264	William Nesfield	1814		24 Feb. 1814					1815	
265	Edward Davenport	1814		30 Mar. 1814					1816	On reduction of 2nd Batt.
266	James M. Noble	1814		31 Mar. 1814					1819	
267	Wm. Horne Dougan	1814	4 Feb. 1814	14 Apl. 1814					1826	
268	Wm. Nesbitt Orange	1814	5 Feb. 1814	21 Aug. 1817					1820	
269	John Mac Donald	1814	6 Feb. 1814						1823	
270	Edward Kenny	1814	17 June 1812	26 June 1819					1851	Retired 1851. Died 1879
271	Thomas Lewis	1814	12 May 1814	1 Nov. 1819	4 Dec. 1832	26 Feb. 1845			1815	
272	Felix Smith	1814	11 Aug. 1814						1820	
273	James Imlach	1814	27 Oct. 1814						1815	
274	R. Mockler	1815			31 May 1810				1816	On reduction of 2nd Batt.
275	W. E. Ellis	1815		9 June 1812					1816	On reduction of 2nd Batt.
276	Frederick Skinner	1815		25 Aug. 1814					1816	On reduction of 2nd Batt.
277	Chas. Soarlin Naylor	1815	25 *Dec.* 1812	25 Dec. 1815	9 May 1834				1835	
278	Lawrence Graeme	1815	16 Mar. 1815	13 Dec. 1821					1823	
278	— Strange	1815	23 May 1815						1816	On reduction of 2nd Batt.
280	John Hope	1815	24 May 1815						1816	On reduction of 2nd Batt.
281	J. Gillespie	1815	25 May 1815						1816	On reduction of 2nd Batt.
282	J. Masters	1815	9 Mar,						1816	On reduction of 2nd Batt.
283	James Dawson	1815	10 Oct. 1815						1816	On reduction of 2nd Batt.
284	G. D. Roberson	1816				1 *Jan.* 1805	25 July 1810		1817	Retired on half pay 1817 Died 25th Feb., 1818
285	John Carroll	1816	16 May 1816	28 Mar. 1816					1816	On reduction of 2nd Batt.
286	C. F. Henley	1816	16 May 1816						1818	On reduction of 2nd Batt.
287	John Wm. Tottenham	1817	3 Mar. 1817						1823	
288	C. Augustus Thursby	1817	27 Nov. 1817						1820	
289	Thomas Van-Buerle	1817		11 Mar. 1812					1825	
290	R. Manners Lockwood	1818		28 Apl. 1814					1821	
291	Sir George Beckwith	1818						21 Sept. 1818	1823	

APPENDIX.

Succession Number.	Name.	Date of Joining.	Ensign.	Lieutenant.	Captain.	Major.	Lieut.-Col.	Colonel.	Date of Leaving.	Remarks.
292	Wm. Henry Rainsford	1818		26 Apl. 1810			1 Nov. 1817		1833	
293	Patrick Kelly	1819		25 Sept. 1807					1820	
294	John Snow	1819					12 Aug. 1819		1820	
295	Edward Miles	1819							1833	Died 4th Dec. 1848
296	Joseph Moore	1819		22 July 1813					1832	
297	R. B. Freer	1819		21 Aug. 1810					1820	
298	James Murray McLean	1819	26 Dec. 1815	25 Dec. 1824					1831	
299	Amos R. C. Norcott	1819	27 May 1819						1821	
300	Thomas Forbes	1819	27 June 1816	19 Oct. 1824					1832	
301	Wybrant Olpherts	1819	8 Dec. 1819	8 Mar. 1825					1826	
302	Robert Vincent	1820		1 Feb. 1815					1825	
303	William John King	1820	1 *Mar.* 1817	29 Jan. 1820					1832	
304	Charles Gerard King	1820	2 *Mar.* 1817	3 June 1820	1 Nov. 1838				1839	
305	Thomas Beckham	1820		28 Feb. 1813					1821	
306	James Buchanan	1820		21 Oct. 1814					1821	
307	Lambert Cowell	1820		22 Dec. 1818					1824	
308	Henry Duncan Keith	1820		14 Aug. 1815					1824	
309	J. W. Malet	1821		25 Oct. 1805			9 Aug. 1821		1826	
310	J. W. Campbell	1821		8 July 1820					1823	Exchanged to 28rd Dragoons
311	S. G. Bagshaw	1821							1825	
312	William Kennedy	1821		2 Mar. 1820					1824	Died of wounds received at the capture of Fort Mergui, 6th Oct. 1824
313	C. O'Neil	1821		11 Nov. 1813					1826	
314	William Thomas	1821		22 Nov. 1821					1823	
315	Edmund Worsley	1821		14 Sept. 1813					1823	
316	James Currie	1821	1 Oct. 1817	31 Aug. 1824					1826	
317	Charles Arrow	1821	16 Oct. 1820	9 Mar. 1825					1828	
318	T. Prendergast	1821	17 Oct. 1820	22 Apl. 1825					1828	
319	T. P. Gordon	1822	17 Jan. 1822						1826	
320	T. W. Edwards	1822	Qr.-Mr. —1822						1832	
321	John Holland	1822		21 Oct. 1818					1829	To 86th Regt.
322	J. L. Moloney	1822	7 Nov. 1822	20 Apl. 1814					1826	
323	John Robinson	1822							1826	

APPENDIX. 197

Succession Number.	Name.	Date of Joining.	Ensign.	Lieutenant.	Captain.	Major.	Lieut.-Col.	Colonel.	Date of Leaving.	Remarks.
324	Sir Robert Macfarlane	1823						24 Mar. 1823	1837	
325	Patrick McKie	1823							1826	
326	William Cary	1823							1823	
327	John Macleod	1823		30 Sept. 1813					1826	
328	H. S. La Roche	1823	2 Dec. 1821	11 Apl. 1816					1816	
329	Arthur Schiel	1823		23 Dec. 1822					1833	
330	Henry Harding	1823		16 Sept. 1813					1825	
331	W. Campbell	1823	26 Mar. 1813						1825	
332	E. G. Smith	1824		24 June 1813	29 May 1817				1825	
333	W. H. Phibbs	1824		25 Jan. 1825					1825	
334	John Thomas	1825		27 Jan. 1825					1825	
335	Hon. C. D. Blayney	1825			18 Aug. 1825	21 May 1841	26 Feb. 1846		1840	Exchanged to 44th Regt.
336	Edward Thorp	1825	7 *Mar.* 1811	26 *Jan.* 1813	13 Oct. 1825				1836	
337	Francis Hawkins	1825							1839	Died at Antigua, of Yellow Fever 1839
338	J. McCausland	1825		9 Sept. 1818						
339	Walter Butler	1825		27 Jan. 1807					1826	
340	John J. Peck	1825		24 May 1821					1826	
341	J. H. Palmer	1825		3 May 1815					1826	
342	J. Gray	1825	31 Aug. 1824	4 May 1826					1829	
343	C. Macan	1825	19 Oct. 1824	18 Apl. 1827					1828	
344	J. Graham	1825	22 Apl. 1825	19 Apl. 1827	19 Apl. 1833	10 Jan. 1851	20 June 1854		1865	Died 1878
345	H. Wilson	1825	21 July 1825	29 Nov. 1827					1831	
346	Edward S. Miles	1825	10 Nov. 1825	21 Sept. 1826					1828	
347	George H. Layard	1825	11 Nov. 1825						1831	
348	J. McCaskill	1826					31 Aug. 1826		1832	
349	William S. Forbes	1826				8 June 1826			1833	
350	Robert Stanford	1826	7 *Apl.* 1825	5 Nov. 1825					1852	
351	Robert Lewis	1826		2 Mar. 1826	12 Feb. 1828	16 June 1843			1851	
352	J. M. Russell	1826		27 Mar. 1826					1832	
353	T. W. Stroud	1826		14 Jan. 1826					1832	
354	Thomas G. Twigg	1826		8 Sept. 1812					1830	
355	James Barrett	1826		30 Oct. 1812					1827	
356	St. Ives Sutton	1826		16 Nov. 1826					1827	
357	Henry J. Dewes	1826	8 May 1826						1832	Died 1882
358	Christopher Lee	1826	4 May 1826	17 Mar. 1832					1835	

APPENDIX.

Succession Number.	Name.	Date of Joining.	Ensign.	Lieutenant.	Captain.	Major.	Lieut.-Col.	Colonel.	Date of Leaving.	Remarks.
359	William Glover	1826	23 Aug. 1826						1833	Exchanged with Blythe from unattached Captaincy.
360	Mundy Pole	1826	21 Sept. 1826	21 June 1827	24 Dec. 1833				1841	
361	J. L. Kingston	1827		19 Sept. 1826					1835	
362	Charles Knox	1827		9 Aug. 1827					1829	
363	H. T. Griffiths	1827	19 Apl. 1827						1832	
364	W. H. Bayntun	1827	15 May 1827	4 Dec. 1832					1834	
365	W. Hope	1827	12 Apl. 1826						1831	
366	James White	1828		7 Oct. 1824					1830	
367	T. Collins	1828		7 July 1825					1831	
368	Hector McCaskill	1828	27 Nov. 1827						1831	
369	Archibald Hay	1828	10 July 1828	29 Mar. 1833					1836	
370	W. A. Poppleton	1831	12 June 1830	19 Apl. 1833	7 July 1839				1840	
371	P. L. Campbell	1831	13 June 1830						1832	
372	F. W. Johnson	1832			15 June 1830				1835	
373	R. T. Healey	1832		8 June 1830	24 Apl. 1835				1837	
374	Charles James	1832		20 Jan. 1829	9 Oct. 1835				1838	
375	R. J. Falconer Miles	1832	6 Apl. 1832	24 Dec. 1833					1835	
376	Caledon. Rd. Egerton	1832	15 June 1832	28 Mar. 1834	15 Mar. 1839	5 Dec. 1861	9 Mar. 1855	20 Feb. 1874	1856	Died May 1874
377	Fredk. Chas. Aylmer	1832	4 Dec. 1832	26 July 1834	20 May 1840	30 Dec. 1864	2 Nov. 1855		1856	
378	G. W. Blunt	1832	2 Nov. 1832	30 May 1834					1888	Died of Yellow Fever at Trinidad 1888
379	James Dukes	1832	Qr.-Master 1832						1848	
380	W. O. Rochfort	1833		18 Oct. 1831					1834	
381	F. Roger Palmer	1833	15 Mar. 1833	24 Mar. 1835					1836	
382	Claude Robert Bozzi Granville	1833	29 Mar. 1833	5 June 1835					1836	
383	Norman Cowley	1833	26 Apl. 1833	19 June 1835					1837	
384	William A. Devraynes	1833	18 Oct. 1833	2 Oct. 1835					1836	
385	Pennington Grant Need	1833	24 Dec. 1833	9 Oct. 1835					1888	Died of Yellow Fever at Trinidad 1888
386	James W. Crowdy	1834	28 Mar. 1834	8 Apl. 1836					1887	
387	G. Galvert Clarke	1834	30 May 1834	7 Oct. 1836	20 Sep. 1839				1845	

APPENDIX.

Succession Number.	Name.	Date of Joining.	Ensign.	Lieutenant.	Captain.	Major.	Lieut.-Col.	Colonel.	Date of Leaving.	Remarks.
388	Charles Daly		1834 25 July 1834	17 Feb. 1837	31 Dec. 1839	29 Dec. 1854			1855	Died of Disease in the Crimea 1855
389	Richard Doherty		1835				4 Sept. 1835		1838	To be Governor of Sierra Leone
390	John Spence		1835 30 *Sept.* 1830	12 Apl. 1833	14 Apl. 1843				1849	
391	C. Montague Walker		1835 10 Apl. 1835	10 Mar. 1837					1841	
392	Arthur Pigott		1835 24 Apl. 1835	2 July 1838	25 Aug. 1843				1851	
393	George Horne		1835 19 June 1835	28 Aug. 1838					1839	
394	W. H. Thornton		1835 30 June 1835	1 Nov. 1838					1845	
395	Henry Crawford		1835 9 June 1835	8 Nov. 1838	23 Jan. 1846				1851	
396	H. R. Hartley		1835 37¼ *Foot*	2 *Sept.* 1813	29 *Nov.* 1821	8 *Nov.* 1827	12 Apl. 1831		1835	Retired on half pay
397	J. B. Pearson		1835		4 Dec. 1835				1838	Died of Yellow Fever, at Trinidad 1838
398	Thomas Wright		1836	4 Dec. 1832					1837	
399	M. M. Dillon		1836	1 July 1836					1842	Retired, Dec. 1842
400	Henry Edmunds		1836 8 Apl. 1836	16 Mar. 1839	20 Oct. 1846				1847	
401	R. Macdonald		1836 7 Oct. 1836	13 May 1839					1841	
402	Sir C. BulkeleyEgerton		1837		22 *Apl.* 1795	1 June 1798	14 Nov. 1802	26 Sept. 1837	1857	Served in the Regt. until 1809, afterwards given the Colonelcy in 1837
403	Fowke Moore		1837		17 Apl. 1835				1839	
404	G. Hughes Messiter		1837 17 Feb. 1837	26 Sept. 1834					1838	
405	Charles Sandes		1837	20 Sept. 1839					1840	
406	T. Hutchinson		1837 10 Mar. 1837	28 June 1839					1840	
407	John Gray		1838		20 Apl. 1826				1830	Died of Yellow Fever in 1839 at Antigua
408	J. D. Macdonald		1888	13 June 1834	16 June 1843	20 June 1854			1855	Died of Disease in the Crimea 1855
409	W. J. D. C. Aplin		1839 7 July 1839	20 May 1840					1843	
410	Robert B. Hawley		1839 28 Aug. 1839	31 Dec. 1839	10 Jan. 1851	2 Nov. 1855			1855	
411	John Newbury		1839 28 Dec. 1839	21 Aug. 1841					1844	
412	J. Quintus Wall		1839		23 Aug. 1839				1840	
413	Oliver Creagh O'Brien		1839 28 Dec. 1839	15 May 1840					1844	
414	J. C. Romer		1839 15 Mar. 1839	20 Nov. 1840					1814	
415	C. Doyle Patterson		1839 21 June 1839	4 Oct. 1841					1842	
416	Frederick W. Oakley		1839 28 June 1839						1841	

APPENDIX.

Succession Number	Name	Date of Joining	Ensign.	Lieutenant.	Captain.	Major.	Lieut.-Col.	Colonel.	Date of Leaving.	Remarks.
417	George Augustus F. Ruxton	1839	2 Aug. 1839	27 Dec. 1842					1843	
418	Thos. Dopping Buchanan D'Arcy	1840	10 Jan. 1840	14 Apl. 1843					1848	
419	F. Y. J. Stewart	1840	15 May 1840	18 June 1843					1852	
420	G. D. Robertson	1840	4 Aug. 1840						1843	
421	William Huntley Mills	1840	20 Nov. 1840	25 Aug. 1843					1844	
422	Henry Wynyard	1841			21 May 1841				1846	
423	J. D. Blythe	1841			1 Dec. 1837				1843	
424	Ralph Dudgeon	1841	19 Mar. 1841						1842	
425	Arundel Edmund Hill	1841	7 Sept. 1841	27 Oct. 1843	3 Oct. 1846				1855	Died of wounds received during the Siege of Sevastopol
426	Macartney Hume Oldfield	1841	26 Nov. 1841						1844	
427	William Augustus Gaussen	1842		8 Apl. 1842					1847	
428	Alexander McGeachy Alleyne	1842	14 May 1842	17 May 1844					1848	
429	William Duff	1842	27 Dec. 1842	11 Sept. 1844					1847	
430	James W. Bouverie	1843					14 July 1843		1845	Died in Canada,Feb. 1845
431	Richard Pennefather	1843		18 Feb. 1843					1845	
432	Dunbar Douglas Muter	1843	14 Apl. 1843						1845	
433	Robert Blair Kennedy	1843	16 June 1843	26 Feb. 1844					1847	
434	James Shuter	1843	25 Aug. 1843						1845	
435	Edward Collingwood Cuppage	1843	8 Feb. 1842						1845	
436	John Macdonald	1843	10 Nov. 1843	8 Aug. 1845	29 Dec. 1854	23 Apl. 1861			1865	To 96th Regiment.
437	John F. Fitz Giffard Myrton	1844		27 May 1845					1845	
438	G. L. D. Amiel	1844		1 July 1845					1845	
439	C. Richardson	1844	15 Mar. 1844						1846	
440	A. E. Mulloy	1844	17 May 1844	20 Oct. 1846					1848	
441	Chas. Hy. Elphinstone Holloway	1844	11 Oct. 1844	1 Oct. 1847					1851	

APPENDIX. 201

Succession Number	Name	Date of Joining	Ensign	Lieutenant	Captain	Major	Lieut.-Col.	Colonel	Date of Leaving	Remarks
442	Hugh M. Campbell	1845	1845		31 Dec. 1844				1846	
443	J. T. Stanley	1845	1845		27 June 1845				1847	
444	G. Marshall Knipe	1845	22 Feb. 1839	20 May 1842					1854	Retired on half pay
445	Leslie Skynner	1845	26 Oct. 1841	14 July 1843	2 Feb. 1846	27 Mar. 1855	17 Nov. 1857		1858	Died of Fever at Ahmedabad, 8th May 1858
446	Butler Dunboyne Moore	1845	17 Jan. 1845	22 Oct. 1847	5 Dec. 1851				1852	
447	Bowes Mein	1845	28 Mar. 1845	24 Dec. 1847					1848	
448	Horatio Nelson Kippen	1845	18 Apl. 1845	3 Mar. 1849					1846	
449	T. R. J. G. Thompson	1845	11 July 1845						1853	
450	G. Pinckney Atkinson	1845	8 Aug. 1845						1846	
451	J. Lewes Phillips	1846	22 Jan. 1842	19 Dec. 1845	2 Mar. 1849	9 Sept. 1856			1859	Died 12th Oct. 1859
452	Ed. Jonathan Head	1846	20 Feb. 1843	3 Oct. 1845					1853	Paymaster to Regt. 1851
453	Frederick A. Hardy	1846	24 Jan. 1845						1846	
454	Edward Buller Thorp	1846	12 June 1846	3 Feb. 1849	11 Mar. 1853	9 May 1858	15 Feb. 1874		1876	
455	Frederick J. Isaacke	1847			28 Apl. 1842				1848	
456	C. Tindal Griffiths	1847			23 Apl. 1847				1848	
457	Carrick Darby	1847	3 Sep. 1847	2 Mar. 1849	29 Dec. 1854				1855	Died on his way home from Crimea of disease
458	William Drummond	1847	1 Oct. 1847	3 Aug. 1849					1852	
459	John Atkinson	1847	22 Oct. 1847	17 Jan. 1851	4 Aug. 1854	13 Oct. 1859			1861	Died 1861
460	Leopold Brown	1847	28 Apl. 1846						1850	
461	Henry W. Palmer	1846	11 Jan. 1839	22 July 1842	25 Jan. 1846				1849	
462	Hans Robert White	1846	22 Jan. 1843	19 Dec. 1845	5 Dec. 1851	2 Nov. 1855			1856	
463	T. Hobbs Williams	1846	20 May 1842	14 Apl. 1846					1849	
464	Alexander Campbell	1846	7 May 1847	16 June 1848	20 Feb. 1852				1853	
465	Alfred Nixon	1848	3 Mar. 1848	5 Dec. 1851	29 Dec. 1854				1858	Died in India 1858
466	Charles Heycock	1848	31 Mar. 1848	5 Dec. 1851	30 Dec. 1854				1860	
467	Robert Selby	1848	3 Oct. 1848	20 Feb. 1852	16 Jan. 1855				1863	Died at Moolkan, 17th Aug. 1863
468	William Watson	1846	Qr.-Mr. 25 Apl. 1848						1855	
469	W. Cecil George Pery	1849	2 Feb. 1849	6 Aug. 1852	26 Jan. 1855				1862	Retired by sale of Commission
470	R. Rowland Conyers	1849	2 Mar. 1849	31 Oct. 1852	27 Mar. 1855				1858	Retired by sale of Commission

APPENDIX.

Succession Number	Name.	Date of joining.	Ensign.	Lieutenant.	Captain.	Major.	Lieut.-Col.	Colonel.	Date of Leaving.	Remarks.
471	Augustus H. Ferryman	1849 27 June	1834	30 June 1837	16 Apl. 1841	22 Dec. 1849	24 Nov. 1848	28 Nov. 1854	1860	Exchanged to 75th Regt.
472	Edmund Alleyne Dawes	1849 6 July	1849	8 Nov. 1852					1853	
473	William Boyle	1850 5 Dec.	1850	21 May 1851	14 Jan. 1850	17 Nov. 1857	13 Oct. 1858	13 Oct. 1863	1874	Died Feb. 1874
474	Maurice Cane	1850 15 July	1850	7 Sept. 1851	1 Sep. 1849				1861	
475	George Cresswell	1850 16 Aug.	1850	11 Mar. 1853	31 Mar. 1855				1857	
476	Arthur H. Hastead Mercer	1851 30 Apl.	1841	1 Nov. 1842	29 Dec. 1854				1857	
477	John Gray	1851 1 Jan.	1847	17 May 1849					1852	
478	Edmund Morris	1851 13 Dec.	1851	11 Mar. 1853	7 Sept. 1855				1858	Died at the Depot 1858
479	John Longfield	1851 5 Dec.	1851	6 June 1854					1855	Died on way home from Crimea of disease
480	Francis Knatchbull	1851 5 Dec.	1851	6 June 1854	17 Nov. 1857	5 July 1872			1874	Died 1856
481	Geo. Harmer Pering	1852 12 Mar.	1852	11 Aug. 1854					1858	
482	John Waldron Gray	1852 17 Aug.	1852	18 Aug. 1854					1856	
483	Barnes Slyfield Robinson	1852 17 Dec.	1852	8 Dec. 1854	9 May 1855	12 Aug. 1876	1 July. 1881	12 Aug. 1884	1885	Retired on half pay. Died 26th Oct., 1887.
484	Savage Hall	1853 21 Jan.	1853	8 Dec. 1854					1857	
485	Richard Edward Beck	1853 18 Mar.	1853	8 Dec. 1854	10 Aug. 1858				1860	Retired 1860 by sale of Commission. Died October 1887.
486	Augustus Breedon	1863 19 Mar.	1863	29 Dec. 1854	13 Oct. 1858				1859	
487	Rd. Francis Holmes	1853 26 Sept.	1846	8 Apl. 1853	28 Aug. 1857				1870	
488	Daniel Tom	1853 7 June	1844	28 June 1849	9 Aug., 1860				1858	Retired 1858 by sale of Commission
489	Montifort H. Trant Lloyd	1854 6 June	1854	16 June 1855	23 Apl. 1861				1867	
490	John Arthur Barstow	1854 18 Aug.	1854	26 Jan. 1856	10 Dec. 1858				1872	
491	Henry Lewis Harvest	1854 13 Oct.	1854	9 Feb. 1855	18 Aug. 1863	1 July 1881			1884	Retired 1884
492	Hafed Lamont	1855 23 Nov.	1851	23 Nov. 1852					1858	Died in India 1858
493	Simpson Hackett Hobbs	1865 19 Nov.	1852	6 Apl. 1855	6 Nov. 1863				1860	
494	Montague C. Browning	1855 14 Jan.	1865	27 Mar. 1855	10 Dec. 1858				1861	To 87th Regiment 1861

APPENDIX.   203

Succession Number.	Name.	Date of Joining.	Ensign.	Lieutenant.	Captain.	Major.	Lieut.-Col.	Colonel.	Date of Leaving.	Remarks.
495	William Drage	1855	15 Jan. 1855	31 Mar. 1854	4 Sep. 1860				1864	Retired by sale of Commission 1862
496	Robert Johnston	1855	16 Jan. 1855	7 Sept. 1855					1862	Retired 12th Aug. 1887
497	Josias Dunn	1855	9 Feb. 1855	21 Oct. 1855	11 Apl. 1862	20 Aug. 1879	12 Aug. 1881	12 Aug. 1885	1887	
498	Joshua James Bowness	1855	2 Mar. 1855	23 Oct. 1855					1850	
499	Burohall Helme	1855	9 Mar. 1855	23 Oct. 1855	24 Mar. 1863				1867	Retired by sale of Commission 1867
500	W. Norcott Manners	1855	16 Mar. 1855	23 Oct. 1855					1857	
501	Netherville J. Barron	1855	22 Mar. 1855	22 Dec. 1855					1857	
502	John Cordeiro Warne	1855	23 Mar. 1855						1856	
503	G. Francis Dowdeswell	1855	24 May 1855	26 Feb. 1856					1866	Retired by sale of Commission 1866
504	H. Latham Brownrigg	1855	25 May 1855	17 Nov. 1857					1858	
505	Robert Bulkeley Baldwin	1855	1 June 1855	17 July 1857					1870	
506	Henry Bishop	1855	15 June 1855						1862	
507	Alexander Dixon Grier	1855	6 July 1855	10 Aug. 1858	9 Nov. 1867				1872	
508	Robert G. Newbigging	1855	20 July 1855	13 Oct. 1858					1870	Adjutant from 1858 to 1870
509	Henry Burton Dunn	1855	7 Sept. 1855						1857	Resigned Commission 1857
510	William Sibbald	1855	Qr.-Mr. 14 Sept. 1855						1864	To 51st Regiment
511	Owen H. Strong	1855	22 Oct. 1855						1858	
512	William Sealy	1855	23 Oct. 1855	25 Mar. 1869	11 Sept. 1872				1876	Retired by sale of Commission 1876
513	Francis Warburton	1855	9 Nov. 1855						1858	Died in India 1858
514	Robert F. Harrison	1855	28 Dec. 1855						1859	Died March 1859
515	F. W. Adam Parsons	1856	10 Aug. 1848	20 Oct. 1849					1857	Retired by sale of Commission
516	William Pott	1856	8 Jan. 1856	10 Dec. 1856	7 Dec. 1887				1869	
517	William Montague Cochrane									
518	William Greaves Blake	1856	26 Feb. 1856						1857	
		1856	27 Feb. 1856						1857	
519	James T. Nugent	1856	28 Feb. 1856						1857	

APPENDIX.

Succession Number	Name	Date of Joining	Ensign	Lieutenant	Captain	Major	Lieut.-Col.	Colonel	Date of Leaving	Remarks
520	Charles George James Arbuthnot	1857	26 *Dec.* 1816		16 *Mar.* 1820	8 July 1823	1 *Oct.* 1825	28 *June* 1838 Major-Gen. 11 Nov. 1851	1864	To 91st Regiment
521	W. Sheffield Hardinge	1857	24 Apl. 1855						1858	
522	William Atthill	1857	29 Dec. 1857	4 Sept. 1860					1864	Retired by sale of Commission 1864
523	F. H. Digby Marsh	1858	31 *Mar.* 1848	4 *Sept.* 1851	27 Sept. 1858					1863	Retired by sale of Commission 1863
524	James Shaw Hay	1858	17 Sept. 1858	3 Apl. 1861						1867	Retired by sale of Commission 1867
525	R. Nathan Hubbersty	1858	24 Sept. 1858	23 Apl. 1861	23 June 1869	1 July 1881				1885	Retired 1885. Died 1886
526	William H. Rudall	1858	8 Oct. 1858	11 Oct. 1862						1866	Retired by sale of Commission.
527	George D. Dickson	1858	9 Oct. 1858							1859	Died Sep. 1859 from an accidental fall at Calcutta
528	Augustus Wm. Price	1858	26 Nov. 1858	24 June 1862						1869	
529	Wm. Grenfeld Ostler	1859	11 Jan. 1859							1860	Retired by sale of Commission
530	George J. Whitaker Hayward	1859	12 Jan. 1859	24 *Mar.* 1863						1864	To 79th Regiment
531	De Vic Valpy	1859	20 *Oct.* 1848	5 *Oct.* 1849	26 Mar. 1858					1867	Retired by sale of Commission
532	Stephen Wm. Sewell	1859	9 *Nov.* 1855	28 Sept. 1858						1861	Died at Umballa 1861, from effects of a fall from horseback
533	Charles Wm. Burton	1859	29 July 1859	18 Aug. 1863						1868	
534	Chas. Vernon Hassall	1859	28 Oct. 1859	6 Nov. 1863	23 June 1869					1873	
535	Legendre Chas. Bourchier	1860	5 *Apl.* 1833	12 *May* 1836	20 *July* 1838	12 *Dec.* 1851	9 Oct. 1859			1865	Retired on half pay
536	Thomas Parnell Green	1860	30 Dec. 1859	3 June 1864						1865	Died on the voyage home from India 1865
537	Luke Henry Jones	1860	21 Sept. 1860							1865	
538	Robert Gibson	1861	3 *Apl.* 1849	22 *Feb.* 1850	18 *Feb.* 1859	16 Apl. 1861	6 Nov. 1863			1863	Was Qr.-Mr. 87th Regt. from '47. Retired 1863

APPENDIX.

Succession Number.	Name.	Date of Joining.	Ensign.	Lieutenant.	Captain.	Major.	Lieut.-Col.	Colonel.	Date of Leaving.	Remarks.
539	Duncan Campbell	1861	15 Jan. 1861	3 Aug. 1866	27 Aug. 1873				1874	Retired on half pay
540	James King	1861	21 Sept. 1860						1863	Retired by sale of Commission
541	Henry J. K. Grenville	1861	2 July 1861	1 Feb. 1867					1867	Retired by sale of Commission
542	Alexander G. Fraser	1862	29 July 1859	15 Oct. 1861					1866	Retired by sale of Commission
543	Alfred Godwin-Austen	1862	11 Apl. 1862	6 Nov. 1867	15 Feb. 1874				1875	To 24th Regt.
544	Irwin Charles Maling	1862	6 Aug. 1861						1869	
545	Henry T. Pycroft	1863	24 Mar. 1863						1866	Retired by sale of Commission
546	William Maitland Meacham	1863	17 Apl. 1862							
547	George Daniel Hall Brookes	1863	22 May 1863						1866	
548	Acheson W. Smyth	1863	17 Nov. 1863						1865	
549	Charles Gascoigne	1864	7 Dec. 1820	30 Jan. 1823	31 Dec. 1825	23 Aug. 1831	22 Oct. 1839 Hon. Col. 1864	11 Nov. 1851	1867	Retired by sale of Commission
550	Henry W. Somerville Carew	1864	21 Aug. 1849	20 June 1854	22 Mar. 1864				1870	
551	Christopher Garsia	1864	23 Mar. 1858	11 Oct. 1860					1868	
552	Henry Caddell	1864	3 June 1864	9 Nov. 1867	3 June 1874	9 Jan. 1882			1888	Retired, Jan. 1888
553	Francis W. Osborne	1864	19 July 1864 Qr.-Mr.						1873	Died at Bangalore, 2nd Oct. 1873
554	James Buchanan Kirk	1865			31 Dec. 1867	21 Feb. 1865			1869	
555	Erasmus Harris Vaughton		5 Feb. 1865						1870	
556	George Coates	1865	4 Aug. 1865						1868	
557	Montagne Fawkes	1866	5 Sept. 1862	22 Sept. 1865	22 Oct. 1870	1 July 1881				
558	John Browne Ribbon	1866	30 Mar. 1866	7 Dec. 1867					1872	
559	Alfred James Hesketh Daubeny	1866	29 July 1862	10 Nov. 1865					1873	
560	Arthur William Carter	1866	3 Aug. 1866						1869	
561	John Cuthbert	1867	1 Feb. 1866	23 June 1869	12 Aug. 1876				1880	Died 9th Sep. 1880

Succession Number	Name	Date of Joining	Ensign	Lieutenant	Captain	Major	Lieut.-Col.	Colonel	Date of Leaving	Remarks
562	J. Wharton Harrel	1867			1 Jan. 1868				1870	Retired on half pay
563	Hardinge Cornwallis Hogg								1868	
564	Charles Arundel Barker	1867	12 Oct. 1867							
565	Alfred John Le Cornu	1867	6 Nov. 1867	23 June 1869	23 Apl. 1877	14 May 1884			1870	Retired
566	Alexander Macaulay	1867	9 Nov. 1867	29 Dec. 1869					1871	
567	Richard Hovil	1867	7 Dec. 1867	14 Sept. 1870					1870	
568	Patrick David Boyle	1868	2 Sep. 1868						1870	
569	John Penton	1868	16 Sept. 1868						1869	
570	Kenelm Digby Murray	1869	6 *June* 1861	13 *Sept.* 1853	22 *Aug.* 1858	5 Apl. 1864	12 Aug. 1876	28 Mar. 1879	1881	Retired on half pay
571	William Paul Barry Brereton	1869	4 *Sept.* 1860	28 *Feb.* 1864	30 June 1869	1 July 1881	30 June 1886	18 Nov. 1886	1886	To 1st Battalion.
572	John Gordon	1869	17 *July* 1863	6 May 1868	16 June 1877				1881	Retired 1881. Died 1886
		1869	23 Jan. 1869	28 Oct. 1871	9 Sept. 1880	12 Aug. 1885			1885	To 87th Regt. 1885, Died July 1887
573	John Alexander Maylin Vipan	1869	23 June 1869	7 Dec. 1870	20 Aug. 1879				1880	Retired by sale of Commission.
574	Edgar Cubitt Brown	1869	24 June 1869	28 Oct. 1871	2 Mar. 1881				1888	Died at Malta 10th April 1883
575	Robert Hawkes Ellis	1869	25 June 1869	27 Oct. 1871	23 June 1880				1870	
576	James Boyle	1869	9 Oct. 1869		23 Feb. 1870				1885	Retired 1885
577	Ramsay Stewart	1870	8 *Aug.* 1868	22 June 1870	14 Sept. 1878				1870	
578	Joseph R. McMurray	1870							1890	Retired with Gratuity
579	Ormsby Cox	1870	9 *Nov.* 1858	6 Sept. 1861					1875	Died 9th December 1875
580	Alexander Henry Gibbs Anton	1870	9 Apl. 1870	28 Oct. 1871	1 Dec. 1880		22 Oct. 1870		1880	Promoted Captain in 94th Regiment
581	Sir John Garvock	1870							1874	
582	Christopher Neeld Jones	1870	7 Dec. 1870	28 Oct. 1871	1 Dec. 1890				1880	To 94th Regt. Killed at Tel el Kebir Sept. 1882
583	G. Osborne Smith	1871	13 *July* 1871	12 Dec. 1868	6 Mar. 1880	11 Apl. 1886			1880	To 94th Regiment
584	Henry R. A. Ellis	1871	4 Jan. 1871	28 Oct. 1871	1 Dec. 1890					

APPENDIX. 207

Succession Number	Name.	Date of joining.	Ensign or Sub Lieut.	Lieutenant.	Captain.	Major.	Lieut.-Col.	Colonel.	Date of Leaving.	Remarks.
585	Arthur Gorham Howard Hayne	1872	*Sub Lieut.* 3 Feb, 1872	3 Feb, 1875					1877	To Madras Staff Corps
586	Edwd. James Nicholls Fasken	1872	2 Nov, 1872						1877	To Bengal Staff Corps
587	Malcolm E. Haleman O. Welsh	1873	20 July 1870	28 Oct. 1871					1875	To Bengal Staff Corps
588	Malcolm John Meade	1873	*Sub Lieut.* 9 Aug. 1873						1878	To Bengal Staff Corps
589	John de Courcy Dashwood Meade	1873	*Sub Lieut.* 9 Aug. 1873						1880	To Bengal Staff Corps
590	James Edward Bell	1874	Qr.-Master 24 Jan, 1874							
591	Robert Hutchison Campbell Tufnell	1874	*Sub Lieut.* 23 Apl. 1873						1876	To 76th Foot
592	Lord H. Hugh Manvers Percy V.C., K.C.B.	1841	July 1836	*Lt. & Capt.* 29 Dec. 1840	*Capt. & Lt.-Colonel* 7 Mar, 1851				1878	To Madras Staff Corps
593	C. Caldwell Grantham	1874	16 Sept. 1845	23 Oct. 1847	23 July 1858	8 May 1872	16 Sept. 1878	Major-Gen. 10 Feb, 1865 Lieut-Gen. 29 May 1873	1877	
594	Rd. Oliffe Richbmond	1874	2 July 1858	6 May 1863	1 Apl. 1874				1879	Retired
595	Edmund Geo. Barrow	1874		30 Dec. 1871					1878	To Pay Department
596	Josiah Erskine Collins	1875	16 Aug. 1861	8 June 1867	27 Apl. 1870				1879	To Bengal Staff Corps
									1891	To Half Pay, then to 53rd Regt, and then to the 67th Regt.
597	Walter Cave	1875	8 June 1861	28 Dec. 1865	20 Aug. 1871	12 May 1881			1886	To 1st Batt. Retired Aug. 1888
598	Chas. Edwd. Harrman	1875	*Sub Lieut.* 21 Sept. 1874	21 Sept. 1875	30 Mar. 1881				1881	To 94th Regiment
599	Herbert Augustine Christopher Harrison	1876	*Sub Lieut.* 12 Feb, 1876	12 Feb. 1877						
600	Jas. Douglas Standen	1876	28 Apl. 1875	28 Apl. 1877	14 May 1884				1877	To 94th Regiment
601	James Archer	1876	Qr.-Master 1876						1879	Died at Rangoon 21st Jan, 1879
602	Walter Cook	1876	10 Sept. 1875						1879	To Bengal Staff Corps

APPENDIX.

Succession Number	Name.	Date of Joining.	Ensign, Sub-Lieut., or 2nd Lieut.	Lieutenant.	Captain.	Major.	Lt.-Col.	Colonel.	Date of Leaving.	Remarks.
603	Louis Robert Meredith Maxwell	1876	11 Sept. 1876	11 Sept. 1876	21 Feb. 1883				1883	Exchanged to 64th Regt.
604	Fredk. Henry Munn	1876	11 Sept. 1876	11 Sept. 1876	30 Mar. 1883	1 July 1888			1888	To 1st Batt.
605	George Cortlandt Childe Shakespear	1876	11 Sept. 1876	11 Sept. 1876					1883	To Indian Staff Corps
606	Stanley Wolferston Jervis	1877	10 Sept. 1875						1879	To Indian Staff Corps
607	Claude Rainer Rogers	1877	24 June 1876	24 June 1876	28 Aug. 1883					
608	Malcolm Henry Stanley Grover	1877	11 Sept. 1876						1880	To Madras Staff Corps
609	Hugh James Alexander Davidson	1877	15 Aug. 1877	3 Dec. 1878					1879	Transferred to 94th Regt.
610	Sir Henry Percival De Bathe	1877	1 Nov. 1839	Lt. & Capt. 14 Feb. 1845		Capt. & Lt.-Col.	17 Feb. 1854	28 Nov. 1854 Lieut.-Gen. 8 Oct. 1876 Gen. 1 Jan. 1879.	1880	To 85th Regt.
611	William Fremantle Cahusac	1878	30 Jan. 1878	9 Sept. 1880					1881	To Bombay Staff Corps
612	Herbert Hugh Dobbie	1878	1 May 1878	1 Dec. 1880					1881	To Bombay Staff Corps
613	Stephen Neary	1878	4 Dec. 1878	1 Dec. 1880					1879	To 44th Regt.
614	Charles Irwin Fry	1879	22 Jan. 1879	1 Dec. 1880					1883	To Bombay Staff Corps
615	John Watkins	1879		Lieut. & Qr.-Mr. 30 April 1879	Capt. & Qr.-Mr. 6 Nov. 1886					
616	Alexander McDonnell Moore	1879	23 July 1879	1 Dec. 1880	12 Aug. 1885					
617	Reginald Eric Duncan Campbell	1879	11 Oct. 1879	11 April 1881	12 Aug. 1887					
618	Felix Frederick Hill	1880	14 Jan. 1880	13 April 1881	25 Jan. 1888					

APPENDIX. 209

Succession Number	Name.	Date of Joining.	Ensign, Sub-Lieut., or 2nd Lieut.	Lieutenant.	Captain.	Major.	Lieut.-Col.	Colonel.	Date of Leaving.	Remarks.
619	John Arthur Lambert	1880	10 *July* 1835	*Lt. & Capt.* 1 July 1881	11 *Sept.* 1840	*Capt. & Lt.-Colonel*	15 *Nov.* 1860	28 *Nov.* 1854 *Major-Gen.* 27 *Dec.* 1864 *Lieut.-Gen.* 28 *May* 1873 General 1 Oct. 1877	1887	Died 21 Sept., 1887
620	William Pearson Davison	1880	23 Oct. 1880	1 July 1881						
621	Francis Marwood Hext	1880	23 Oct. 1880	1 July 1881	23 Feb. 1881				1884	To Bombay Staff Corps
622	Charles George Nurse	1881	22 Jan. 1881	1 July 1881	1 July 1888					
623	Rowland Brinckman	1881	22 Jan. 1881	1 July 1881	1 July 1888					
624	Frederick Jno. Angell	1881	22 Jan. 1881	1 July 1881					1886	To the Ordnance Store Department 1st Apl., 1886.
625	Frederick Thesiger Williams	1881	22 Jan. 1881	1 July 1881					1884	To Madras Staff Corps

APPENDIX.

On the 1st July, 1881, the 89th Regiment was amalgamated with the 87th Irish Fusiliers and thus became the

"2nd BATTALION PRINCESS VICTORIA'S (ROYAL IRISH FUSILIERS)."

Succession Number.	Name.	Date of Joining.	2nd Lieut. or Ensign.	Lieutenant.	Captain.	Major.	Lieut.-Col.	Colonel.	Date of Leaving.	Remarks.
626	Wm. Harry Percival Plomer	1881		22 Oct. 1881						
627	Charles Marling Cartwright	1881		22 Oct. 1881					1883	To Bombay Staff Corps
628	Herbert Wm. Laing	1881		22 Oct. 1881					1884	To Madras Staff Corps
629	Edward Branfil Harrison	1881		22 Oct. 1881					1883	To 1st Batt. R.I. Fusiliers. Resigned commission 1887
630	John Reeves	1883		21 *Jan.* 1874	25 June 1881	25 Jan. 1888				
631	Arthur Fredk. Terry	1884	8 *June* 1867	3 *Aug.* 1870	11 Apl. 1885				1887	Retired 1887
632	Herbert Adolphe Coddington	1884		6 Feb. 1884						
633	Wm. Elliott Cairnes	1884		14 May 1885						
634	Rd. Waugh Leeper	1885		6 May 1885						
635	George Cox	1885	4 *Jan.* 1861	12 *July* 1864	22 *June* 1867	1 *July* 1881	12 Aug. 1885	18 Nov. 1886		
636	Arthur Banbury	1885	28 *Oct.* 1876	28 Oct. 1877	10 Mar. 1886				1886	To 1st Battalion
637	Hon. Ed. Barrington Lewis Hy. Stopford	1885	13 *Aug.* 1879	30 Mar. 1881	3 Aug. 1887					
638	Urmston Fitz-Otho Fitzgerald	1885		25 Nov. 1885					1886	To 1st Battalion 1886. Died in India 1886
639	John George Parker	1886		28 Apl. 1886						
640	Richard Tucker Gray	1886		28 Apl. 1886						
641	Walter Barrington Silver	1886		25 Aug. 1886						
642	Montagu Edward Higginson	1886		25 Aug. 1886						
643	G. Kilner Swettenham	1886		10 Nov. 1886						

APPENDIX. 211

Succession Number.	Name.	Date of Joining.	2nd Lieut. or Ensign.	Lieutenant.	Captain.	Major.	Lieut.-Col.	Colonel.	Date of Leaving.	Remarks.
644	Frederick L. Vernon Jenkins	1887	5 Feb, 1887						1887	To 1st Batt.
645	Herbert de Vere Harvest	1887	14 Sept. 1887							
646	Augustus Halifax Ferryman	1887	27 June 1834	30 June 1837	18 April 1841	22 Dec. 1843	24 Nov. 1848	28 Nov. 1854 Gen. 1 Oct. 1877		General Ferryman served in the 80th Regt. 1840 to 1860
647	John E. R. Brush	1888	9 May 1888							
648	Thomas Edwin Scott	1888	9 May 1888							

APPENDIX.

Succession Number.	Name.	Date of Joining.	2nd Lieut. or Ensign.	Lieutenant.	Captain.	Major.	Lieut.-Col.	Colonel.	Date of Leaving.	Remarks.

Succession Number.	Name.	Date of Joining.	2nd Lieut. or Ensign.	Lieutenant.	Captain.	Major.	Lieut.-Col.	Colonel.	Date of Leaving.	Remarks.

ADDENDA TO ROLL OF OFFICERS.

Succession Number.	Name.	Date of Joining.	2nd Lieut. or Ensign.	Lieutenant.	Captain.	Major.	Lieut.-Col.	Colonel.	Date of Leaving.	Remarks.
377	F. C. Aylmer									Retired.
402	H. R. White									Sold Commission.
466	C. Heycock									Retired.
475	G. Cresswell									Retired on half pay.
476	A. H. H. Mercer									Sold Commission.
477	J. Gray									Retired on half pay.
480	F. Knutchbull									To 9th Foot.
493	S. H. Hobbs									Retired.
504	H. L. Brownrigg				1 Apl. 1870					To 84th Foot.
505	R. B. Baldwin				17 Apl. 1870					Half pay, Then to 4th Ft.
508	R. G. Newbigging									To 81st Regt.
510	O. H. Strong									To 10th Foot.
516	W. Pott			8 Oct. 1858						To 27th Regt.
519	J. T. Nugent									To 6th Foot.
533	C. W. Burton									To 12th Foot.
541	L. C. Maling			23 June 1869						To 35th Regt.
546	W. M. Meacham									To 41st Regt.
540	C. Gascoigne									To 72nd Highlanders.
551	C. Garsia									To Bengal Staff Corps.
554	J. H. Kirk		17 Oct. 1851	11 Feb. 1865	29 Dec. 1869					To 91st Highlanders.
555	E. H. Vaughton									To 10th Foot.
556	G. Coates									To C. & T. Department.
559	A. J. H. Daubeny									To 107th Regt. Retd.1884.
560	A. W. Carter									To Madras Staff Corps.
563	H. C. Hogg									To Bombay Staff Corps.
568	P. D. Boyle									To Grenadier Guards.
575	R. H. Ellis									Died 1880.
581	Sir J. Garvock		4 Sept. 1835	31 Dec. 1839	25 Nov. 1842	3 Jul. 1846	22 Dec. 1848			
601	F. H. Munn					1 July 1888			1888	To 10th Foot.
607	C. R. Rogers					12 Aug. 1888			1888	To 1st Battn.
617	R. E. D. Campbell								1888	To 1st Battn.
618	F. F. Hill				12 Aug. 1888				1888	To Ordnance Store Dept.
624	F. J. Angell				7 Sept. 1888				1888	To 1st Battn.
626	W. H. P. Plomer									
643	G. K. Swettenham									
649	Geo. Bloomfield Gough	1888	9 Nov. 1888							
650	Sir Henry Blyth Hill	1888	9 Nov. 1888						1888	To Indian Staff Corps.

ALPHABETICAL INDEX

OF ALL THE

OFFICERS AND NON-COMMISSIONED OFFICERS

MENTIONED IN THE

RECORDS

OF THE

89TH REGIMENT.

Those names in "*italics*" are names of officers mentioned in the "Records," but who did not belong to the 89th Princess Victoria's Regiment.

ALPHABETICAL INDEX.

A

	PAGE
Abbott, Rev. F. J.	138
Abercrombie, Hon. John	10
Abercrombie, Sir Ralph	4
Achmuty, Sir Samuel	10, 12
Agnew, Patrick, (1)	180, 187
Agnew, Patrick, (2)	180, 193
Albemarle, Earl of Lindsay	178, 192
Allen, Ralph	191
Allen, Thomas Lowther	186
Alleyne, Alexander McGeachy	200
Amiel, G. L. D.	200
Anderson, Lieut. —	21, 23
Anderson, Arthur Gore	151, 182
Anderson, George	186
Anderson, J.	182
Angell, Frederick John	158, 160, 209
Annesley, Henry	17, 191
Anton, Alexander Henry Gibbs	146, 152, 154, 206
Aplin, Andrew Snape Hammond	66, 77, 89, 92, 93, 94, 96, 97, 179, 194
Aplin, W. J. D. C.	199
Arbuthnot, Charles George J.	119, 135, 178, 204
Arbuthnot, Sir Thomas	85, 86
Archer, James	152, 153, 154, 155, 181, 207
Armstrong, J.	180, 189
Armstrong, Richard	190
Arrow, Charles	66, 77, 196
Atkin, Christopher	188
Atkinson, John	117, 124, 127, 131, 134, 201
Atkinson, G. Pinckney	201
Atthill, William	128, 129, 204
Austin, Alfred Godwin Godwin	146, 151, 205
Aylmer, Frederick Charles	109, 110, 114, 198
Aylmer, John	186

B

Bacot, Surgeon	134
Bagshawe, S. G.	196
Baines, Thomas Joseph	192

APPENDIX. 217

	PAGE
Baker, John Robert	194
Baldwin, Robert Bulkeley	117, 134, 203
Banbury, Arthur	164, 210
Barker, Charles Arundel	146, 152, 206
Barnes, George West	21, 193
Barney, William	39, 40, 195
Barrett, James	197
Barron, Netterville John	113, 114, 203
Barrow, Edmund George	150, 152, 154, 207
Barrow, Surgeon	152
Barstow, John Arthur	112, 114, 115, 117, 145, 202
Basden, James Lewis	26, 27, 28, 40, 52, 54, 57, 61, 62, 64, 66, [67, 68, 69, 77, 89, 92, 93, 94, 95, 96, 179, 191
Bass, Phillip	190
Battersby, Lieut.-Col. —	37
Bayley, William E. M.	187
Bayntun, W. H.	198
Beatty, John	186
Beck, Richard Edward	112, 114, 115, 117, 202
Beckham, Thomas	196
Beckwith, Sir George	23, 195
Bell, James Edward	181, 207
Bell, John Allen	192
Bell, William	182, 192
Bellassis, Lieut. —	44
Benson, William	186
Birch, Colonel —	83, 84
Birtles, George	195
Bishop, Henry	115, 117, 203
Blagrave, James	192
Blake, Dennis John	187
Blake, William Greaves	203
Blakeney, Sir Edward	88
Blaney, Lord Andrew	7, 9, 179, 186
Blaney, Hon. C. D.	197
Blunt, G. W.	98, 198
Blythe, J. D.	200
Bonnyman, Assistant Surgeon	117
Borton, C.B., Maj.-Gen. A.	149, 150
Bourchier, Legendre Charles	132, 133, 204
Bouverie, James W.	97, 179, 200
Bowen, Hugh	192
Bowness, Joshua James	114, 121, 203
Bowyer, Henry	178, 188
Boxer, Captain —	99
Boyd, James	189
Boyd, Major-General —	19
Boyd, Robert Browne T.	182
Boyle, Hon. Charles	187

Q 2

APPENDIX.

		PAGE
Boyle, James	... ... 146, 151, 152, 156,	206
Boyle, Patrick David ...	... ...	206
Boyle, William	112, 114, 117, 119, 122, 123, 124, 126,	
	[128, 132, 133, 135, 136, 139, 146, 147,	
	[148, 150, 179,	202
Boyton, John	... ...	191
Breedon, Augustus	... ... 112, 121,	202
Brereton, Paul Barry ...	... ... 146, 151, 153, 155,	206
Brice, George Tito	 158,	159
Brickell, James	... ...	188
Brinckman, Rowland ...	158, 160, 162, 165, 180,	209
Broadbelt, F. R.	... ...	187
Brookes, George Daniel Hall	... ...	205
Brown, Captain —	... ...	37
Brown, Edgar Cubitt	146, 152, 156, 158, 159,	206
Brown, Leopold	... ...	201
Brown, Major-General —	 29,	34
Browne, Daniel	... ...	193
Browne, Thomas	 19,	190
Browning, Montague C.	112, 114, 115, 117, 121,	
	[123, 125, 127, 130,	202
Brownrigg, Henry Latham	... ... 114, 117,	203
Brunter, Captain —	... ...	27
Brush, John E. R.	... ...	211
Brush, Oliver	... ...	191
Buchanan, James	... ...	196
Buckingham & Chandos, Duke of ...	... ...	151
Buller, V.C., K.C.M.G., Sir Redvers	... ... 160, 162,	163
Bullock, Hugh	... ...	189
Burchall, William Moore	... ...	190
Burchell, John	... ...	186
Burton, Charles William	... ... 129, 131,	204
Butler, Richard	 10,	187
Butler, Walter	... ...	197

C

Caddell, Henry	... 146, 150, 152, 158, 160, 183,	205
Cahusac, William Fremantle	... ... 153, 156,	208
Cairnes, William Elliot	 164,	210
Campbell, Alexander (1)	 184,	191
Campbell, Alexander (2)	... ...	201
Campbell, Sir Archibald	... 54, 55, 59, 61, 64, 70, 71, 72,	75
Campbell, Captain — ...	... ...	36
Campbell, Colonel — ...	 36,	40
Campbell, Duncan	... ... 134, 138, 146, 148,	205
Campbell, Hugh M.	... ...	201
Campbell, J. W.	... ...	196
Campbell, Major-General	... ...	146

APPENDIX. 219

	PAGE
Campbell, P. L.	198
Campbell, Reignald Eric Duncan	156, 208
Campbell, W.	197
Cameron, Sir John	83
Cameron, John	187
Cane, Maurice	202
Cannon, Charles	52, 58, 62, 64, 66, 68, 180, 191
Carew, Henry W. Somerville	205
Carmichael, Charles Carr	187
Carter, Arthur William	205
Carroll, John	195
Cartwright, Charles Marling	158, 159, 210
Cary, William	197
Cathcart, Lord	8
Caulfield, John	194
Cave, Walter	151, 152, 153, 155, 207
Chambers, David	192
Chaplin, John	187
Chapman, Robert	194
Charleton, Andrew Robert	194
Chauncey, Commodore —	17
Christie, Richard	186
Clarke, G. Calvert	198
Clarke, William Henry	94, 193
Clark, *Sergeant*	162
Clifford, Miller	19, 20, 22, 36, 39, 46, 47, 50, 52, 53, 179, 193
Coates, Charles	53
Coates, George	190, 205
Cochrane, William Montague	203
Coddington, Herbert Adolphe	164, 210
Codrington, K.C.B., Sir William	113
Colley, Patrick	190
Collingwood, Edward	200
Collins, Josiah Erskine	151, 207
Collins, T.	198
Conran, Colonel —	9
Conyers, Robert Rowland	109, 110, 114, 121, 123, 201
Cook, Walter	207
Cooper, John	192
Cooper, W. S.	165, 166
Coore, Major —	40
Coote, K.B., Sir Eyre	178, 189
Cotton, Brigadier-General —	67, 69, 72, 73, 74, 76
Courtney, Samuel	188
Coventry, John	194
Cowel, Lambert	196
Cowell, William	188
Cowley, Norman	198
Cox, George	164, 166, 179, 210

APPENDIX.

	PAGE
Cox, H.	189
Cox, Ormsby	146, 151, 206
Cradock, Major-General	7
Craig, Henry	189
Crawford, Henry	199
Crawford, John	193
Cresswell, George	109, 110, 202
Croker, Charles	190
Croker, John Dillon	191
Crosbie, Lieut —	44
Crosbie, William	1, 178, 186
Crowdy, James W.	198
Cunningham, John	191
Cuppage, John Macdonald	110, 114, 133, 136, 180, 200
Currie, James	66, 68, 196
Curzon, Hon. Ferdinand	195
Cuthbert, John	146, 152, 155, 156, 180, 205

D

Daines, Captain —	23
Dalgetty, Alexander	191
Daly, Hon. Charles	95, 109, 110, 111, 199
Daniel, —	192
Daniel, Thomas	189
Darby, Carrick	109, 110, 111, 201
D'Arcy, Thomas Dopping	200
Daubeny, Albert James Hesketh	146, 151, 183, 205
Davenport, Edward	195
Davidson, Hugh James Alexander	152, 154, 208
Davidson, James	194
Davison, William Pearson	158, 159, 160, 162, 209
Dawes, Edward Alleyne	202
Dawn, R.	52
Dawson, James	195
De Bathe, Sir Henry Percival	156, 178, 208
De Rottenburg, Major-General	17
De Wattville	41
Devaynes, William A.	198
Dewes, Henry J.	197
Dickson, George D.	131, 204
Dillon, John M.	190
Dillon, M. M.	199
Dixon, Robert	188
Dobbie, Herbert Hugh	153, 156, 208
Doherty, Richard	88, 89, 90, 92, 179, 199
Dougan, William Horne	54, 62, 195

APPENDIX.

Dowdall, Aylmer	44, 46, 48, 52, 62, 195
Dowdeswell, George Francis	114, 117, 203
Downie, Nathaniel	187
Dowson, C.	182
Doyle, General —	4
Drage, William	113, 114, 115, 117, 203
Drummond, Lieut.-Col. —	37
Drummond, Lieut.-Gen. G. —	26, 29, 38, 39
Drummond, William	201
Dudgeon, Ralph	200
Duff, William	200
Dukes, James	181
Dunn, Henry Burton	115, 203
Dunn, Josias	113, 114, 117, 146, 148, 152, 154, 155, [156, 157, 158, 164, 165, 166, 179, 203
Dunscomb, Adam	189
Dunscomb, Francis	192
D'Urban, Benjamin	189

E

Edmunds, Henry	180, 199
Edwards, T. W.	66, 77, 181, 196
Eeles, Charles	192
Egerton, Sir Charles Bulkeley	91, 119, 178, 188, 199
Egerton, Richard	188
Egerton, Caledon Richard	84, 109, 110, 112, 113, 114, [141, 150, 178, 180, 198
Elliott, Captain —	35, 38, 40
Ellis, Henry Robert Alfred	154, 155, 206
Ellis, Robert Hawkes	146, 206
Ellis, W. E.	195
Elphinstone, Lord	117
Emright, —	187
England, K.C.B., Sir Richard	110
Evans, Henry Eyre	188
Evans, Major —	37, 40
Evatt, J. H.	194
Eyre, K.C.B., Sir William	113

F

Fallon, *Private* T.	123
Fasken, Edward James Nicholls	148, 207
Fawkes, Montague	146, 156, 205
Ferryman, Augustus Halifax	107, 108, 109, 110, 114, 115, 117, 118, [128, 132, 166, 178, 179, 202, 211

APPENDIX.

				PAGE
Fischer, Lieut.-Col. —	...	...	...	39, 40
Fisher, *Private* John	...	...	...	114
Fitz-Clarence, Lord Frederick	...	...	...	104
Fitz-Gerald, Urmston Fitz-Otho	...	...	...	210
Fleming, Hugh	...	...	...	189
Fogherty, Surgeon	...	...	...	155
Forbes, Thomas C.	...	...	62, 64, 66,	196
Forbes, William S.	...	...	...	197
Forster, Archibald Cochrane	...	151, 152, 154, 156,	182
Fortescue, William L.	...	...	...	191
Francis, Christian	...	...	...	186
Fraser Alexander George	...	...	134,	205
Fraser, Lieut. —	...	...	...	36
Freer, R. B.	...	...	...	196
French, Richard (1)	...	...	11, 12, 15,	188
French, Richard (2)	...	...	...	191
Fry, Charles Irwin	...	...	154, 156, 159,	208

G

Garden, Robert	...	...	...	9, 179,	192
Gardner, Charles	...	...	...	...	191
Garrett, K.C.B., Sir R.	...	...	...	...	136
Garroway, Captain —	...	...	...	...	48
Garsia, Christopher	...	...	...	...	205
Garvock, Sir John	...	...	...	147, 178,	206
Gascoigne, Charles	...	...	135, 139, 147, 178,	205
Gaussen, William Augustus	...	...	...	...	200
Gibbs, William	...	...	...	...	192
Gibson, Robert	...	...	...	134,	204
Gilborne, Richard	...	...	...	110, 115,	117
Gilchrist, John	...	...	...	...	191
Gillespie, J.	...	...	...	...	195
Gillespie, Joshua	...	...	...	...	193
Gillespie, Major-General —	...	...	...	...	11
Gledstanes, George	...	...	...	...	186
Glegg, Major —	...	...	...	...	35
Gleig, Rev. G. R.	...	...	...	...	138
Glew, Captain —	...	...	...	...	36, 38
Glover, William	...	...	...	...	198
Godwin, Colonel —	...	...	...	...	66
Goodall, Nathaniel	...	...	...	184,	190
Goodwin, John	...	...	...	...	195
Gordon, Andrew	...	...	...	178,	187
Gordon, John	...	...	146, 160, 161, 162, 163,	206
Gordon, Lieut.-Col. —	...	...	...	27, 37,	40
Gordon, Richard	...	...	...	...	193
Gordon, T. P.	...	...	...	...	196
Gore, Henry Ross	...	...	52, 54, 62, 66, 72, 77,	189

APPENDIX.

	PAGE
Govan, C. M.	157
Graeme, Lawrence	195
Graeme, Patrick	28, 193
Graham, Colonel —	4
Graham, V.C., K.C.B., Sir Gerald	160, 161, 163
Graham, James (1)	187
Graham, James (2)	197
Grant, Sir J. Hope	137
Grant, James	66, 77, 182
Grant, John	181, 182, 186
Grant, *Sergeant* J.	113
Grantham, Charles Caldwell	151, 153, 154, 155, 207
Granville, Charles Robert Bozzi	180, 198
Gray, Sir George	117
Gray, Hugh	187
Gray, J.	64, 66, 77, 197
Gray, John (1)	93, 199
Gray, John (2)	202
Gray, John Waldron	109, 202
Gray, Richard Tucker	165, 210
Gray, William	194
Greaves, G. F.	194
Green, Thomas Parnell	204
Grenville, Henry John K.	134, 138, 205
Grier, Alexander Dixon	115, 117, 146, 203
Grier, Stephen	190
Griffiths, C. Tindal	201
Griffiths, H. T.	198
Grimes, Major —	120, 122
Grover, Malcolm Henry Stanley	208
Gwyn, William	193

H

	PAGE
Hagerman, Lieut. —	23
Haines, K.C.B., Sir Frederick P.	149, 151
Hall, Samuel	9, 14, 15, 42, 45, 46, 186
Hall, Savage	112, 114, 115, 202
Hamilton, *Corporal*	58
Hamilton, Lieut.-Col. —	34, 37
Hampton, General —	18
Handcock, Matthew	194
Handfield, Charles (1)	1, 179, 186
Handfield, Charles (2)	187
Hanna, Rev. Richard	83
Harding, Henry	197
Hardinge, Hon. Arthur E.	159

APPENDIX.

	PAGE
Hardinge, William Sheffield	... 204
Hardy, Captain —	... 60
Hardy, Frederick A.	... 201
Harman, Charles Edward	151, 152, 154, 155, 156, 157, 180, 207
Harrel, James Wharton	... 206
Harriot, Major —	20, 21, 22
Harrison, Edward Branfill	158, 210
Harrison, Herbert Aug. Christopher	... 207
Harrison, Robert	123, 131, 203
Hartly, H. R.	87, 88, 179, 199
Harvest, H. de Vere	166, 211
Harvest, Henry Lewis	112, 146, 150, 152, 155, 156, 202
Harvey, Lieut.-Col.	20, 22, 35
Harvey, Sir J. —	... 103
Hassall, Charles Vernon	134, 146, 204
Hatch, Major —	... 124
Hawkins, Francis	... 197
Hawley, Robert B.	110, 112, 114, 180, 199
Hay, Archibald	... 198
Hay, James Shaw	131, 183, 204
Hay, Philip	... 189
Hayne, Arthur Gorham Howard	... 207
Hayward, George J. Whitaker	134, 204
Head, Edward Jonathan	182, 201
Healey, R. T.	... 198
Healy, Surgeon Major	... 155
Heffernan, Private W.	... 113
Helme, Burchall	113, 114, 131, 183, 203
Hemphill, Colonel —	... 36
Henley, C. F.	... 195
Heycock, Charles	112, 114, 115, 117, 120, 121, [123, 124, 125, 126, 135, 201
Hewson, John	... 193
Hewson, John Milliquet	52, 62, 77, 194
Hext, Francis Marwood	158, 160, 162, 209
Higginson, Montagu Edward	165, 210
Hilden, Robert Ongley	... 188
Hill, Arundel Edward	109, 110, 111, 200
Hill, Felix Frederick	156, 159, 160, 162, 208
Hill, Lord	83, 87
Hill, William	... 194
Hilliard, William (1)	9, 186
Hilliard, William (2)	... 191
Hobart, Lord	... 151
Hobbs, Simpson Hackett	114, 115, 117, 133, 202
Hogg, Hardinge Cornwallis	... 206
Holland, Captain	36, 38
Holland, John	... 196
Holloway, Charles Henry Elphinstone	... 200

APPENDIX.

	PAGE
Holmes, Colonel —	122
Holmes, Richard Francis	112, 114, 115, 117, 126, 129, 135, 180, 202
Hope, Captain —	100
Hope, Sir James	98, 99
Hope, John	195
Hope, William	77, 198
Hopper, George	184, 193
Horne, George	199
Horsford, K.C.B., Sir Alfred	136
Hovil, Richard	206
Hubbersty, Richard Nathan	131, 146, 152, 154, 156, 204
Hunt, Arthur	186
Hutchinson, Captain —	44
Hutchinson, T.	199

I

Ingall, Captain —	100
Imlach, James	195
Irwin, Thomas Hastings	188
Isacke, Frederick J.	201

J

Jackson, Captain —	22
Jackson, K.C.B., Sir Richard	98
James, Charles	198
James, John	192
Jenkins, F. L. Vernon	166, 211
Jenkins, G.	117
Jervis, Stanley Wolferston	208
Jervoise, Captain —	30, 35, 38
Jervoise, William	190
Johnson, F. W.	198
Johnston, Francis Hutchinson M.	194
Johnston, Robert	113, 117, 203
Jones, Christopher Neeld	147, 151, 152, 155, 206
Jones, George E.	56, 62, 85, 87, 166, 179, 191
Jones, K.C.B., Sir Harry	112
Jones, Luke Henry	134, 136, 204
Jones, Mortimer	194

K

Kay, James	187
Keatley, —	192
Kier, Sir William Grant	46, 47, 49
Keith, H. D.	196

APPENDIX.

				PAGE
Kelly, Patrick	...	...	...	... 196
Kennedy, Robert Blair	...	...	...	... 200
Kennedy, William	...	...	52, 56, 57, 58,	196
Kenny, Edward	...	52, 58, 62, 64, 66, 92, 180,	195
King, C. Gerald	...	52, 58, 62, 64, 66, 68, 77,	196
King, James	...	...	...	134, 205
King, James Tynte	...	...	...	... 188
King, Robert	...	...	...	... 186
King, W. J.	...	...	52, 62, 66, 68,	196
Kingston, J. L.	...	...	...	... 198
Kinnealy, *Private* P.	...	...	...	... 113
Kippen, Horatio Nelson	...	...	...	... 201
Kirby, Major —	...	...	...	... 36
Kirk, James Buchanan	...	...	...	138, 205
Kirkwood, Surgeon	...	...	...	... 156
Knatchbull, Francis	...	109, 110, 114, 117, 126, 146, 150,	202
Knipe, George Marshall	...	...	...	109, 201
Knox, Charles	...	...	...	... 198
Knox-Gore, Major-General	...	...	152, 153, 154,	156

L

Lacey, *Private* John	...	...	...	... 58
Laing, Herbert William	...	...	...	158, 159, 210
Lake, Lord	...	...	...	... 3
Lambert, John Arthur	...	...	156, 166, 178,	209
Lamont, Hafed	...	...	112, 114, 115, 125,	202
Lancaster, William	...	...	...	... 193
La Roche, H. S.	...	...	...	... 197
Latham, John Henry	...	...	...	... 194
Lawrenson, Edward	...	...	...	... 190
Layard, George H.	...	...	...	... 197
Leader, William	...	...	...	19, 194
Le Breton, Lieut. —	...	...	...	... 35
Le Cornu, Alfred John	...	...	...	... 206
Lee, Christopher	...	...	...	180, 197
Leeper, Richard Waugh	...	...	...	164, 210
Legge, L.	...	...	...	... 187
Leith, Alexander	...	...	...	... 189
Le Mesurier, John	...	...	...	... 187
Le Mesurier, Peter	...	...	...	... 190
Lenaghan, *Private* D.	...	...	...	... 113
Leonard, Captain —	...	...	...	... 37
Leslie, John William	...	...	...	... 194
Lewis, Henry Ogle	...	...	...	... 194
Lewis, Robert	...	...	...	... 197
Lewis, Thomas	...	...	...	... 195
Lindsay, (Bertie) Earl of	...	...	...	178, 192

APPENDIX. 227

	PAGE
Lisle, Major —	27, 36
Lloyd, Montifort H. Trant	112, 114, 115, 117, 129, 202
Lloyd, Robert	194
Lloyd, Thomas Prince	182
Lockwood, Robert Manners	195
Long, Assistant Surgeon	146
Long, William Nethersole	186
Longfield, John	109, 110, 111, 202
Loring, Captain —	35, 36
Low, Abraham	190
Lowrey, James	192
Lynch, Hugh	191

M

Macan, C.	197
Macaulay, Alexander	206
Macdonald, John	195
Macdonald, John Duntze	109, 110, 111, 199
Macdonald, J. R.	199
Macfarlane, Sir Robert	91, 178, 197
Mackenzie, Colin	193
Mackonachie, Captain —	37
Macleod, John	62, 64, 66, 197
Madden, George	195
Magdala, G.C.B., G.C.S.I., Lord Napier of	149
Magrath, Hamilton	188
Magrath, Mark	186
Maguire, John	191
Maister, Lieut.-General —	94
Maling, Irwin Charles	205
Malet, J. W.	50, 54, 196
Malone, H.	192
Maloney, Richard P.	192
Manners, William Norcott	113, 114, 203
Marsh, Francis Henry Digby	204
Masters, J.	195
Matthews, E. Kilby	186
Maule, Francis	192
Maule, Major-General	35
Maxwell, Louis Robert Meredith	152, 208
McBean, Donald	9, 10, 189
McBean, General —	54
McBeath, George	189
McCaskill, Hector	198
McCaskill, J.	79, 80, 179, 197
McCausland, J.	93, 197
McClure, Robert	187
McCrohan, James	190

APPENDIX.

	PAGE
McDonald, Archibald	186
McDonald, Sir John	83
McDonald, John	187
McDouall, James	187
McDowall, James (1)	186
McDowall, James (2)	187
McDowell, Major —	61
McKay, Hugh	187
McKeand, Robert	187
McKie, Patrick	52, 58, 62, 66, 197
McLaughlin, Captain	37
McLean, J. M.	52, 54, 56, 66, 196
McMillan, Quintin	187
McMurray, Joseph Robert	146, 152, 154, 155, 180, 206
Meacham, William Maitland	205
Meade, John de Courcy, Dashwood	148, 152, 207
Meade, Malcolm John	148, 207
Mein, Bowes	201
Mercer, Arthur H. Hastead	109, 110, 202
Meredith, Joshua	186
Meredith, Richard	182
Messiter, George Hughes	199
Michel, Sir J.	127
Miles, Edward	50, 51, 55, 56, 57, 59, 65, 82, 84, 85, 179, 196
Miles, Edward S.	197
Miles, Francis	184, 194
Miles, R. J. Falconer	84, 198
Mills, William Huntley	200
Mockler, R.	195
Moira, Lord	1, 14
Molony, J. L.	52, 196
Montresor, Thomas Gage	188
Moore, Alexander McDonnell	154, 160, 162, 208
Moore, Butler Dunboyne	201
Moore, Fowke	199
Moore, Gustavus	186
Moore, Joseph	52, 196
Moorson, Lieut. —	35
Morris, Edmund	112, 114, 125, 202
Morrison, Joseph	16, 18, 19, 20, 24, 31, 36, 39, 184, 190
Moulson, Edward	193
Mulcaster, Captain —	18
Mulloy, A. E.	200
Munn, Frederick Henry	155, 157, 158, 160, 162, 183, 208
Munro, Hector	194
Murphy, *Pte.* Andrew	58
Murray, Kenelm Digby	146, 150, 206
Murray, *Sergt.-Major*	153
Muter, Dunbar Douglas	200

APPENDIX. 229

	PAGE
Mytton, John F. FitzGiffard	200

N

Napier, John	186
Napier of Magdala, G.C.B., G.C.S.I., Lord	149
Napier, K.C.B., Sir R.	128
Naylor, Charles Scarlin	46, 48, 180, 195
Neary, Stephen	208
Need, Pennington Grant	93, 198
Nesfield, William	195
Newbigging, Robert G.	115, 117, 180, 203
Newbury, John	199
Nixon, Alfred	109, 110, 114, 115, 117, 125, 201
Noble, James M.	195
Norcott, A. R. C.	196
Nugent, James Thomas	203
Nunn, Lorenzo	188
Nurse, Charles George	158, 160, 162, 209

O

Oakes, Lawrence	10, 180, 188
Oakley, Fred. W.	199
O'Brien, Oliver Creagh	199
O'Connell, Richard	187
O'Donoghue, Daniel	190
O'Donoghue, Lieut.-Col.	67, 69, 70
Ogilvie, James	178, 189
O'Kelly, George	190
Oldfield, Macauley Hume	200
Olpherts, Wybrow	52, 62, 64, 196
O'Malley, George	190
O'Neil, C.	56, 62, 64, 66, 196
Orange, William Nesbitt	195
Ord, George Frederick	192
Orr, John	194
Orr, Surgeon	66, 77, 93
Osborne, Francis W.	146, 148, 181, 205
Ostler, William Grenfield	131, 204
Oughton, James	194
Owen, W. G.	149

P

Palmer, F. Roger	198
Palmer, Henry W.	201

APPENDIX.

	PAGE
Palmer, J. H.	197
Parke, Brig. Gen. —	124
Parker, John George	165, 210
Parry, Lieut.-Col. —	36
Parsons, Fred. William Adam	203
Patterson, Charles Doyle	199
Patterson, William	190
Paulet, Lord W.	137
Payne, Joseph	189
Pearse, Walter	48, 52, 54, 62, 64, 66, 77, 88, 89, 90, 93, 94, 192
Pearson, J. B.	93, 199
Pearson, Lieut.-Col.	20, 21, 22, 37, 40
Peck, John J.	197
Peel, J. H.	193
Pennefather, Richard	200
Penton, John	146, 151, 152, 154, 155, 156, 157, 158, 179, 206
Percival, William	188
Percy, George	190
Percy, V.C., K.C.B., Lord Henry Hugh Manvers	150, 178, 207
Pering, George Harmer	109, 110, 117, 183, 202
Perry, John Taylor	187
Perry, William	180, 187
Pery, W. Cecil George	109, 110, 112, 114, 123, 127, 201
Peshall, Charles John	187
Petry, John	194
Phibbs, W. H.	197
Philan, Lieut. —	44
Philan, W. W.	194
Phillips, John Lewes	109, 110, 119, 121, 123, 179, 201
Pick, Vesian	190
Pigott, Arthur	91, 199
Pigott, General —	4
Plenderleath, Charles	20, 22, 187
Plomer, William Harry Percival	158, 160, 162, 183, 210
Podmore, Thomas	192
Poe, Emmanuel T.	194
Pole, Mundy	92, 94, 198
Poppleton, W. A.	198
Pott, William	127, 203
Powell, Matthew	193
Power, George	186
Prendergast, T.	77, 196
Price, Asst. Surgeon	121, 129
Price, Augustus William	131, 183, 204
Pritchard, Lieut.-Col. —	100
Prother, Lieut.-Col.	42, 43, 46, 49
Provost, Sir George	17, 24, 30
Pycroft, Henry Thomas	205
Pym, Colonel —	83, 84

APPENDIX.

R

	PAGE
Radcliffe, Gerard	187
Raglan, Lord	114
Raikes, C.B., Lieut.-General	151
Rainsford, W. H.	25, 42, 50, 179, 196
Ramsay, Thomas	190
Raymond, William	188
Redmond, Charles	52, 62, 66, 192
Reed, Samuel	189
Reeves, John	160, 162, 210
Reynolds, J. Smith	193
Riall, Major-General	26, 28, 33, 35
Ribton, John Browne	146, 205
Rice, James Arthur	188
Richards, Captain —	129
Richardson, C.	200
Richmond, Richard Oliffe	151, 152, 154, 207
Ricketts, Phillip	192
Roberts, Major-General —	121, 122
Roberts, Surgeon	110
Robertson, G. D. (1)	195
Robertson, G. D. (2)	200
Robinson, Barnes Slyfield	112, 114, 118, 127, 129, 152, 155 156, [158, 160, 162, 163, 164, 179, 202
Robinson, John	196
Robinson, Lieut.-Colonel	36, 38
Rochfort, W. C.	198
Roddy, Charles Packenham	181, 184, 188
Roe, Asst. Surgeon	112, 114, 115, 117
Rogers, Claude Rainier	152, 155, 156, 157, 160, 162, 165, 180, 208
Rogers, Rev. E. J.	138, 141
Romer, J. C.	199
Roome, Captain —	129
Rorke, Major —	125
Rose, G.C.B., Sir Hugh	134
Rose, Richard, Croker	43, 44, 52, 62, 64, 66, 68 189
Ross, Alexander	178, 188
Rosse, Rt. Hon. the Earl of	107
Routh, Surgeon	156
Rowe, Francis Richard	190
Rudall, William H.	131, 204
Russell, J. M.	197
Ruxton, George Augustus F.	200

S

Sanderson, Robert	48, 192
Sandos, Charles	199

APPENDIX.

	PAGE
Saunders, William	194
Savage, Francis	190
Scarlett, K.C.B., Sir James Yorke	137, 142
Schiel, Arthur	197
Scott, Colonel —	28, 34, 37
Scott, General —	34
Scott, James	189
Scott, Sergeant Patrick	114
Scott, Robert	110, 114, 115, 117, 182
Scott, Thomas Edwin	211
Scully, Walter	191
Sealy, William	121, 129, 146, 148, 152, 180, 203
Selby, Robert	109, 110, 117, 122, 135, 201
Selway, H.	180, 181, 190
Selway, Henry R.	191
Sewell, John	193
Sewell, Robert	14, 179, 193
Sewell, Stephen William	133, 134, 204
Shakespear, George C. Childe	159, 208
Shakespear, Lieut. —	99
Shakespeare, Sir R.	120
Shand, J. M.	184, 189
Sheehey, Roger	191
Sheridan, Thomas	181, 184, 191
Sherlock, William	190
Sherwin, William	186
Shuter, James	200
Sibbald, *Color-Sergeant*	52
Sibbald, William	114, 115, 117, 181, 203
Silver, Walter Barrington	165, 210
Simpson, Lancelot	186
Simpson, Major —	126
Simpson, Robert	192
Sinclair, John	187
Skinner, Captain —	23
Skinner, Frederick	195
Skynner, Leslie	109, 110, 114, 115, 116, 117, 118, 119, 120, [179, 201
Smelt, Major—	37
Smith, Edward Colthard	189
Smith, E. G.	197
Smith, Felix	195
Smith, George Osborne	151, 156, 157, 158, 160, 162, 183, 206
Smith, Sir Lionel	89
Smith, Surgeon	133
Smith, Walter Bartelot	190
Smyth, Acheson William	205
Snow, John	196
Somerset, Brigadier-General —	127

APPENDIX. 233

	PAGE
Spence, John	199
Sparrow, Surgeon	146, 151, 152
Spicer, Captain —	60
Spunner, Robert	194
Standen, James Douglas	152, 154, 155, 156, 207
Stanford, Robert	197
Stanley, J. T.	201
Stanton, Henry	190
Stawell, Bernard	186
Steel, Watson A.	184, 192
Stewart, Captain —	37
Stewart, F. Y. John	200
Stewart, Ramsay	206
Stewart, William	3, 5, 7, 86, 179, 187
St. Leger, Johnston	11, 188
Strange, —	195
Strathnairn, Lord	143
Strong, Owen H.	115, 117, 203
Stopford, Hon. Edward B. L. H.	164, 210
Stroud, T. W.	197
Stuart, Allen	193
Stubbington, Sergeant	161
Sutton, St. Ives	197
Swettenham, George Kilner	165, 210

T

Taylor, Abraham B.	48, 62, 63, 66, 194
Taylor, Thomas	193
Terry, Arthur F.	164, 210
Thomas, John	197
Thomas, William	196
Thompson, George William	194
Thompson, John	192
Thompson, Thomas, R. J. G.	201
Thornton, William	187
Thornton, W. H.	199
Thorp, Edward	90, 96, 97, 99, 101, 103, 104, 105, 107, 179, 197
Thorp, Edward Buller	111, 113, 114, 115, 117, 118, 120, 123, [126, 128, 131, 132, 135, 138, 144, [146, 148, 149, 150, 152, 179, 201
Thursby, C. Augustus	195
Toln, Thomas	181, 191
Tom, Daniel	112, 114, 115, 117, 202
Tompkins, Lieut. —	37
Torrens, Henry	192
Tottenham, John William	195
Trenwith, *Corporal*, J....	113

	PAGE
Tucker, Lieut. Col. —	31, 39
Tuckey, Thomas	190
Tufnell, Robert Hutchinson C.	150, 207
Twigg, Thomas G.	197
Tyrry, Michael Gould	193

V

Vallette, Major	40
Valpy, De Vic	204
Van Buerle, Thomas	195
Vaughton, Erasmus Harris	205
Vennell, Henry	186
Vennell, William	187
Vincent, Brig.-Gen. —	17
Vincent, Robert	196
Vipan, John Alexander Mayhew	146, 151, 152, 154, 155, 206
Vivian, Sir Hussey	85

W

Waddy, Cadwallader	190
Walker, Lieut.-Col. —	99
Walker, C. Montague	199
Walker, Thomas	180, 186
Wall, J. Quintus	199
Wall, Richard	110, 192
Walsh, Surgeon	62, 64, 66
Warburton, Captain —	99
Warburton, Francis	121, 125, 203
Ward, Asst. Surgeon	146
Ward, Lieut.-Col. —	99
Warne, John Cordeiro	114, 203
Warre, Sir William	106
Waters, Surgeon Major	156
Watkins, John	155, 156, 160, 161, 162, 165, 181, 208
Watson, Major —	100, 103
Watson, W.	110, 181, 201
Watt, William	192
Watts, Osman Charles	193
Welch, Malcolm Ed. Haleman Owen	148, 207
White, Hans Robert	112, 114, 201
White, J.	182
White, James	198
White, L. Luke Esmond	182
Whitelocke, John	9, 178, 191
Whittingham, Sir Samford	93
Wilde, Ralph	193

APPENDIX. 235

		PAGE
Wiles, Asst. Surgeon	...	112, 114
Wilkinson, General —	...	17, 19, 28
Williams, Frederick Thesiger	...	158, 160, 162, 209
Williams, Thomas Hobbs	...	201
Willis, Sir George	...	164
Wilson, H.	...	197
Wilson, M. William	...	182
Wilson, Samuel	...	189
Wingfield, Richard J.	...	188
Worsley, *Edmund*	...	196
Worsley, Henry	...	190
Wright, Thomas	...	199
Wynyard, Henry	...	200

Y

Young, Plomer 60, 77, 191

www.ingramcontent.com/pod-product-compliance
Lightning Source LLC
Chambersburg PA
CBHW052048220426
43663CB00012B/2481